"Lori is an amazing coach. She has assisted me in so many ways. She is very insightful, intuitive, discerning, creative, caring, helpful, giving, and so much more, but all in one package. I needed someone who was unbiased to give perspective and support in my life. Family and friends mean well, but are sometimes unable to provide the kind of reflection that a coach, like Lori, can provide. I thought I would just try coaching for three months, but I have found Lori to be such an amazing support and value to me that our coaching experience has extended to nine months and continues. I am a mom, recording artist, and professional in healthcare. I really desired to define success strategies to pursue goals at a greater level. She has kept me on track and allowed me to experience her cheerleading too. She is faithful, responsive, and demonstrates lots of integrity with all her interactions. Well, that is just a little about my high regards for Lori's services. I highly recommend Lori." *Marluta Correll — Englewood, OH (Work-at-home Mom of 2)*

"I was a stay-at-home Mom stuck in the trenches. I was bogged down with day-to-day tasks of kids and home, and needed to find myself. Lori helped me discover my needs and identify the activities that would make me feel better about myself as a Woman, not just a Mom. Most importantly, Lori helped me to brainstorm, to commit to new things, and she held me accountable so that I kept the promises I made to myself. Life went from busy to fulfilling as I started activities just for me, used babysitters more and took time to do the things I had been thinking about but never put into action! Within a couple months I was building new friendships, taking classes, and getting through the whole day with a smile. Through the experience of rediscovering my dreams and hearing the encouragement from Lori to just do it, I found more joy in all the things I do, even laundry, because I know time for me is scheduled too. Lori is a great listener with a can-do attitude and that rubbed off on me. Thank you Lori!"
Sheila Marino — Littleton, CO (Stay-at-home Mother of 2)

"Coach Lori is wonderful to work with: honest, professional and caring, with a great deal of expertise. It's hard to put into words the inner balance and peace I have achieved from working with Lori. I am happier, more relaxed, and more focused on my goals in all areas of my life. I think the most helpful thing about working with Lori is the supportive and knowledgeable way she assists me on a path of increased self-awareness. I've grown from my work with Lori in many ways. I'm better at realizing my wants and needs and

working towards them; I'm better at setting limits and saying "no" if I need to; I'm better at balancing all areas of my life to find harmony. One of my favorite pieces of advice from Coach Lori is to be "in the moment". Sounds simple, but it's not easy to do with conflicting demands and pressures. My coaching sessions have allowed me to work towards "being in the moment" and enjoying life to the fullest."
Kristen Osterhaus — Aurora, IL (Work-at-home Mother of 1)

"Lori is a very knowledgeable, well-rounded and supportive coach. She is working with me on a wide range of both day-to-day and "big picture" issues. She offers everything from practical techniques to better manage my time and discipline my two-year-old to approaches to spark my creativity and help me articulate my needs and passions in life. I really enjoy our sessions and leave each one with useful advice and tools that I can use every day." *Dana R. — Naperville, IL (Working Mother of 1)*

"Working with Lori has made a tremendous difference in my life. She makes me feel so supported without any judgments. It is a lot to go on the journey to live an authentic life and knowing that she's my companion, cheerleader and confidante is so, so heartening. She champions me and helps me to see hope and possibility when I doubt myself. She holds my best self up for me to see when I start to forget or doubt who I am. Lori is so sincere and so happy for me when I reach a milestone. I know, no matter what, that she's really there for me and wants to see me live out my truth."
Debbie H. — Montclair, NJ (Work-at-home and Single Mom of 1)

"Working with Lori has been extraordinary. I have been able to accomplish goals that I had not been able to accomplish on my own. I have been able to be more disciplined in my daily life and I feel better about myself as a result. Thank you Lori!" *Danielle K. — Roselle, IL (Work-at-home Mom of 1)*

"I came to Lori in search of a "balanced life", having difficulty finding time for all parts of my life including myself. Having to reestablish and focus on priorities with her in a non-judgmental way has been a wonderful experience. At every meeting with her, Lori helps eliminate or tackle any obstacles in our path. I'd strongly encourage anyone to work with Lori interested in reducing stress, in overcoming challenges, and simply leading a happier life." *Lydia Burch — Naperville, IL (Working Mother of 2)*

"Lori has helped me sort through my very busy life and all the "stuff" that surrounds us – family, friends, neighbors, to do's, bills, jobs, etc. Coaching has helped me pull out and keep what is important to me: my inner being and my priorities. After a call, I feel renewed in the direction I am taking to fulfill my personal goals. I feel I know "who I am" much more. I am a calmer, happier person." *Maureen McCoy – Elmhurst, IL (Stay-at-home Mother of 4)*

"Working with Lori Radun as my coach has made a dramatic change in my life. We worked together to set specific, achievable goals in the areas I identified as needy. Together, we developed a step-by-step plan to achieve those goals. Lori assisted me in seeing both the 'big picture' and the weekly 'little steps' that would get me to where I wanted to be.

What I especially appreciate in Lori is her psychology background. She is able to ask me the 'tough' questions, to guide me through the maze of my own mental roadblocks to accomplishing my goals. She is a cheerleader when I move forward and a problem-solver when I'm stuck.

Another aspect of working with Lori that I appreciate is her availability. Whether by phone, e-mail or in person - she is 100% focused on my situation and me. I receive prompt callbacks or e-mail responses that indicate there is a caring, supportive person at the other end, who is truly in my corner!" *Janet K. – Naperville, IL (Empty Nester Mom of 3)*

"Lori is a great coach to work with. No matter what obstacle I felt was in my path, Lori helped me figure out what steps I could take to make the changes I desired. Whether it was with my kids (she's got lots of great tips for parents!), my spouse, or figuring out my next career path, Lori has a way of asking just the right thought provoking question to help me see other possibilities. She's extremely supportive and genuinely interested in my success. In the short time I've worked with her, I have gone from feeling like I was mired in a deep rut to feeling optimistic about my plans for the future. I feel like it was Lori's support and encouragement that helped me make that transition." *Christy P. – Fishers, IN (Working Mom of 3)*

"Lori is a loving and caring coach while being a person of integrity and strength. She has been such an inspiration to me, as a coach and as a speaker, for her ability to stay with the plan and create results, while inspiring and motivating others to grow. I recommend her services to anyone who is looking for a coach who will create the necessary action to make things happen." *Aline V. – Naperville, IL*

"I just wanted to write a short note of thanks for providing me with a valu-able, insightful, and inspirational coaching experience. You were always able to see the best in me, even when I did not see the best in myself. Through your positive and empowering process, you were able to keep me on track with my goals and stretch me to reach higher. Your spiritual strength provided a wonderful reinforcement to my own faith, and helped me explore how I can draw on my faith as a foundation and as a guide. And to top it off, we had a lot of fun in the process!" *Rick L. – Michigan (Entrepreneur Dad of 2)*

THE Momnificent! LIFE

*Healthy and Balanced Living
for Busy Moms*

Lori Radun, CEC, AELC

The Momnificent™ Life
Healthy and Balanced Living for Busy Moms

by Lori Radun

Library of Congress Control Number: 2009923980

ISBN 978-0-97438232-4-8

...itional copies of this book are available at www.momnificent.com

...ished by Mom Coach Press, A Wyatt-MacKenzie Imprint
Aurora, IL

Mom Coach Press
A Wyatt-MacKenzie Imprint

...nformation visit www.wymacpublishing.com

*To my mom, Roxie Lear — my first and only example
of what it means to be a mom.*

*To my beautiful boys, Kai and Ian — may my love for you
bless your lives forever.*

ACKNOWLEDGEMENTS
⭐

First, and foremost, I thank God for blessing me in all the ways He has and does every day of my life.

I want to thank my husband, Rick, for being an amazing support to me in so many different ways. Thank you to Kai and Ian, my children, for allowing me to learn and teach about parenting by practicing on you. Thank you Mom for believing in me and encouraging me in everything I do. Thanks to Brad, my brother and fellow entrepreneur. I want to thank all my friends (and you know who you are) for always supporting me, through the good, the bad, and everything in between.

As a life coach, I am grateful to iPEC Coaching for the phenomenal training I received. Thank you to all my coach friends and peers for being on this journey with me. I am especially grateful for all my former and current clients. You have trusted me to be your partner on your personal growth journey, and that is an honor. This book would not be possible without everything I have learned from each and every one of you. While I share stories from my clients' lives, names and other pieces of information have been changed to protect identities. The stories, however, are real and not fabricated.

Thank you to Nancy Cleary from Wyatt-MacKenzie Publishing for all your help in bringing this book into the world of moms. You are a true joy to work with, and I look forward to a continued relationship for years to come.

START A MOMNIFICENT!™ LIFE GROUP
☆

Moms need and want to be in community with other moms. The Momnificent!™ Life is a great book for moms' groups, book clubs, or other women's clubs. If you have an existing group you are part of, leverage the power and accountability of group support while working on this book together.

How you structure your group is completely up to you, but here are some general guidelines for using this book in a group format.

- Read and work on one particular section of the book before moving on to another section.

- Have each group member read the chapters and complete the take action assignments individually before opening up for a group share.

- Have an open discussion about what group members want to create for that particular area of their life.

- Help each other set goals pertaining to a particular area of life.

- Assign a time frame to work on goals.

- Follow up with a group share on successes, struggles and celebration of individual goals.

For more resources on starting or joining a Momnificent!™ Life group, please visit our website at www.momnificent.com.

THE MOMNIFICENT!™ LIFE
Healthy and Balanced Living for Busy Moms

INTRODUCTION

★

When I first introduced the concept of "Momnificent" to my newsletter list of moms, I asked them one simple question. How do you feel about the term "Momnificent"? I purposely did not define the word for them because I wanted to see what the initial reaction would be. Over 60% of moms who answered this question said they loved it — they wanted to *be* momnificent! This was an encouraging number since moms didn't truly know what it meant. Nine percent were confused by the term "momnificent." One mom said, "What does it mean? Mom inefficient?" Although I could certainly understand her interpretation, I had to smile because that suggested definition was not even remotely close to what my intended message was.

The fact that you are reading this book tells me you are momnificent. Momnificent is simply a concept that describes moms who *value* living positive, healthy and balanced lives. You don't have to live your life perfectly, nor do you need to have all the answers. My goal with the concept of "momnificent" is to equip you with the tools you need to create a magnificent life as a mom.

That being said, there are eight components to living a momnificent life. I realize that many moms struggle with at least one, probably more of these different components. I, myself, can be challenged at times by each of these components. However, I keep trying to master these ideas because I know they are the keys to living a momnificent life. My hope is you will embrace the components of the momnificent life so you can begin creating, maintaining and living a magnificent life.

The first component of a momnificent life is **confidence**. Confidence is about knowing who you are and being accepting of who you are, limits and all. Confidence in all areas of your life will help you be successful as a mom, a woman, a wife, or in any other role you decide to identify with. Almost any chapter in this book can help you develop confidence, depending on in what areas you wish to grow. As we grow and become clear about who we are as individuals, our confidence will blossom. When we practice new skills and live more fully into who we wish to be, our confidence is developed.

The second component of a momnificent life is the **ability to set healthy boundaries**. Healthy boundaries in our lives protect what is most important to us. Boundaries help us decide what we are willing to tolerate and what we are not. They provide the walls around our life that enable us to maintain a positive and healthy life; a life that is specifically designed to work for us. An introduction to boundaries and the seven types of boundaries is located in the relationships section of this book. Once you understand the various boundaries, you will find other chapters that speak specifically to your boundary needs.

Thirdly, a momnificent life enables us to have **positive energy** for ourselves, as well as positive energy to give to our families and the world. To have positive energy, we must manage all the energy drains in our lives. Energy drains are different for every mom. They range from clutter in our environments and holding onto negative emotions to draining friendships and financial worries. The other component of maintaining positive energy is about finding those things that refuel you, and making a commitment to engage in those activities on a regular basis. Again, you will find chapters throughout the book that will help you eliminate energy drains and assist you in finding ideas for refueling your energy.

The fourth component of a momnificent life is having **healthy and supportive relationships**. We cannot successfully manage life alone. You absolutely need to be in relationship with other people, and healthy and supportive relationships will go a long way in helping you cope with the everyday ups and downs of life. Obviously, a great place to work on relationships is with the chapters in the relationships section. However, having healthy and supportive relationships also includes having a relationship with our self, our money, or a Divine power. So you will find chapters to help you with these relationships in Personal Development, Spirituality, Fun and Enjoyment and Personal Finance.

Fifth, **life balance** is a significant component of the momnificent life. Life balance is explained in detail in Chapter 1. You will have the opportunity to evaluate your current life balance with specific exercises in this chapter. I think sometimes moms are confused by what life balance actually means. Many moms believe that you are balanced when you are spending equal attention to all areas of your life. However, life balance takes a much more custom approach to life. It's really about aligning the way you live your life with your truest self. Start with Chapter 1 and based on what you learn there, you can then decide what section to turn to next.

The sixth component of a momnificent life is having a **spiritual foundation**. Having a connection to something spiritual grounds us and helps us feel secure with the uncertainties of life. It is this spiritual connection that enables us to feel peace and surrender much of what is, in reality, beyond our control. Spirituality has a different meaning for everyone. Some of us embrace religion. Others rely on a connection to God, Spirit, the Divine or some other spiritual force. Some moms spend time in nature, in quiet solitude or doing yoga and meditation to experience spiritual renewal. Whatever way you choose to nurture your spiritual well-being is okay with me. I will refer to God at times throughout this book, or I will mention prayer and other forms of spiritual connection. Substitute whatever fits your personal definition of spirituality. Keep an open mind to how the Spirit may speak to you through the chapters in this book.

Practicing self-care is the seventh component of a momnificent life. Without regular self-care, it is difficult to be your best. Regular self-care will help you be a better mom, and without it, you will eventually reach burn out. Self-care involves taking care of your physical, emotional, mental and spiritual well being. It means you will give your body, mind and soul what it needs to feel renewed and refreshed. It's what enables you to continue giving in a way that most moms can truly understand. Self-care is a significant component of living a magnificent life.

Last, you could not live a momnificent life without being a **nurturing and effective parent**. It's the one element you can't get away from as long as you are a mom. Parenting your children is a significant part of your life and almost always dominates your time. Living into our own personal definition of what it means to be a "good mom" is the central focus of our existence while our children are in our home. It is important to acknowledge, however, that being a mom is not our entire identity. We were women before we became moms, and we will always be women. We are friends and daughters, and some of us are wives and career professionals. Being a mom is a part, and a very important part, but certainly not the whole of who we are. While you can turn to the section on Home and Family to develop yourself as a parent, developing other areas of yourself will make you a better mom as well.

As I continue on my own personal journey through motherhood, my hope is that you will allow me to share what I've learned from being a mom, a wife, a friend, a daughter, and most recently, a life coach. It is my prayer that you will live a momnificent life. You are momnificent and you deserve it!

CHAPTER 1
✳
Life Balance is a Process

"The concept of balance defines our Universe. The cosmos, our planet, the seasons, water, wind, fire and Earth are all in perfect balance. We humans are the only exception." —Wayne Dyer

✳

Have you ever watched children walk along a curb, or along the railway ties lining the local playground? They walk with their arms straight out, placing one foot in front of the other, as they teeter from side to side. They have to stay focused in order to keep their balance. As parents, we also need to focus on balance in our lives or we may end up falling off – not off a curb or a railway tie, but off our path in life.

What does it mean to live a balanced life? Well, let's start by defining life balance. Life balance occurs when *who you are, what you want* to do in life, and *what you value* are aligned with your *thoughts, activities and choices.* When your life is balanced, you are at peace with yourself and your life. You are energized in life versus stressed and tired. A person in balance is satisfied with all areas of their life. Life may not be perfect, but they certainly don't feel dissatisfied with their life. Balanced individuals are growing as human beings, and they feel a sense of purpose in life.

Let me give you a personal picture of what balanced living looks like for me. By paying attention to who I am and what's important to me, I craft a life that reflects these values. It is important to me to exercise, so I work out four times a week. I value my family, so I regularly spend time with my children and husband. Because spiritual growth is important to me, I regularly attend church where I serve as a worship leader for our children's ministry. My career as a life coach reflects my passion for personal growth. Not every moment of my life is balanced, but I am always making choices that help me live the life that is important to me.

Finding balance in life is different for everyone. Some of us want to slow life down a little and lighten our load. Others may love the fast-paced lifestyle of the "Energizer Bunny," as they go-go-go. It is important for each of us to think about how we want to spend our lives and about what is most important to us as individuals. If you find yourself driven by circumstances and not exercising your power of choice, you are probably living "out of balance."

Balance in our lives enables us to make choices that are right for us — for the right reasons. We learn to say "no" to things we don't want to do. Or to change our attitude about those things that really must be done. We become willing to look honestly at what is not working in our lives. For some, it may be as simple as handing over household chores to a housekeeper in order to pursue a hobby. Others may find that seeking out a biking partner helps motivate them to exercise. Keeping balance may require saying no to a child's extracurricular activity to make time for a family night. Trying out new ideas one at a time can help each of us achieve the balance and fulfillment that may be missing from our lives.

Balance and time go hand in hand. We make choices about our time to create the balance we are looking for. When we are spending our time doing the things that are most important to us, time is not an issue. We become frustrated with time when we aren't choosing the right activities for our life and our personality. On Monday, I spoke to a woman named Kathy. Kathy was frustrated with the lack of time in her life. She explained to me that she never got anything done because every day she spent her time picking up all the clutter in the house. The real reason Kathy was frustrated was not because she wasn't getting anything done. She was, in fact, getting things done. She was not, however, doing the things she wanted to do. By shifting her energy and focusing more on tasks that brought her pleasure, or tasks that were more important to her, her frustration with time would diminish.

Analyzing Your Own Life Balance

In this section, I'm going to help you assess the current balance and satisfaction in your own life. Below is a picture of The Wheel of Life. We are going to use this wheel to give you a big picture look at your current life.

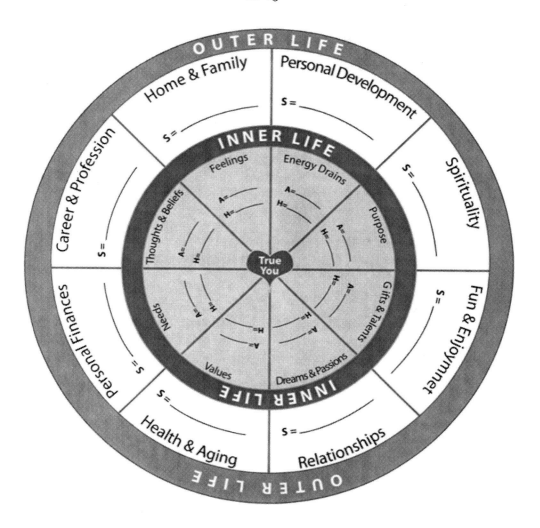

Outer Life

You'll notice there are eight major areas of the outer life, and each area has a place for you to fill in a value under "S =." For each of the eight areas in the outer part of the wheel, I want you to rate your current level of satisfaction on a scale of 1 to 10. A rating of 1 means you are completely dissatisfied and a rating of 10 means you are completely satisfied; nothing could be better. As you contemplate your level of satisfaction, please reflect on these questions for each area. Use these questions along with your own interpretation of these life areas to guide your decision.

PERSONAL DEVELOPMENT

How do you view your current level of self-esteem? How well do you feel you are handling your inner life? How satisfied are you with your personal growth?

SPIRITUALITY

How comfortable are you with the meaning of spirituality in your life? Are you regularly engaging in spiritual practice according to your definition? Do you feel you are using your gifts and talents for the greater good of the Universe?

FUN AND ENJOYMENT

Are you engaging in regular fun in life, participating in activities that you enjoy? Do you regularly take time to refuel?

RELATIONSHIPS

How satisfied are you with the quality of relationships in your life, including marriage and friendships? Are you growing in each of your relationships? How satisfied are you with the quantity of relationships in your life? Are your relationships meeting your needs?

HEALTH AND AGING

How comfortable are you with your relationship with food and exercise in your life? Do you have a healthy body image? Are you experiencing good health according to your definition of "good health"? Are you comfortable with the process of aging?

PERSONAL FINANCE

How satisfied are you with both your long term and short term financial picture? How comfortable are you with yourself as a money manager? Do you have healthy views of money and abundance?

CAREER AND PROFESSION

How satisfied are you with your current choice of career? How happy are you with your current position and current employer? How well are you managing the demands of your job? (Note: If you are a stay at home mom or stay at home dad, your profession is motherhood or fatherhood — yes, it is a real job!)

HOME AND FAMILY

How satisfied are you with your family environment? Your environment includes your home environment as well as the various relationships that exist in your home. How comfortable are you with the roles you carry in the home? How well are you managing the demands of maintaining a home and family?

Inner Life

For each section of the inner life, you will have two ratings. Both ratings are on a scale of 1 to 5, 1 being low and 5 being high. The **"A" rating** is your **awareness** level, and the **"H" rating** is how well you are **honoring** this particular item in your life. Please consider these questions when deciding your rating level in each section.

ENERGY DRAINS

Awareness: How aware are you of the various things in your life that drain your emotional and physical energy? (A rating of 5 means you are very aware.)

Honoring: How well are you honoring yourself by having a plan in place to eliminate energy drains or to regularly refuel? (A rating of 5 means you have eliminated your energy drains or are regularly refueling.)

PURPOSE

Awareness: How aware are you of your life purpose – your reason for being here on Earth?

Honoring: How well are you honoring your life purpose by actually living into it?

GIFTS AND TALENTS

Awareness: How aware are you of the various gifts and talents you have been blessed with – those special qualities that make you "unique"?

Honoring: How well are you honoring yourself by actually using your gifts and talents?

DREAMS AND PASSIONS

Awareness: How aware are you of what you are passionate about and what you dream of doing or being?

Honoring: How well are you honoring yourself by engaging in your passions and working toward your dreams?

VALUES

Awareness: How aware are you of the important values you want to live your life by?

Honoring: How well are you honoring yourself by living your life in alignment with your values?

NEEDS

Awareness: How aware are you of what your personal emotional needs are? (e.g., need to be loved, need to accomplish, need to feel safe)

Honoring: How well are you honoring yourself by making sure your personal needs are getting met?

THOUGHTS AND BELIEFS

Awareness: How aware are you of the various thoughts that run through your head at any given moment? How aware are you of the beliefs that are guiding your life?

Honoring: How well are you honoring yourself by keeping your thoughts positive and your beliefs empowering?

FEELINGS

Awareness: How aware are you of what you are feeling at any given moment? (e.g., anger, sadness, guilt, etc.)

Honoring: How well are you honoring yourself by expressing your feelings and doing what you can to release negative feelings?

Interpreting Your Results

A lot of information can be gathered from this exercise. First, let's look at the overall big picture of your life. Add up all the numbers from both the outer and inner life. The maximum score is 160. With a score of 160, life is perfect and you do a darn good job knowing and honoring your true self! Since that score is a bit unrealistic, look at where you might fall.

128 and above	Life is good, and you love it!
104 – 127	Life is decent. It has its up and downs, but you're generally happy.
80 – 103	Your satisfaction with life is average. Some aspects of your life could be improved.
49 – 79	Life is just okay. It certainly is not what you want it to be.
48 and below	Your life needs some serious work, and you probably feel pretty miserable.

Now I am not a research psychologist, so don't get too hung up on the numbers. Rating numbers are very subjective. An eight for one person means something completely different for another. You know how you feel about your life. The purpose of this exercise is to help you be honest about your life, and to think of things you might not normally think of.

Another way to interpret the results of this exercise is to measure your life balance based on your ratings in the outer section of the wheel. If your rating levels are dramatically different in each of the areas, you probably feel unbalanced. Below is an example of a balanced life versus an unbalanced one.

Life Area	Balanced Life	Unbalanced Life
Personal Development	7	5
Spirituality	7	7
Fun and Enjoyment	8	3
Relationships	8	6
Health and Aging	7	3
Personal Finance	8	2
Career and Profession	7	6
Home and Family	8	8

You'll notice in the example of an unbalanced life, the ratings are all over the board. This person is happy with home and family, but is very dissatisfied with their personal finance, health, and fun and enjoyment. Large discrepancies between the different areas indicate you need to work more on balancing your life.

Last, you can use your rating levels to help you identify what areas of your life you want to work on. For instance, if you rated your awareness of energy drains in your life at a five, but your honoring rating is only a two, this gives you a clue that life could be better for you if you worked on eliminating some of your energy drains.

Now it is entirely possible that some areas of the wheel are not important to you. Some people don't have a desire to understand their life purpose. While it can certainly make life more fulfilling, it may not be something you are interested in focusing on right now. This is your life and you get to decide what you need and want to change to create a better quality of life.

Secrets to Living a Balanced Life

It is important to remember that balance is a process and is constantly changing, just as our lives are constantly changing. Balance is not some static goal that we achieve and then move on. We achieve balance in the moment, understanding that in the next moment everything may change.

Put this book down for a moment and stand on one foot for a period of three minutes or until you lose your balance. What did you notice about your body while you were trying to stay balanced? You leg and foot muscles are working to keep you still. Your might crunch your toes to try and grab onto the floor. You'll feel the muscles in your leg flex if you start to lose balance. You might even have to throw your arms out to the side, teeter from side to side, or bend forward to keep from falling. Your body was making adjustments, some small and possibly even bigger ones to keep you balanced. Maintaining life balance is handled in the same way. When you feel yourself feeling stressed and unbalanced, it's time to make an adjustment in your life. Here are 10 secrets or adjustments you can work on to maintain a balanced life.

1. *Discover your true self*

Remember our definition of balance.

> *"Balance occurs* when *who you are, what you want* to do in life,
> and *what you value* are aligned with your *thoughts,*
> *activities* and *choices."*

Who you are, what you want, and what you value require you to know yourself well. When I was 20, I began my journey in self-discovery. Like most 20 year olds, I was trying to navigate my way through life, not truly understanding who I was or what made me happy. The only beliefs I really knew about life were the ones I learned from childhood. It didn't take me long to figure out I was not well equipped to create a happy life for myself.

The process of healing and becoming aware of me started with therapy and mountains of self-help books. Also, at this time, I began an entry-level career in business. After 10 years of hard work both in my career and on myself, I felt more mature, and I was established as a manager in business.

To the outside world, I was successful. I was married and had a beautiful little boy. My career path was on the rise, and I had achieved financial independence. However, I was not happy. My marriage did not honor who I was, and neither did my career in business.

Following a painful divorce, my life direction began to change. I started to honor who I truly am. I went back to school and earned my degree in Psychology. It was a fascinating and fun experience. As a single parent, I began to envision what I truly wanted from life for my son and for myself. The most important thing to me was to do the things I loved and surround myself with people who honored my authenticity.

Getting remarried to a wonderful man, who shared my values, honored a big part of myself. However, I still felt stuck in my business career; my heart just wasn't in it. Deciding to have another baby was my ticket to freedom (I just didn't know it). I arranged a part-time work-at-home option with my employer so I could be close to my two boys.

After two years working from home, a Divine Power stepped in. I was laid off from my work-at-home position and offered a full-time position back in the office. I followed my heart and my Creator's plan for me. I declined the position and began my search for the career that fit my true being. Once again, I was hit over the head when someone very dear to me suggested I would make a great life coach.

"Coaching?" I said. "What is that?" As I began to research the field, an overwhelming passion, connection, and excitement took over me. I enrolled in coaching school and began an even bigger process of understanding and honoring my true self. My first required exercise for my coaching certification was to complete a life review that consisted of 18 pages of questions about me and my life.

The list of questions continued on for what seemed like forever. Does everyone need to go through this same process for understanding who they are? I don't think so, but discovering our true self does require us to do some honest soul searching. Most of us learn more about ourselves from the various life experiences we go through. Each experience in our life teaches us more about who we are and who we are not. Self discovery is a practice that leads to helping each of us make better decisions about our life and our time.

Below is an exercise that will help you identify your most important values. Your values make up the foundation of who you are as an individual. When you align your life with your values, happiness, balance and fulfillment is the result.

Values Exercise

Complete this exercise alone. If you have a spouse, ask him or her to do this exercise as well. Circle all the values from this list that are important to you. From the list of circled values, pick out your top five and write them on the lines provided. Compare your list to your spouse's list. How might they be the same or different? How does your life currently reflect these values? Where might your life be conflicting with these values?

Accomplishment	Family	Kindness	Romance
Abundance	Fidelity	Leadership	Security
Achievement	Flexibility	Love	Self-care
Adventure	Freedom	Loyalty	Self-discipline
Beauty	Friendship	Mercy	Self-expression
Clarity	Fulfillment	Moderation	Self-mastery
Commitment	Fun	Nature	Self-realization
Communication	Gratitude	Openness	Sensitivity
Community	Hard Work	Orderliness	Service
Connecting to Others	Holistic Living	Partnership	Spirituality
Courage	Honesty	Peace	Trust
Creativity	Humor	Personal Growth	Uniqueness
Dependability	Integrity	Physical Appearance	Unselfishness
Emotional Health	Intimacy	Privacy	Vitality
Environment	Family	Professionalism	
Excellence	Joy	Respect	

List your top 5 values:

1. _____

2. _____

3. _____

4. _____

5. _____

2. Know what you want

What do you want for your life, and how do you see yourself? What are the desires of your heart? Do you have a crystal clear vision, and the belief it takes to realize your goals?

Are you setting goals in your life and taking steps to achieve your goals? Living a balanced life may require you to make changes in your life. If you are not satisfied with a particular area of your life, it means your choices and activities do not support what's important to you. It's hard to feel balanced when you're not living your life in integrity with who you are. When I first started my coach training and was asked to rate my current level of satisfaction in the area of Fun and Enjoyment, I gave myself a rating of 3. I was embarrassed to see how little effort I was making to experience fun in my life. As a result of being more proactive and setting goals in the area of fun and enjoyment, I am pleased to say my rating has significantly increased.

Go back to your wheel of life and reflect on it for a moment. Which area stands out for you as needing attention?

_____

What changes need to take place to increase your satisfaction in this area? Write down 2 changes you would like to make.

1._____

2._____

What goals do you need to set to achieve these changes? For instance, if you want to increase your satisfaction with your personal finances, one change you might want to make is to make more money. Goals that would support this change would be looking for a higher paying job, applying for a promotion, or getting a better education.

Write your goals down on a piece of paper and keep them in a place where you will look at them often. I keep two goal lists on the wall in front of my desk. One list is the personal goals I am working on for the year, and the other is a list of my business goals. Everything I do needs to support the attainment of my goals.

3. Analyze where you spend your time

Living a life of balance requires us to spend our time in the areas that are most important to us. Not everyone places equal value on each area of the wheel. Some people value health over relationships, while others value family over spirituality. You do not need to spend equal time in each area of your life to live a balanced life. The level of importance and the amount of time you spend need to be closely related. Analyze your time by completing this next exercise.

Level of Importance

5 – Very Important

3 – Moderately Important

1 – Not Important

Amount of Time

5 – Spend a Great Amount of Time

3 – Spend a Moderate Amount of Time

1 – Spend Little Amount of Time

Area of Life Wheel	Level of Importance	Amount of Time
Personal Development		
Spirituality		
Fun and Enjoyment		
Relationships		
Health and Aging		
Personal Finance		
Career and Profession		
Home and Family		

Where are your discrepancies between your level of importance and the amount of time you spend nurturing this area? For instance, if personal development is very important to you, and you spend very little time developing yourself, you are going to feel unhappy. If spirituality is not important to you and you spend little to no time engaging in spiritual practice, then you are living in integrity with what you want. If all of these eight areas are important to you, then you will need to divide your time fairly equally between the different areas.

4. *Prioritize daily*

Maintaining balance means we ask ourselves daily what we want to focus on. We pay attention to what we need to feel balanced. Some days it might mean we need to focus on getting our home organized. Other days we may have a need to take care of our body and relax. Look for signs of stress in your life and ask yourself what you need.

Make a list of tasks you would like to accomplish in a given day. Stick to three or four of your most important tasks – the tasks that will bring about peace and harmony in your life. Build in a constant awareness of all the areas of your life that need attention and make daily adjustments according to your need for balance.

Learn to say NO to protect what's most important to you. If you need one or two hours to catch up on laundry or take a nap and read a good book, then protect that time. Do not let anything or anyone else monopolize that time.

5. *Simplify your life*

The more activities and the more stuff you have to manage, the more unbalanced your life will feel. Too much of anything can lead to stress, so learn to live with the basics. When my friend's husband was a bachelor, instead of doing laundry, he would just buy more clothes. Now he has more clothes than his closets and drawers can handle. Fewer clothes make laundry much easier. Clean-up is much faster with only a modest amount of toys. A lot of stuff complicates your life unnecessarily.

Avoid over-committing. There is nothing worse than feeling like you are constantly on the go, rushing from one activity to the next. Many moms tell me they can't fit one more thing into their life – clearly a sign of being over-scheduled. Do you have a significant amount of down time in your life? Are there weekends when nothing is scheduled and you just spend time at home doing whatever you want? By simplifying your life, you can avoid the frenzied state that so many moms live in.

6. *Recognize and manage your internal conflicts*

Our internal balance is disturbed when we are in conflict with ourselves. Just this morning my client Maggie called me wrestling with internal guilt and shame she felt from making the same mistake yet again. Every Monday morning she goes to exercise class while her husband gets the children ready. He is supposed to drop off the little girls at the gym so they can play while mommy exercises. However, this morning, Maggie took the minivan and the car seats her husband needed to transport her girls. This wasn't the first time she made this mistake so she was being particularly hard on herself. There was a part of her that understood that the mistake is normal and human and another part of her that wanted to believe she was not a dependable mother. This internal conflict Maggie was experiencing was disrupting her state of balance.

Many moms struggle with feeling internal peace. They feel guilty if they make mistakes. They worry about whether or not they are raising their children "correctly." Moms wrestle with tasks they have to do or feel they should do when they don't want to do them. They feel guilty engaging in self-care activities. Some moms are plagued with self-doubt and look for external sources to validate them, and feel frustrated when the affirmation is absent.

We must recognize and manage our internal conflicts so we can experience peace of mind. Tell the truth about who you really are and don't be afraid to be different than the norm. Keep an open mind to different perspectives, but choose which perspectives feel right to you. Internal conflict occurs when we aren't clear about who we are or when we are not living life according to our core beliefs. So be crystal clear about what you believe and honor your beliefs.

7. *Live in the moment*

I love what Eckhart Tolle has to say about living in the moment, or the NOW as he calls it. He says: "What you think of the past is a memory trace of a former NOW. When you remember the past, you reactivate a memory trace — and you do so now. The future is an imagined NOW, a projection of the mind.

When the future comes, it comes as the NOW. When you think about the future, you do it now. Past and future obviously have no reality of their own." In other words, the past is over and the future has yet to come, so enjoy the present moment.

Worrying about the future and dredging up the past for the purpose of reliving pain will block your energy. To stay balanced, you need to keep the energy flowing in your body. Practice experiencing the moment and everything that it entails. Allow yourself to feel whatever feelings come up for you. If you feel angry, feel the anger. If joy is your primary emotion, embrace it wholeheartedly. Do not stuff your feelings or try to make negative feelings go away. Just be in the moment and you will naturally move through the feelings. Balance requires flexibility and the ability to roll with whatever life hands us. Fighting with life will disrupt the flow.

8. *Make choices that move you toward balance*

For every YES you say in life, you are saying NO to something else. If you say yes to sleep, you may be saying no to working out or taking quiet time alone. If you say no to cleaning, you might be saying yes to spending time with the children.

Say yes to the tasks, activities, or situations that make you feel more alive and no to the ones that drain you. When my teenager wants to engage me in an argument or debate, I say no because I know it will drain my emotional energy. I walk away to protect the balance I want to experience in my life. When I am feeling tired and worn out, I say no to more work and yes to a fun or relaxing activity.

Pay attention to the choices you make and how they affect all areas of your life. You might choose to take on a promotion at work, but do it only after you've assessed whether or not it will affect the balance in your life. Will you be required to work longer hours or travel away from home several times per month? How will that affect your family and your health? Is the extra money worth the sacrifices you might have to make? The increase in finances, however, may allow you to take more vacations. Make decisions in your life by weighing the effects these choices have on your entire life.

To maintain balance, what is one thing you want to say YES to?

What is one thing you need to say NO to?

_____

9. *You must have love in your life*

Balance is next to impossible without love. Whether you love yourself, love other people, love your community, love your life or love the Universe, you must experience love in your life. Love is the opposite of hate, and underneath the hate is fear. Love balances every negative emotion that we feel — anger, guilt, sadness, fear, etc.

Mary J. Blige, singer and songwriter, wrote a song called "What Love Is." In her song she talks about love being joy and pain, sunshine and rain, an excuse for dying, and a reason to live. In these examples of opposites, you can't have one without the other. Because life is full of ups and downs, you must have love to maintain that balance.

10. *Resources and support system*

To maintain balance in your life, often we need additional resources and a strong support system. Resources include things like money, facilities, out of the box thinking, time, books, and people. Your support system includes all the people in your life plus the ones you haven't met yet. Did you hear that? All the people you haven't met yet are part of your support system. That means you may need to reach out and meet new people if you need additional support.

We are not expected to go through life alone. Sometimes we need help. It takes money to survive and pay for the activities that are important to us. Sometimes we can use a brainstorming partner to see other possibilities in our life. Time is always a precious commodity that if managed wisely, can greatly meet our need for balance. Books help us learn about new ways to grow. And people, of course, are our number one resource for helping us create the life we want to live. People support us, love us, mentor us and teach us.

Balance is a fluid state — it changes from day to day. So assess balance in your life over a period of time. One or two chaotic days does not mean you are living out of balance, but if chaos is the norm for you, you could be yearning for some life balance. Don't make balance a goal. Instead, look at whether you are moving toward or away from balance in your life.

In the remainder of this book, you will notice the chapters are divided by the eight areas of the life wheel. It is not necessary to read this book from beginning to end; rather it is designed for you to skip around, depending on your needs. You can focus on a section at a time or you can choose a topic that addresses your concerns in the moment. Each chapter will help you grow in a different way and every chapter has a take action assignment you can use to reinforce what you've learned and further your growth. To get the most out of this book, please don't skip the assignments. You will learn a lot about yourself from these exercises.

Enjoy your journey!

PERSONAL DEVELOPMENT

CHAPTER 2
✳
Vision and Belief Are Like Cookies and (Chocolate) Milk

"Keep your dreams alive. Understand to achieve anything requires faith and belief in yourself, vision, hard work, determination, and dedication. Remember all things are possible for those who believe." —Gail Devers

✳

Maybe you would disagree, but to me, cookies and milk is a match made in heaven. They just go together. Can you enjoy cookies without milk? Sure, as long as they are Oreos or homemade chocolate chip cookies. Is a glass of milk refreshing by itself? Personally, I can't drink plain white milk, so it must be chocolate milk. Cookies and milk are good by themselves, but put them together, and you have a perfect recipe for a satisfying dessert or snack. A little sugar, a little chocolate, some protein, and added calcium for our bones. Can't beat it!

Vision and belief is another perfect match in life. Without a vision, you don't know where you are going. Even if you believe in yourself, you will still wander around with no direction. Likewise, if you have a vision, but don't believe you can get there, you won't move very far. You need both vision and belief.

What is your vision? Vision is your ability to clearly see what you want in your life. Getting clear happens when we focus on what is important to us, and tap into who we are, with all our dreams and passions. Some of us have a business vision. Others have a vision of how they want their marriage or family to look. Maybe you have a plan for what you want to accomplish in the next day, week, or month. Our vision can be a short term or long term picture, or both.

For example, as a parent, I have a vision of who I want my child to be when he goes off to college in another two years. I picture him being responsible with his academics, able to take care of himself, and having the skills he needs to function in an adult world, without my supervision. Without this vision, I cannot see what I need to do as a parent to prepare him for the future. Does he know how to wash and iron his clothes? Can he fix himself a nutritious meal? Are his study habits and choices going to ensure him reasonable success in college? If not, I have some work to do. With a vision, you can see where you are today compared to where you want to be in the future. A vision highlights the gaps, and helps you set forward-moving goals.

Belief is what gives you the confidence that you can realize your vision. Do you believe in yourself and have faith that you can accomplish whatever you set your mind to? If not, you will get stuck or sabotage your success. Belief requires us to take an honest look at our strengths, and own them. It is not going to be helpful to focus on what we believe we lack. The world will deliver to you exactly what you believe you deserve. If you believe you deserve to be paid $50,000 for your skills and expertise, and you act as if you truly believe it, someone will pay you $50,000.

My son is a naturally talented baseball player. He has speed, the ability to hit on both sides of the plate, and his coach says he has a "cannon" at the end of his arm. His peers on the football team recently commented, "You know Kai is a really good baseball player, but he needs to have more confidence in himself." People will pick up on a lack of belief — we act different when we feel insecure, and our energy reflects that. I always tell my son, "You have to visualize walking up to the plate, see the ball thrown from the pitcher's hand, and picture yourself crushing the ball into a gap in the outfield. You have to believe, in the deepest part of your soul, that you can hit the ball."

Creating Your Vision – First Things First

Before you begin working on your vision, it is important that you are in a completely relaxed state. Do whatever you need to do to set aside distractions. Go to a place where you can be quiet and reflective. It's not necessary to complete your vision in one sitting. Take your time and do your best to think deeply about what you truly want. The vision process below will guide you through everything you need to think about when creating your vision. You will need paper and a pen or pencil for this exercise.

As you think about your answers to these questions, beware of the tendency to censor your thoughts. It is completely normal to interrupt yourself with negative thoughts such as these:

- What I want is impossible.
- I can't have what I want.
- It doesn't matter what I want.
- I can't create the kind of life I want.
- I don't know what I want.
- I don't know how to create what I want.
- I'm afraid I can't make these changes.

Do your best to free your mind of these defeating thoughts and see yourself as capable of creating and having whatever you want. Pretend there are no obstacles in your way.

The Visioning Exercise

For this exercise, I want you to imagine that you are looking at your life and you have achieved the magnificent life you want. Close your eyes and focus hard on your vision – making it present day reality. Describe on paper the experience you have imagined, using the present tense, as if it is happening right now. Use statements such as "I am", "I have" and "I feel" to answer these questions.

- What does your life look like?
- How does your life feel to you?
- What words or images would you use to describe your life?

You are now going to deepen and expand your vision. For this next set of questions, I want you to assume you are now living an extraordinary life. You have achieved everything you could ever hope. Imagine that other people are interested in what you have to say about your extraordinary life. Using present tense language, answer the following questions in as much detail as you can.

Home:
Where do you live?
What does your home look like?
How do you live?
How are chores being handled at home?

Example: I live in Florida in a 3 bedroom ranch home. My home is clean and organized to fit our lifestyle, etc.

Self-Image:
What kind of Mom (Dad) are you?
What kind of wife (husband) are you?
What personal qualities do you possess?
How do you feel about yourself?

Tangibles:
What material things do you own?
What material things do your children have?

Health:
What is your current state of health?
What is your desire for fitness and athletics in your life?
What is your body image?

Relationships (answer the questions that are relevant to your life):
What does your marital relationship look like?
What are the siblings relationships like?
Describe your relationship with each of your children.
Describe your spouse's relationship with each of the children.
What types of friendships do you and your children have?
Describe your extended family relationships.
What is your relationship with yourself like?

Work:
How are you making money?
Do you work?
If so, what is your ideal profession?
At what type of company do you work?
If you are a stay-at-home mom, what do you see as your work?

Fun and Enjoyment:
What ways do you have fun?
What pursuits or hobbies are you involved in?
How do you create the time for fun and enjoyment?
What do you do with your spouse to have fun?
How do you have fun with your children?
How often do you vacation?

Finances:
What is the total household income?

How much money is being saved for the future?
How is your money invested?
Who takes care of the finances in the home?
How do you resolve financial matters in the home?

Values and Beliefs:
What are your core values?
What are your beliefs about your life purpose?
How are your values and beliefs being expressed in your life?

Community:
How involved are you in the community?
What community activities do you participate in?

Spirituality:
What are your spiritual beliefs?
How are your spiritual beliefs being expressed?

Other:
What else, in any area of your life, would you like to create?

Clarifying and Expanding Your Vision

Now go back and reread the vision you created. Think about what aspects of that vision are closest to your deepest desires. Consider each section of your vision. Ask yourself these two questions to dig deeper, clarify what you think, and eliminate things you truly don't want or value.

• **If you could have this vision now, would you take it?**
• **If you had it, what would it bring you?**

Highlight the areas that are very important to you, and revise your vision if necessary.

Deepening Your Belief in Achieving Your Vision

If you truly want to realize your vision, you must believe you can. As many times as you can (daily, weekly or at a minimum, monthly), read your vision out loud with as much passion and emotion as you can muster. Spend time imagining yourself living the magnificent life you have outlined for yourself. When you feel comfortable, share your vision with as many people as you can trust to hear it without judgment. Use your vision to set goals in your life and develop an action plan for achieving your goals. Take steps on a regular basis to help you move toward your goals. As you begin to realize your dreams by achieving some of your goals, your belief will deepen. This deeper belief will give you the forward momentum you need to stay focused on your vision. As you go through your life, your feelings and your vision may change. Revise your vision and change your goals as needed, but don't ever stop believing that you can have the extraordinary life you want.

TAKE ACTION ASSIGNMENT

Do everything that is outlined in this chapter. Create your vision. Read your vision regularly with emotion and passion. Set goals to realize your vision. Believe, without a doubt, you can achieve your dreams!

CHAPTER 3
✳
There is Fulfillment in Personal Growth

"Get over the idea that only children should spend their time in study. Be a student so long as you still have something to learn, and this will mean all your life." —Henry L. Doherty

✳

I'll never forget this one particular day during my coach training. The whole class was split up into small groups of seven, and we were practicing the coach skills that had been introduced to us earlier. Each of us took turns being the coach and the client. When it was my turn to coach, I started out by asking my client empowering questions about her situation. Every question I asked turned up a dead end — in other words, I was not able to move her toward any kind of resolution. My frustration was mounting because I was struggling with the new skills I was trying to learn. When the mentor coach said "Time's up!" I burst into tears. I remember feeling like such a failure because I couldn't get anywhere with my client. I wanted so badly to succeed that I forgot that I was learning something new, and growth takes time. The same skills that were so difficult for me during my training are second nature to me today. The more I practiced the skills, the more confident I was in my ability to be a good coach.

Learning new skills or developing existing ones is a great way to boost your self-confidence. Rather than staying stuck in the same place, you are growing and becoming better at skills that are important to you. As you learn and grow into your full potential, your self-esteem increases. You feel good about yourself and you will find more fulfillment in what you do.

Suzanne came to me feeling kind of stuck in the humdrum of everyday life. She was having difficulty creating time to improve skills that were important to her. While her children were a priority for her, she still had a strong desire to be growing as a woman. Suzanne had a dream to write children's books and she wanted to learn how to operate her digital camera better. The number of skills one can work on is endless. Here is a small list to help you begin brainstorming ways in which you might want to grow.

Character Skills:	patience, courage, discipline, consistency
Relationship Skills:	listening, showing affection, communication
Artistic Skills:	writing, drawing, painting, singing
Athletic Skills:	running, tennis, golf, volleyball
Job Skills:	creating presentations, new computer skills, management
Hobby Skills:	scrap booking, photography, ceramics
Home Skills:	cooking, building things, gardening, decorating
Professional Skills:	teaching, coaching, nursing, marketing
Technical Skills:	electrical, computer design, drafting, computer programming
Money Skills:	budgeting, investing, saving, accounting
Spiritual Skills:	mercy, grace, forgiveness, love

After helping Suzanne start developing new skills and interests, she expressed to me how that changed her life. She told me how taking time to grow helped her go through her whole day with a smile. She even found joy in everything she did, including activities that earlier she viewed as boring and draining.

There are a number of sources for developing the skills you want:

EDUCATION

Your educational system provides excellent opportunities to learn new skills. Whether it is through a university, community college, or technical school, the number of classes available continues to grow. A good community college not only offers classes needed for a specific degree program, but they also offer many continuing education classes like Voice, Organization, Personal Finance and Investing. It's never too late to go back to school, even if you only take one class. One of my coaching peers recently took an online fiction writing class. She worked at her own pace to complete the course. More and more universities and colleges are recognizing the need for convenience and flexibility. Even busy moms can invest in their growth, without ever leaving their home.

SELF-HELP

Some people prefer to teach themselves. Go into any bookstore and you'll see the number of "how to" books has exploded. There is not a shortage of self-help books, evident in the number of books in the "For Dummies" series. I was curious so I checked on Amazon.com to see what topics were available in this series. Here are just a few of the titles I found.

Personal Finance for Dummies
Buzz Marketing with Blogs for Dummies
The Civil War for Dummies
Sex for Dummies
Job Interviews for Dummies
Getting Your Book Published for Dummies
Digital Photography for Dummies
Stress Management for Dummies
Home Based Business for Dummies
The Bible for Dummies
Flipping Houses for Dummies

"Flipping Houses for Dummies"? What the heck is that? Is this a book that teaches you how to flip your house over? You get my point. You can probably find a book on just about anything. If you are self-disciplined and enjoy independent learning, this is the way to go for you. Self-help materials are available in book format, electronically in the form of e-Books or eCourses, audio programs and even educational videos.

I have taught myself a number of new skills needed for growing my business. Some of the courses and e-Books I have purchased pertain to creating a blog, building my coaching practice, writing an e-Book, developing an internet sales letter, and increasing my newsletter subscriber list. I make a point to invest in my education and personal growth on a regular basis.

MENTORS

A mentor is an excellent source for learning. It's always nice to receive first hand experience from someone who has "been there and done that." A mentor has already encountered the obstacles and found ways to overcome them. He or she probably knows what works and what doesn't. A mentor can guide you and give you real world experience.

I once worked with a client who wanted to start her own business. She really looked up to me and wanted to learn all she could from someone who had already started her own business. She would ask me a lot of questions and listen to my experiential advice.

Where do you find a mentor? Mentors are everywhere: in business, in the education field, in church, scattered all around the world. Through networking with different people and spending time around people who know what you want to learn, you will find a mentor. Barbara Stanney wrote a book called *Secrets of Six Figure Women*. At the time, she was trying to build her own writing business, and she was curious about how other women built their earnings to six figures and more. By interviewing many women that achieved this level of income, she was receiving mentoring about how to do something she was interested in doing. Mentoring does require time and energy, so make sure you ask someone first before you assign them the task of mentoring you.

PRACTICE

Another tried and true way to develop skills is through practice. If you want to get better at playing a musical instrument, you must practice. Lately, my husband and I have been trying to learn a new way of communicating with each other. The more we practice the methods we've been taught, the smoother our communications. Before we know it, this style will become natural for us and we will both be better communicators. Have patience when you're learning a new skill. It takes time and perseverance.

It doesn't matter if you choose personal, spiritual, or professional skills to learn; the idea is that you keep growing. By making a commitment to continually grow, your life will be more interesting and rewarding. Not only will personal growth increase your confidence as a woman, it will give you personal fulfillment as well. When we remain stuck in the same place, we are not using the resources that are available to us in this world. There is so much to learn; so many exciting ways we can live more fully into our best selves. Be your best and live your best life!

TAKE ACTION ASSIGNMENT

Review the various categories of skills listed in this chapter. Pick one new skill you would like to learn, and one skill you need to develop. Decide which way of learning works best for you, and commit to working on these two skills over the next six months. When you feel confident about these skills, pick two new ones. Repeat this process until you have learned everything you need or want to learn. You'll probably be learning for a lifetime.

CHAPTER 4

✳

Face and Embrace Change

"The doors we open and close each day decide the lives we live."
—Flora Whittemore

✳

David Zinn, a wise man I know, once said, "If we don't change, we aren't growing, and if we aren't growing, we are dying." Isn't that so true? Some change is welcomed into your life: a new hairstyle, a promotion you've been wanting, or a remodeled kitchen. Sometimes change is handed to you without your consent...a layoff, a divorce, or even the death of a loved one. And there's always self-created change that you still resist...losing weight, expressing your feelings appropriately or pursuing your dream job. The world and everything in it is constantly changing.

So many of us focus on changing other people around us, even though we know deep down this doesn't work. Or we stay stuck in a rut, complaining about how miserable life is to us. In fact, there is so much resistance to change that a book was written called *Why Should I Be the First to Change?* There are many answers to this question. First, you will be happier if you are continually growing and learning. Second, you are the only person that is responsible for changing you. Third, you're wasting your valuable time and energy waiting for others to change. When you change, people will follow. Lastly, by living your life to the fullest, you contribute to making the world a better place to live for yourself and others.

Then why is change so hard? And how can you learn to face change head on and embrace it wholeheartedly? Let's examine five key reasons we resist change and explore five new ways to learn to embrace change. By choosing to modify our perspective or outlook on change, change can become our friend and not our enemy.

Fear vs. Courage

One of the main reasons we resist change is fear. Sometimes it can be scary to change. The list of fears is endless: fear of failure or success, fear of being alone, fear of making mistakes, fear of rejection and certainly, fear of the unknown. It is normal to feel fear, but yet it is so crippling. Having courage does not mean we don't feel fear. It means we push through the fear and do it anyway. Ask any public speaker, extreme sports enthusiast or successful business entrepreneur. You have to take risks if you want to grow and feel fulfilled in life.

Jennifer was a single mom of two children who, for years, was a hair stylist. Reaching a point in her life when she wanted to make a career change, she had to make some difficult phone calls. Many of her clients had come to rely on her, but she didn't want to do their hair anymore. Jennifer was terrified of calling her clients to let them know she was changing careers. She imagined them being angry with her, or worse, not wanting to let her go. She felt trapped in her career because her time was being monopolized by hair clients. As one of her assignments, I asked Jennifer to clear her weekend by canceling all her hair appointments. She was to let each of her clients know that she was no longer going to be able to do their hair because she was moving on to something else. This seemingly simple task was not carried out because Jennifer was paralyzed by fear. So we made the phone calls together. After hanging up from her last client, I asked her how she felt. She was so relieved, but yet surprised that her clients did not react at all the way she had imagined they would. The fear Jennifer was experiencing was all in her mind.

When faced with fear, take baby steps. Oftentimes, we discover the change was not as difficult as we had imagined it to be. Each time we confront our apprehension and act courageously, we gain more power over our fear.

Status Quo vs. Opportunities

When I asked Becky what stopped her from leaving a miserable marriage, she told me it was comfortable. The marriage itself was not comfortable, but the life she lived was familiar, bringing her a sense of security. Let's face it. Humans are creatures of habit. Some people float through life behaving in the same way every day. Change never even occurs to them. The same argument occurs over and over, and their reactions are never any different. Or they stay in the same unsatisfying job year after year and become best friends with depression.

What about the opportunities that are being missed? There is a lot for people to experience in this world if they only open their eyes to change. Maybe a healthier friend or a dream career awaits them. Whenever my clients tell me how things are going to be, I always ask them "what if" you are wrong and "this" happens instead. It's important to explore what could be gained from change. Perhaps you don't see the golden opportunity ahead of you, but at the very least, by resisting change, you are missing the opportunity to learn what life has to teach. I am a firm believer that when you close the door, a new and better door opens.

Negative Thinking vs. Positive Thinking

Imagine your best friend invites you to join her for the local writer's club meeting. She knows you secretly wish you could write a book. You reply, "I can't go to a writer's club. I don't write well enough for that. People will judge me because I'm not a writer." She tries again the next three months, only to listen to your endless self-defeating remarks. Eventually she stops asking and so you never try your hand at writing. You never write a book and this just proves that you are not a writer. The self-fulfilling prophecy was manifested – you created exactly what you thought.

Let's roll the tape back. What if your response was, "I would love to go. I've always wanted to try and write. This will be a great experience for me." You and your friend go every month and at the end of the year, you publish your first book. Your brain will agree with anything you tell it. If you feed your brain negative thoughts, you will create negativity. Giving your brain affirmative food for thought will create the positive change you desire. A Native American elder once described his own inner struggles in this manner. "Inside of me there are two dogs. One of the dogs is mean and evil. The other dog is good. The mean dog fights the good dog all the time." When asked which dog wins he reflected for a moment and replied, "The one I feed the most."

Doing It Alone vs. Getting Support

Some change is so challenging or overwhelming that even the thought of trying is debilitating. When I think of parents who lose a child or the woman who needs to lose 150 pounds, my heart goes out to them. One can only imagine the monumental adjustment that lies ahead. Even smaller changes, like transitioning through a divorce or a job loss, can be difficult when you feel you are alone through the process.

Change requires supportive people. You need people who believe in you and who will encourage you on your journey. Sometimes you need someone to hold you accountable for what you say you're going to do. You need friends and family members who won't let you give up. You need love and understanding when you are struggling. Surround yourself with loving and helpful people, and call on a Source greater than yourself. Some changes are so difficult, but all things are possible with Divine intervention.

Control vs. Letting Go

It is human nature to control – our emotions, other people, our money, our life. However, much of change, which occurs in life, is uncontrollable. Our world is changing at an extremely fast pace, leaving us spinning our wheels as we attempt to adapt. Whether it's a natural disaster like Hurricane Katrina, a giant merger, or skyrocketing gas prices, it's all happening to us. Stress and resistance is the natural reaction to change.

If we can learn to let go and accept what we cannot control, life is smoother and change can be embraced. We don't know what greater plan is at work. When I first started my business, I worked extremely hard to control my success. As my fear of failure escalated, I fought harder and a vicious cycle began. Just when I had decided to give up (for the day or week), a tiny door opened. It didn't take long for me to figure out that I am not in charge here. God had a different plan for me and my timing was certainly not His. When I learned to let go and put my faith in God, opportunities for change and growth came out of nowhere. He blessed me in ways I would never have imagined.

One thing is certain. Change stops for no one. We can choose to resist and make life much harder, or we can face and embrace change, resulting in a life that cultivates and strengthens our character.

TAKE ACTION ASSIGNMENT

What change are you resisting in your life right now? What are your fears around this change? Name 5 benefits of making this change. What negative thoughts need to be eliminated to support this change? And who can support you through this change? Take two baby steps this week to embrace this change.

CHAPTER 5

✵

Truth Telling – The Pathway to a Life of Integrity

"One isn't necessarily born with courage, but one is born with potential. Without courage, we cannot practice any other virtue with consistency. We can't be kind, true, merciful, generous, or honest." —Maya Angelou

✵

At face value, it may seem easy to tell the truth. However, what if telling the truth hurts another person? Or maybe you're not sure what the truth is? Perhaps you're trying to ignore the truth because it means you might have to make some changes. Truth telling can be hard. It makes us feel vulnerable. However, by telling the truth, you live a life of the highest integrity. Living a life of integrity helps you love yourself and other people. Although I think a life of integrity is the #1 reason to tell the truth, here are 10 other reasons truth telling is beneficial:

1. Telling the truth helps us feel good about ourselves. We don't have to live with a guilty conscience.

2. Telling the truth puts us on the road to acceptance – acceptance of ourselves and others.

3. Telling the truth helps us get our needs met.

4. Telling the truth creates greater intimacy and lets others know who we are.

5. Telling the truth helps us know ourselves better.

6. Telling the truth signals necessary change.

7. Telling the truth gives you and others freedom to make the right choices.

8. Telling the truth makes you more trustworthy.

9. Telling the truth helps others grow.

10. Telling the truth is pleasing to God.

The Essential Ingredients for Telling the Truth

· First, it takes a very *strong commitment* to make integrity and honesty one of your top values. Without a devoted attitude, you will have a tendency to slip back into hiding the truth.

· Second, you need to surround yourself with *people who can hear the truth* without negative repercussions. Having non-judgmental friends and family members is crucial. You also need people who will help draw the truth out — people who are not afraid to ask the tough questions.

· Third, it takes *courage* to tell the truth. You might be afraid of how people will respond or what they will think. Telling the truth may mean you have to make some tough decisions that cause you pain initially.

· Fourth, you need to know how to deliver the truth tactfully. Even though the truth may hurt your loves ones at times, if you present the truth with *love*, it is much easier to hear. Telling the truth must come from your heart. There should be no traces of a vindictive attitude when telling people the truth.

· Lastly, telling the truth takes *practice*. You must be willing to keep trying until it gets easier. Practice different ways of telling the truth until you find it is comfortable for you.

Areas to Practice Truth Telling

What do you tell the truth about? *Tell the truth about who you are and what works for you.* Years ago, when I worked in the business world, I was a manager over six women. For the most part, everyone worked well together, but there were a couple of women who were very difficult to please. They had a tendency to carry around a negative attitude, which in a small office can be quite infectious. I was the type of person who took my job seriously and I worked hard to make sure everyone was treated fairly. It bothered me that these women were never happy. It was a constant struggle to keep the morale in the office positive.

I had been a manager for years, and for many of those years, I was miserable. Because I was a people pleaser by nature, my personality was not cut out for management. So I went to the owners of the company and I spoke the truth about who I was. I told them that management did not fit for me. I did not like what came with the territory of being a manager. I told them I was not happy and asked to resign from the position. The owners of the company thought I was a great manager, but I knew the truth. I was fighting an internal battle that I no longer wished to fight. Telling the truth freed me from that internal conflict.

Tell the truth about what you are feeling. So often, we try and hide our negative feelings. Maybe you were taught it's wrong to feel and express anger. Or perhaps you were made to feel weak if you expressed sadness through tears. There is only one way to experience freedom from your emotions – allow yourself to feel them. Your feelings tell you a lot about yourself.

- If you're feeling angry, it's a signal that something is wrong. Someone has stepped over your boundaries or maybe there is an issue in your life that remains unresolved. Perhaps you need to forgive.

- Sadness is an indication that you are disappointed about something or perhaps you are grieving the loss of something or someone important to you.

- Jealousy tells you that you want something you currently don't have.

- Guilt is a sign that you have behaved in a way you disagree with or you are still living by rules that you don't believe in.

- Whatever you are feeling, tell the truth so you can release the hold of negative emotions.

Tell the truth about what you like and dislike. If someone asks you what you think of something, tell the truth, even if you don't like it. How will people come to trust you if you don't communicate with honesty? There are always tactful ways to speak the truth.

My husband asks me all the time what I think of his hair or his choice of clothing. If he's having a good hair day, I tell him. When he's having a bad hair day, I tactfully tell him his hair is sticking up in the back or I help him make his hair look better.

Be honest with yourself about what you like and dislike. You will not get your needs met if you don't tell the truth. I don't care for that restaurant. Would you mind if we changed the radio station? I don't feel comfortable with that solution. These are all ways in which you can communicate your likes and dislikes.

When my younger son was two, he had a brilliant way of expressing his truth. Whenever we made a suggestion that he disapproved, he would say, "I don't like that good idea." We can learn from children about speaking our truth.

Tell the truth about your strengths and weaknesses. We all have our positive and negative qualities. Both should be out in the open. It does us no good to deny our strengths or weaknesses. They are part of who we are. Your strengths tell you and others where you excel and what gifts you have to offer the world. Your weaknesses tell you and others where you need work or help from other people. You cannot change what you don't acknowledge. To be at your best, you need to capitalize on your strengths and compensate for your weaknesses.

For instance, maintaining structure and consistency in the home is one of my struggles. At a time when my younger son was attending physical therapy for a broken leg, I was responsible for making sure he did his exercises at home three times per week. I would start off every week with great intentions to initiate and supervise his exercises. And at the end of every week, I realized we had only done his exercises once. After several weeks of the repeated pattern, I decided to transfer the responsibility to my husband. He loves structure! I could now focus my energies where I excelled. Had I not told the truth about my aversion to structure, the cycle would never have been broken.

When you begin telling the truth in every area of your life, you create a life that is fully aligned with your truest self. As Brian Tracy says, "When your inner and outer life are in complete alignment (only achieved through truth telling), you feel terrific about yourself. You enjoy high self-esteem and your self confidence soars." So there is one more good reason to start telling the truth.

TAKE ACTION ASSIGNMENT

Name one area of your life in which you are not telling the complete truth. Start by expressing your truth in private by acknowledging it in your thoughts or writing in a journal. Take your truth one step further and share it with a trusted friend, family member or professional. Breathe while you listen to their reaction. Congratulate yourself for telling the truth.

CHAPTER 6

✳

The Transitional Roller Coaster

"Disenchantment, whether it is a minor disappointment or a major shock,
is the signal that things are moving into transition in our lives."
—William Bridges

✳

Everywhere I turn, moms are in transition. Transitions are all around us, some of which are more recognizable than others. Here are some typical transitions or changes moms can experience. Are any of these recognizable to you?

· Learning to be a single mommy and divorcee
· Navigating through menopause
· Developing a new business vision
· Starting a new job or re-entering the workforce
· Leaving the workforce to be a stay-at-home mom
· A child entering a new developmental phase (e.g., the terrible twos or the teenage years)
· Getting remarried
· Finding out that another child is on the way (planned or unplanned)
· Changing preschools or daycare providers
· Contemplating or making a career change
· Moving into different living arrangements (a new home in the same city or a different state or country)
· Entering a new phase of marriage
· Going back to school
· Changing churches
· Reinventing yourself

Sometimes we ease into a transition, but other times we're thrown in, leaving us struggling to find the life preserver. Some transitions are short, while others make us wonder if the end will ever come. Transitions can be unwelcome and unexpected; transitions can also be a planned breath of fresh air. No matter how we get into a transitional period of our lives, here are some tips to help us navigate our way through transitions, and make change a friend instead of an enemy.

Ride the Wave

A transition is like a roller coaster, with its ups and downs. Get your balance and integrate the changes into your daily life. Take it slow so you don't fall down and overwhelm yourself. Give yourself some time to get used to the wave — we don't learn to surf overnight. And you won't transition in one or two days. Expect the waters to be a little rough at first; this will help you adjust your expectations.

Look For and Embrace the Highs

Every transition, wanted or not, has positive moments or outcomes. Your job is to search for and recognize them. There were tears during my son's kindergarten transition, but we celebrated each moment of progress and joy. He made a new friend or he didn't cry at recess today. Embracing the positive gives us the energy to muddle through the lows.

Accept the Muck

How about that duck in the truck who's stuck in the muck? It's pretty yucky in the muck, but certainly a necessary and normal part of transitions. If we don't wade through the muck, how can we appreciate its opposite — getting clear? Confusion is often a part of transitions that most people would rather avoid. But if you can relax and accept the confusion for what it is, clarity will come. Use the confusion to search your soul and discover new things about yourself and life. The mucky water will soon become crystal clear.

Make it a Lesson in Learning

What can you learn from a transition? As you struggle to deal with your two year old's newfound independence, what are you learning about yourself as a parent? What do you know about two year olds, and what is yet to learn? Transitions are great opportunities to learn more about who we are and who we aren't. It's a chance to grow and stretch ourselves. Sure, it can be uncomfortable at first, but the end result is a better you, a more mature outlook, an expanded vision of life, or a transformative revelation. A transition is merely another chapter in your life's lesson book.

Out With the Old and In With the New

Whenever I deal with uncomfortable change in my life, I always remember that when an old door closes, a new door opens up. When you get rid of what no longer works in your life, opportunities open up for new and exciting changes to take place. Use the transitional period to clear out old stuff that is dragging you down. It could be old clothes, dying relationships, or bad habits that interfere with the process of change. Take time to rejuvenate and take care of yourself. Soak in bubble baths or take a weekend vacation. Try reorganizing your life; it simplifies, energizes and generally makes life run smoother. Try on a new focus by thinking about how you can grow during this transition.

Transitions Require Change

It is nearly impossible to get through a transition without growing and changing in some way. Embrace change as a normal part of life and use these tips for navigating your way through personal change.

• **Take Action.** You can read every self-help book, attend seminars, or talk with people about how they've made changes, but unless you actually take action, nothing is going to happen. Of course gaining knowledge helps. However, it's only the first step to change. Our mothers group at church once read a book called She's Gonna Blow. In that book, there were hundreds of suggestions on how moms can better manage anger with their children. If a mom is dealing with frequent anger at her children, then she must take some of the principles and actually apply them to her life. Maybe it means she has to resolve anger from her past, count to 10 before she responds, or reserve daily relaxation time for herself. She must do something different if she is going to conquer her anger issues. And you must do something different if you are going to move through a transition.

• **Focus.** To focus, you need a vision and a plan. How do you want your life to be different and what is your plan to change it? This is one thing I have learned from starting my own business. I have a tendency to have a million (well, not quite) ideas about what I want to do to grow my business. I will start to work on one idea and then jump to the next, and then on to something else. Pretty soon I am wondering what exactly I am accomplishing. Is my business actually growing or am I just doing a lot of tasks that don't produce results? For every change you are trying to make, pick two or three things you can do to support that change and stick to them. Try those things for a substantial period of time before you try something new.

• **Have Discipline.** This is what will carry you through when the going gets tough. Anyone can stick to change for a week or two. It takes a disciplined mindset to make lasting change. You have to be able to pick yourself up when you fall down, brush yourself off, and try again. For two years, my older son, Kai, played travel baseball. Then he encountered a long hitting slump and he was no longer a superstar. His dad and I kept telling him he needed to be practicing or his hitting would not improve. It took two years of crushing disappointment from not making the travel team for Kai to learn discipline. He now faithfully practices his hitting at least five times per week. It totally comes from him and his desire to succeed. His discipline has developed a lifestyle change for him that has tremendously improved his hitting and his confidence. Discipline will help you stay strong during a transitional period of your life.

• **Be Courageous.** The number one reason we resist change is fear. Sometimes it can be scary to change. It is much more comfortable to remain status quo. It is normal to feel fear, but yet it is so crippling. To have courage is to not feel fear, but to push through the fear. I have always had a dream of singing on the music team at church. Singing on our church music team meant I had to go through an extensive and frightening audition. I could have easily sat on the sidelines and never taken that risk. Instead, I mustered the courage to try out. It was one of the most nerve wracking experiences I've had. Even though I didn't make the team, I learned something about myself. I am capable of conquering fear, and I lived to tell about it. If you don't conquer your fear, you will remain stuck in your life.

There is a Light at the End of the Tunnel

Transitions do not last forever. It's true we can get stuck for awhile, but eventually there is a light at the end of the tunnel. A two year old turns three. The pain of divorce goes away. The learning curve at the beginning of a new job fades and is replaced with routine. The new house in the new town becomes "home." And you don't have to wait until the transition is over to experience the "light." The "light" can come in the form of support throughout your transitional time. Your light is your hope that things can be "normal" again.

There is one thing for sure. If you're not in a transition today, you will be eventually. Ride the wave, hold on to the highs, accept the muck, and capture the lessons. Transitions are an opportunity for a new beginning, so embrace the changes. Change is a normal and necessary part of life, and you *will* get through it.

TAKE ACTION ASSIGNMENT

Which of the seven tips for managing transitions do you struggle with most? Take some time this week to talk with a trusted friend about your struggles. Brainstorm together solutions for overcoming your struggles. Then take the action that will help you move more smoothly through your transition.

CHAPTER 7
*
Wouldn't it be Nice if Time Grew on Trees?

"Time is free, but it's priceless. You can't own it, but you can use it. You can't keep it, but you can spend it. Once you've lost it you can never get it back."
—Harvey MacKay

*

Over and over, I hear moms saying "I don't have time." I don't have time for myself. I don't have to time to read that. I don't have time to declutter. I don't spend enough time with my children because there is so much to do. When I hear the words, "I don't have time," what I really hear is "That's not important to me," "There are other things more important" or "I don't and can't have control over my time."

On Thursday, I asked my teenager how he did on his chemistry test. I thought it was sort of odd that he didn't mention it to me. Normally, he would be rushing to tell me that he received a 43 out of 48, which equates to a 93.75%. This particular chemistry test was a rather large test that spanned a period of three days. Determined to help him to do well, I took the time to study with him for the first part of the test. The other two parts he was on his own.

It soon became apparent why my son was not eager to share his grade. For part 1, the part we studied together, he received an A! For parts 2 and 3 of the exam, studied by him independently (or not), he received an F and another F. The culprit for these failing grades was TIME! When I asked him why he didn't study more for this test, he explained to me that he didn't have time. Time, as if it has two legs, had run away again! Yes, my son Kai is a busy guy. He is busy playing football, texting his friends, talking on the phone to his girlfriend, listening to his favorite music on iTunes, and of course, eating. No teenager would deny that these are all important aspects of his life.

We all fall victim to time, yet time is not a criminal. Time just is. It keeps going on and on, oblivious to anyone or anything around it. Time doesn't stop for anyone, nor does it run out. Although time doesn't grow on trees, there is plenty of it available. So why do we act as if time has control over us? I think because it gives us something to blame for our own inability to manage our time.

As I sit here in silence at my desk writing about time, I listen to only the ticking of the black and gray clock above me. I have 40 minutes before I have to leave to pick up my other son from kindergarten. There are a number of things I could do in these 40 minutes. I can keep writing. I can fold the clothes that are in the dryer. Downstairs, in the basement, I have a treadmill and an exercise bike. I could get in a 30 minute workout. Or I could complain that I only have 36 minutes left before my time is taken away. I'm not sure how that attitude would help me, but I can choose to view time in that way.

What if you were to stop thinking of time in terms of something you have no control over? What might you have to face if you accepted full responsibility for your time? If time were no longer a valid excuse for why your life is not exactly the way you want it to be, what would have to change? The answer to all three questions is that you have to look at how you contribute to your lack of "time."

Maybe you would have to admit that you dawdle a lot and have a hard time staying focused. With time being removed from the list of excuses, perhaps you have to see how your procrastinating ways might need to be changed. None of us manage our time perfectly. We can all be caught flying by the seat of our pants instead of planning appropriately, or wasting time searching for something because of our lack of organization. Sometimes our poor time management is the result of over scheduling because we don't know how to say no, or taking on all the responsibility because no one can do it better than us.

Just this week, as a matter of fact, I mismanaged my time. I did a presentation at a local park district on Guilt-free Parenting. The class was supposed to run from 7:00 to 8:00 PM. At 7:02, only 2 of the class participants were present. Wanting to wait for everyone to arrive, I waited another 5 minutes. Surely, people would show up by 7:07. Surely not. By 7:10, I was still missing several attendees that had signed up for the class, but I decided to get started anyway. Another person showed up at 7:20. Everyone left at 8:23. I know this because I picked up the evaluation sheets, read a comment that said, "The program started late and ended late," and then glanced at the clock. She was right. But everyone else was late so I was trying to be nice by waiting for them. Although that may be true, the real problem lies in the fact that I did not start the program or end the program on time. The onus is on me and no one else, especially not Ms. Time.

I understand there may be some resistance to letting go of this notion that you have no control over your time. And I know it sometimes feels like we are at the mercy of everyone else. My boss expects me to work 60 hours a week, and I'm afraid if I don't he will replace me. I have three children and all their activities rob me of my time. My job requires me to travel and be away from home all week, so I am inundated with a huge to do list when I get home. No one is stepping up to help at church or school, so someone has to do it. These are all very real life situations and they require very real thought about how they do affect our time. However, by failing to see and act on the choices we have, we give away our power to control our time. By using these ideas to make different choices regarding your time, you can begin to capitalize on this precious commodity.

Prioritize, Schedule and Focus. Make a list of all the things you have to do and want to do for a given time period. Prioritize each of the items on your list. Assign high priority, moderate priority or low priority to each item. What are the most important activities or tasks to you? Spend most of your energy and time on your high priority items and schedule the moderate and low priority items around your main concerns. Stay focused by scheduling only 3-5 items per day on your to do list. A big ongoing to do list is overwhelming and interferes with your ability to focus and complete tasks.

Eliminate Some "Have To's" in your Life. There are things in life that we want to do and have to do. Some "have to's" simply can't be eliminated such as laundry, cleaning the house or grocery shopping. Other "have to's" are negotiable. You don't have to volunteer your time every time someone needs it. You don't have to participate in all social activities. Look closely at all the "have to's" in your life. Which ones can you drop?

Pay Attention to Time Stealers. Can you identify the activities or tasks in your life that steal your time? Maybe it's a friend who calls to chat. Next thing you know 30 minutes have gone by. What about the internet? I don't know about you but I can spend hours surfing the net. In line with the internet are e-mails. Responding to junk e-mail is a real time stealer. Some people spend hours vegetating in front of the television. Poor communication, disorganization, perfectionism and procrastination can rob you of precious hours of time. Manage your time stealers wisely so they don't manage you.

Delegate Tasks. Not everything has to be handled by you. Sometimes it's helpful to let go of the notion that you are the only person that can manage a particular task. Children as young as three can help around the house. Husbands can run errands and do chores as well. Friends and family members can lend a helping hand. If money permits, consider hiring help.

The 5 E's - Quick Guide to Time Management

The ME Items

The ME items are those tasks that can only be handled by you. If you think through the course of your day, you'll probably find there are not a lot of ME items, but there certainly are some. In my business life, my ME items are coaching, speaking and writing. Although I could hire a ghostwriter, I choose not to. All other items like marketing, administrative tasks, billing, public relations and website design don't have to be handled by me. At home, my ME items include being a mom to my children, a wife to my husband, and any task involving self-care. I've thought about outsourcing my exercise, but I don't think that would be too effective. Make a list of the ME items in your life.

The WE Items

The WE items are tasks you can share responsibility with another person. For instance, my husband and I work together on paying bills, running errands and taking care of the children. Depending on the time constraints we both have, we pitch in and share these tasks. Now, there are certain tasks that belong to one person. My husband can count on me to do laundry and I know I can count on him to do the dishes. Where ever there is the opportunity, enlist the help of a spouse, child, trusted co-worker or other family member. Have an agreement that the WE items will be shared.

The HE/SHE Items

Now, let's face it. There are some tasks that you can completely delegate to someone else. You may have to train someone to handle the task and he or she may not handle it exactly the way you would do it. You might even have to pay some money to get the task accomplished, but none the less, it's possible to unload some tasks. And don't get caught in the trap of saying "But eventually I am going to do it." That may be true, but you'll feel much better if you just buckle down and let someone else handle it. Learn to let go of control so you can feel the peace of mind that comes from emptying your plate.

The THREE Items

What three items can you agree will be non-negotiable in your life? A non-negotiable is a rule you set to protect your time - a rule that is never or rarely broken. Some examples of non-negotiable items include:

- Wednesday night is family night - no other commitments allowed on Wednesday nights
- Sunday is a day of rest - no work allowed
- The 1st and 3rd Friday of every month is date night
- Children are allowed to participate in one extracurricular activity per semester
- I will say yes to only one social activity per week
- From 8:00 to 9:00 AM, I will not take phone calls; it's a time to catch up on paperwork

The UGLEE Items

I know. I spelled ugly wrong, but these are the 5 E's. The ugly items are the time wasters that you want to avoid. What are those tasks in your life that are a complete waste of time? Perhaps you use these items to avoid doing other things, or maybe they are just tasks you need to set better boundaries with. For me, it's checking email, surfing the internet, and personal phone calls. It's not that these tasks are not important at times; it's just that there needs to be a limit...a strict limit. Remember managing our time is about making choices with our time in every moment. Always ask yourself, "Is this the best use of my time right now?"

Teenagers love to make money. Many tasks such as housecleaning, laundry, ironing, organization, lawn care, and home projects can be farmed out to the professionals.

Cut Back on Commitments. With so many activities to choose from, it's easy to over schedule your time. The church and community offer many opportunities to volunteer. Children are involved in sports, music, dance and school activities. Friends and family members are often good at booking your social calendar. Add home and work commitments and you have to start using multiple calendars to keep track of everything. Consider limiting the amount of activities you and family members are involved in. Cut out volunteering for a period of time. Limit children's extracurricular activities to one per semester. Carefully select which social activities you want to attend. It's okay to say no to protect your time.

Increase Organization. Believe it or not, lack of organization eats up a lot of time. You spend time looking for things. Eliminate clutter from your life and organize the rest of your belongings. Simplifying increases organization and gives you more time. Poor planning results in mismanaged time. Keep a calendar and "to do" list. Set up daily routines that help your family run more efficiently. To maximize your time, take 15 minutes at the end of each day to plan for the next day.

Conquer Procrastination and Perfectionism. Perfectionists spend way too much time getting things "just right." Procrastinators waste too much time avoiding things they don't want to do. If you fall into either of these categories, making a commitment to tackle these self-management issues will go a long way toward giving you more time.

By understanding you have the power to make different choices regarding your time, you give yourself the freedom to create your life the way you want it to be. Managing your time wisely allows you to spend your time engaging in pleasurable activities with people you love, even yourself.

TAKE ACTION ASSIGNMENT

What do you wish you had more time for in your life? Make a list of the activities you want to make time for. Now that you know that you can create this time, what can you do differently in your life to make time for these activities? Commit to participating in at least one activity from your list every week.

CHAPTER 8

✳

Little Miss Perfect

"Once you accept the fact that you're not perfect, then you develop some confidence." —Rosalynn Carter

✳

She stands exactly 15 1/2 inches tall, beautifully dressed in a pink satin and white lace dress. The pink ribbon on top of her head is in stark contrast to her jet black hair. She has creamy white skin, a slight blush in her cheeks, soft brown eyes and coral colored lips. Little Miss Perfect is her name, and on the surface, she appears to be a porcelain doll. However, in reality she is a symbol of, what coaches call, my Gremlin.

The Gremlin is the voice of negative self-talk or the voice of self-doubt. It is that tiny voice inside us that will do anything to sabotage our success and convince us we are not good enough. We all have a Gremlin; mine happens to be the voice of perfectionism. I am a recovering perfectionist so I am all too familiar with the damaging effects of perfectionism.

The Pros and Cons of Perfectionism

Now, perfectionists have a lot of great qualities. They are usually do it your-selfer type people who are detail oriented, neat and organized. Perfectionists can be high achievers and hard workers. Typically, they are very careful and structured. As long as the negative effects don't outweigh the positive, perfectionism can have some advantages.

If you're plagued with perfectionism, you might recognize some of these problems:

· You believe that what you achieve is who you are.

· You pressure yourself to meet your own high expectations and everyone else's too.

· You're too afraid to take healthy risks because of fear of judgment or fear of failure.

· You're too critical of other people or expect too much from others.

- You live in anxiety over making mistakes or you beat yourself up when you make a mistake.

- You are obsessive about things being done the "right" way.

- The stress of perfectionism is affecting your emotional, relational or physical health.

Causes of Perfectionism

Although knowing the cause of your perfectionism won't cure this often pathological belief, understanding its roots offers an awareness that is needed to begin making changes. More often than not, perfectionism begins in the family of origin. First-born children are often perfectionists, probably due to the anxiety and high expectations new parents often have. As parents, by the 2nd or 3rd child, we are beginning to relax and be more comfortable with our parenting. Just like not all first-born children are perfectionists, there are some children who are not first-born that are plagued with perfectionism.

Sometimes we learn perfectionism from modeling after a perfectionist parent. One mom shared with me that her father was a surgeon, a profession that does not allow for mistakes. His quest for perfectionism in his work spilled over into his family life. Other times a child will develop perfectionism in response to an alcoholic parent. There is this belief, from a child's perspective, that if she is a good girl, she will make her parent happy, and somehow her life might be different.

Perfectionism can arise if we are pushed too hard to achieve as a child. I can clearly remember coming home to show my mom my report card. I had received all A's and one B (or at least that's my memory). My mother informed me, in no uncertain terms, that I was capable of doing better. And she was right. In college, I received straight A's. Nothing less than an A was acceptable to me and I worked hard, cried, and experienced great stress to achieve a 4.0 grade point average.

Some children are rewarded for being a workaholic. A child is considered successful if he can maintain good grades, excel in sports or music, and maintain a multitude of other extracurricular activities. The result is a stressed and overworked child who is reinforced by his achievements. The lack of balance between work and play often fuels perfectionism.

What messages do the media send regarding what's valued in your culture? In America, TV shows, movies and commercials reflect a reality that is often not achievable. Toys such as Barbie don't honor the average looking girl. To be considered beautiful, you must be tall, skinny and full of curves. Glamour magazines send the same message. The distorted media messages make individuals think perfectionism is possible and the only acceptable outcome.

Lastly, perfectionism can be a form of self protection – a way to evade perceived shortcomings. If somehow we believe that we are not good enough the way we are, we will strive to be perfect in as many ways as we can. The belief is that maybe people won't notice our inadequacies.

Overcoming Perfectionism

I wish I could give you a magic pill and overnight you would be cured from perfectionism. Unfortunately, overcoming perfectionism is a process that takes some hard work and time. As I said before, I am a recovering perfectionist, and I can tell you from experience, if you work at it, you can get much better at making sure perfectionism does not dictate your life. Here are some techniques for you to practice with. By changing your thoughts, words, and actions, you will make significant progress.

THINK
- Examine the underlying beliefs you tell yourself that reinforce the perfectionism. Examples include:
    - If I don't do things perfectly, I will lose control.
    - If I make mistakes, people will judge me.
    - There is a right and a wrong way to do things.
- Challenge these beliefs by thinking of experiences that do not support your beliefs.
    - When was the last time life was not perfect, but you still had control?
    - Have you ever made a mistake that no one judged?
    - Can you think of multiple ways to handle the same thing?
- Understand that complete perfectionism is not achievable. It does not exist.
- Acknowledge your fears and other emotions such as anxiety, depression and anger that result from your perfectionism.

SPEAK

- Speak words of affirmation to counteract your unhealthy beliefs. Turn your limiting beliefs into positive and empowering statements; repeat these affirmations many times throughout the day, especially when the limiting belief comes up.
    - Life is never perfect and that is okay.
    - It is okay for me to make mistakes; I am human.
    - Everyone does things in a way that works best for them.
- Speak up for yourself if people try to impose unrealistic expectations on you. Sometimes other perfectionists can trigger our own perfectionism.
- Learn to laugh at your mistakes and at life in general.

ACT

- Strive for excellence instead of perfectionism.
- Set reasonable standards for yourself and others. If you're not sure what reasonable is, ask a few non-perfectionists.
- Face your fears and step out of your perfectionism slowly. Take baby steps.

As a mom, your perfectionism will be passed on to your children if you don't take steps to overcome it. Everyday, I stay conscious of how my perfectionism could rub off on my children. I commend them for B's, even when my urge is to push for A's. When my children are frustrated with their mistakes, I tell them it's okay to make mistakes. And it's okay for you to make mistakes; excellent (not perfect) parenting is good enough.

TAKE ACTION ASSIGNMENT

Pick any one of the *THINK-ACT-SPEAK* techniques and begin practicing it today. It takes time to create a new habit, so continue to practice this technique until it becomes second nature.

CHAPTER 9
✳
Conquering the Procrastination Plague

"Nothing is so fatiguing as the eternal hanging on of an uncompleted task."
—William James

✳

I waited as long as I possibly could to write this chapter. I'm just kidding, but does this sound familiar? Procrastination is one of those habits that afflict us all at times, but it can become a dreadful plague to many. I regularly speak on overcoming procrastination, so I know it is a struggle for a lot of people. When I ask audience members "Who considers themselves a procrastinator?", hands fly up immediately. Procrastinators know, without a doubt, who they are. If you're not a procrastinator, then you can skip this chapter. But chances are, if you've read this far, you know you might benefit from reading on. Either you are a full-fledged procrastinator or you have some experience with procrastinating in some area of your life.

Pro and Cons of Procrastination

On the surface, it may seem there are no advantages for procrastinators. However, if there weren't a payoff, people wouldn't procrastinate. Many times we procrastinate because we don't like doing something. When we put things off, we *don't have to face undesirable tasks.* Sometimes, if we wait long enough, the undesirable *task will even go away.* Procrastinating *enables us to hide behind our fears.* Some tasks are just plain scary. Some people avoid making sales calls because they fear rejection. Others put off a doctor's appointment because they are afraid of what the doctor might find.

Procrastinating allows the *time to do more pleasurable activities* or to *prioritize more important things.* When you procrastinate, you have *time to rest,* and sometimes we need that. Life is not fun if it does not consist of some time for relaxation and play.

The negative effects procrastination has on our lives are much easier to identify. One consequence of procrastination is that you *fail to reap the rewards that come from taking action.* One area that many people procrastinate in is self-care. How many people do you know who say exercise is important to them, but yet they rarely exercise? When we procrastinate, we miss out on the rewards of taking action on the things that we desire. It might be a trimmer body, a more rewarding career, or even a fulfilling relationship. Procrastination interferes with many people living up to their fullest potential. There are so many talented people that never become all they were created to be. It's not just the individuals that are affected; the Universe misses out.

Procrastination *causes stress* in your life. Whether it's the stress of unfinished business or the adrenaline stress that comes from waiting until the last minute, the stress will have an effect on your physical and emotional health. When we are stressed, we are irritable, and it can be difficult to relax and sleep. We might react to the stress by engaging in unhealthy habits like overeating or abusing alcohol. The stress may cause physical illness or chronic pain like lower immune system trouble, headaches, back problems and even depression.

The unfulfilled promises and the chronic lateness that result from procrastinating *erode trust and damage relationships*. Spouses of procrastinators chronically complain their partner never gets things done. They feel their only tool is to nag, and nagging normally doesn't motivate the procrastinator. I once spoke to a husband of a woman that was dragging her feet on eliminating her clutter in the home. It was clear from our very short conversation that he was quite irritated with her procrastination. Some procrastinators have lost their jobs or were passed over for a promotion because of their failure to complete tasks on time. Most people would rather deal with reliable individuals.

Procrastination can be quite an *expensive habit* if it affects our finances. Many procrastinators pay their bills late, resulting in late fees. Or they procrastinate on managing their finances, resulting in overdraft charges from the bank. Sometimes procrastination gets so bad that an individual's credit is severely affected, causing him or her to be unable to purchase a home, a car, or even food for the family.

Lastly, procrastination *withers away our self-esteem*. Most procrastinators carry around a lot of guilt. They feel bad about the choices they are making, but feel unable to stop them. The more their life spirals out of control, the worse they feel about themselves. Projects pile up, tasks go undone, life is unorganized, and the procrastinator feels like a failure. These feelings of failure further complicate the problem by causing exasperation and inaction on the procrastinator's part. Fortunately, there are several ways to conquer the procrastination plague.

Develop an Awareness of Your Style

Before you can begin to conquer procrastination, it is helpful to understand why you typically procrastinate. Having an awareness of your style gives you an idea of what fuels your procrastination. By being aware of your tendencies, it is easier for you to start making changes. Below, I have identified eight different styles of procrastinators, each with a description of typical behaviors and thought processes. Highlight the statements that resonate with you. You may find that one particular style describes you, or you may have traits from many different styles.

Perfect Paula
- Perfectionist
- Fear of Failure
- Fear that your best efforts won't be good enough
- Reluctant to work with others or delegate to people that don't do things your way
- Thinks in terms of black and white
- Tendency to be rigid, stubborn or picky
- Overly preoccupied with details, rules and schedules

Attachment Alice
- Fear of separation
- Don't trust your ability to do things on your own or make your own decisions
- Procrastination is a friend you never say good bye to
- Like to be told what to do
- Uncomfortable in the spotlight
- Don't want to leave a relationship with someone you view as a protector
- Desire to be rescued
- Prefer to stay in your comfort zone
- Worry about the repercussions of change

Separation Sally
- Fear of attachment
- Fear that others will take over your life
- Fear that others will take credit for your accomplishments
- Avoid intimate relationships for fear of being hurt again

- Fear you will hurt other people
- Fear of rejection is so intense that you avoid people

Average Ann
- Fear of success
- Fear that you'll be judged as being too good
- Feel you don't deserve success
- Fear that someone else will be jealous or hurt by your success
- Fear that success will trap you into a life you don't want to live
- Fear of becoming a workaholic

Rebel Ruth
- Have a need to break free from rules that are too confining
- Reaction to authority
- View requests from other people as demands
- Resist people intruding on your time
- Use procrastination as a way to express your anger or get revenge
- High need to fight for your independence and self-respect

Crisis Christy
- Frequently wait until the last minute to do something
- Feeling that life is chaotic
- Your life contains a lot of drama
- Moods change rapidly and dramatically
- Get temporarily and very involved in something and then quickly lose interest
- Preference for action – impatient when things move too slowly
- Enjoy the adrenaline rush of taking risks

Busy Beth
- Always doing things, but never really getting anything accomplished
- Frequently complain of being too busy
- Attention span is short and you move from task to task
- Have difficulty saying no to things you don't want to do
- Get overly involved in other people's problems, postponing addressing your own
- Afraid you might not know what do with yourself if you weren't busy
- Frequently wonder how you got involved in the tasks or projects you're doing

Dreamy Dora
- Think a lot about what you'd like to do, but rarely do them
- Hate details – love creativity
- Dislike difficult tasks
- Want life to be easy and pleasant
- Want to jump from beginning to end without doing anything in between
- Led by your feelings in the moment versus current plans or priorities
- Still wonder what you're going to be when you grow up
- Rarely take an active approach to what you want – wait for things to happen to you

Ideas for Overcoming Procrastination

Overcoming procrastination is a process – it's not going to happen overnight. I will give you a lot of ideas for working on changing this habit, but please understand you are making a major lifestyle change, so it will take some time. Stay with it and don't give up. By using the following Think~Speak~Act techniques, you will begin to conquer procrastination and transform your life.

THINK
- Stop negative thinking – think positively about your ability to change your ways
- Think about your early childhood models and how they may have influenced your procrastination
- Think about the beliefs you hold that reinforce your procrastination
    - I work better under pressure
    - I'll have more time tomorrow
    - I can't do it because I might fail
- Challenge your beliefs and replace them with positive affirmations
    - I do my best work when I have prepared enough time
    - Today is the best day to get things done
    - If I don't try, I'll never know
- Acknowledge your fears and any other emotions you feel
    - Ask yourself the question: "What am I afraid will happen if I _____? (Fill in the blank with the task you are procrastinating on)
- Know who you are and what's important to you
    - Do soul searching on decisions you are procrastinating on – ask yourself why you're on the fence

- Knowing what's important to you enables you to decline activities and tasks that aren't important
- Think about the payoff for procrastinating
    - Ask yourself the question: What benefit am I receiving from not _____? (Fill in the blank with the task you are procrastinating on)

SPEAK

- Speak confidently and positively
    - Avoid words like "can't," "should," "have to," "must" (these words lack energy and motivation)
    - Use words like "can," "could," "want to," and "choose to" (these words shift your energy and change your attitude)
- Learn to say NO at appropriate times — avoid committing to tasks and activities you know you don't want to do
- Speak up and ask for help — having a partner or support motivates us to move forward

ACT

- Get the right people involved to help you
    - Hire professionals to help you with various tasks
    - Hire professionals to help you overcome procrastination
- Stretch yourself by acting with courage
    - Take baby steps — a little action is better than none, and taking action usually propels you forward
- Learn to set boundaries to protect your time and energy
- Set goals using the S.M.A.R.T. process
    - Specific
    - Measurable
    - Achievable
    - Reasonable
    - Time-oriented
- Manage your time wisely
- Reward yourself and celebrate your accomplishments

Conquering the procrastination plague begins with an awareness of your tendencies and understanding the root cause of your behavior. It ends with faithfully working on changing your thoughts, words and actions. With some hard work and commitment, you can make this significant and rewarding lifestyle change.

TAKE ACTION ASSIGNMENT

Pick the area in your life that you procrastinate on the most.
- Household
- Work
- School
- Personal Care
- Social Relationships
- Finances
- Administrative
- Other

What is one change you can make today that will begin to break the cycle of procrastination? Enlist the support of an accountability partner in making this change.

CHAPTER 10
✳
The Dreadful Word: NO

"Knowing your priorities in life leads to easier no-ing when it's time to turn down an opportunity." —Mary M. Byers

✳

Many moms have a hard time learning the essential art of saying "No." It is such a struggle that Mary M. Byers has devoted an entire book, *How to Say No and Live to Tell About It*, and has branded herself as "The No Queen." Sometime between the age of two, when no was our only vocabulary, and becoming an adult woman, we have forgotten the importance of saying no. Perhaps the words of our parents, "You don't tell me NO," have stuck with us and the shame and guilt we feel from asserting our needs and independence lingers on.

Sometimes it is important to say no. Saying no is the equivalent to setting a boundary in your life or telling the truth about who you are. Look at the following examples and reflect on how saying no is essential to fully loving yourself and other people.

· I'm going to say *no* to that invitation because I have too many other things going on this week.
· *No*, you may not speak to me that way. Now, please go to your room.
· *No*, I'm sorry, but I'm not in the mood for sex tonight.
· I'm saying *no* to that big piece of cake because I want to lose weight.
· *No*, I cannot accept that promotion because it requires too much travel.

Saying no enables us to protect what is most important to us. It gives us the freedom to make the right choices for our lives. When we can't say no, we find ourselves in situations we don't want to be in. Life becomes full of situations and people that create dissatisfaction.

When to Say No

You should say no when you don't like something. For example, if you are asked to volunteer at school by doing paperwork, and you hate administrative tasks, then you should say no. Instead, volunteer to do something that better fits what you like to do. When a friend invites you to see a movie you would rather not see, speak up and suggest a different movie.

Oftentimes our uncomfortable feelings can be a sign that we need to say no. Your intuition may be sending you red flags that should not be ignored. How many times have your children asked to do something that did not feel right to you? In these moments, we have a choice to trust our gut and say no, or give in to what makes our children happy.

Has a loved one ever spoken to you in a disrespectful manner while you just stood there and listened to him? When someone steps over your boundary, it is essential to say no. This tells people that you value yourself and will not allow people to mistreat you.

Sometimes we are the ones mistreating ourselves. Maybe you engage in negative self talk or make choices that are damaging to your health. It is critical at this time to practice saying no.

Saying no enables you to protect your time. I recently spoke with a mom who felt guilty because she wasn't spending enough time with her children. She admitted her life was too overbooked with volunteer activities. She needed to say no to things that were occupying her time so she could spend her time doing what she really wanted to do.

When your values are being challenged, you should say no. A friend of mine recently quit her job because the owner of the company was unethical. Choosing to say no to a lie may honor your need to be honest. Saying no enables you to live a life that is in integrity with what is most important to you.

Lastly, sometimes we need to say no when it's the best choice for someone else. We regularly need to say no to our children because they don't always know what is best for them. They do not have the wisdom or the emotional maturity to make all the decisions for their lives. Even adults need to hear no at times. While it may be an extreme example, consider the alcoholic that wants to borrow money to fulfill his addiction or compensate for his lack of responsibility. By learning to say no, we are stopping the process of enabling.

How to Say No

When you first start saying no, it might feel uncomfortable. Your "no" could be expressed in a passive tone of voice. Saying no might also come out in an aggressive way. Anger often disguises fear. It is normal to feel uncertainty and fear. You might wonder how another person will react. You may even know from prior experience that a certain person is going to react negatively. It is true that other people in our life may have negative reactions to us saying no. Our friends and family members may feel disappointed, angry, jealous or sad. Do your best to kindly explain why you need to say no. Let other people have their feelings and understand that you are not responsible for how other people choose to feel. Work on releasing the guilt you feel from choosing what is best for you. An understanding and loving person will want you to take care of yourself, even if it means you have to say no.

The more you practice saying no with an assertive tone of voice, the easier it will become. You will begin to see that people often accept your no very gracefully. What you once dreaded doesn't come true at all. And even when saying no results in discomfort, you begin to learn that you can still survive. You get through the situation without any major crisis. The word no eventually becomes a ticket to freedom.

One of the greatest benefits of saying no is that you get to say yes to something else. This allows you to create a life you want because life is all about choices. Learning to say no enables you to say yes to the people and activities that truly honor you. If I say no to cleaning the house today, I can say yes to having lunch with my girlfriend. By saying no to watching TV, I can say yes to working out. If I want to say yes to spending more time with my husband, I need to say no to working more hours.

Your ideal life is created by making the right choices for you and your family. You can choose to say no just as easily as you can choose to say yes.

TAKE ACTION ASSIGNMENT

List 3 things you need to say no to in your life. How might saying no empower you to live a more authentic life? Commit to releasing these habits, behaviors, activities or people from your life today.

CHAPTER 11
*
Understanding Your Anger

"Do not teach your children never to be angry; teach them how to be angry."
−Lyman Abbott

*

One Saturday morning, my five year old came stomping through the kitchen with a big scowl on his face. He was angry. We had recently developed a schedule board to help Ian plan his day. He loves to follow his schedule, and he was planning on getting ready and dressed for his day from 8:00 to 9:00 in the morning. Mom threw a little monkey wrench in his plan when I told him he needed a bath before he could get dressed. Knowing that mom was working, he raced off to get dad out of bed. Dad, however, had a different agenda. He wanted to sleep in, and he wasn't about to get up to give Ian a bath. Oh no! His plan was messed up and the result was anger. Thankfully, Mom taught him how to rearrange his schedule so that it was playtime between 8:00 and 9:00, and getting ready for his day was now pushed to the 9:00 to 10:00 time slot. A little flexibility and a lot of toy cars, and Ian's anger quickly dissipated. Everyone experiences the feeling of anger from time to time, some more chronically than others.

The Faces of Anger
Anger is a normal human emotion. It is considered the emotion of self-preservation. Anger may appear when someone talks to us in a disrespectful tone of voice, when the bills pile up, or when traffic is causing us to be late for an appointment. Anger shows up when people don't listen to us, don't do what we want them to, and when we're overwhelmed with 100 things to do. You may think of anger as the "screaming and yelling" kind of anger. Anger actually has many more faces: frustration, impatience, annoyance, bitterness, irritability, criticism, temper tantrums, rage, and even depression. A lot of us don't like to talk about anger because it's considered "bad" to be angry. Anger, in and of itself, is not wrong. Mishandling your anger can, however, be harmful to you and others around you.

What is Your Style?
According to Dr. Les Carter, author of *The Anger Trap* and a leading expert on the subject of anger, there are *three styles for handling anger*. Some people are

passive, and they stuff the anger inside, all the while pretending that everything is okay. If your tendency is to turn your anger inward, the result will be depression if you do not release the anger. Depression is repressed anger. Others are *aggressive*. When they are angry, you definitely know because they shout, scream, spew out angry criticisms, and even slam doors and cabinets. People who express their anger aggressively give anger the bad rap that it has. Rage and violence can be byproducts of aggressive expression of anger. The third style of dealing with anger is the *passive-aggressive* approach.[1] When someone is passive-aggressive with their anger, they appear, on the surface, to comply, only to seek revenge in a secretive way. Examples would include people who are nice to your face, but then criticize you behind your back, or people who agree to do something they don't want to do, and then purposely choose not to follow through. The preferred, and the healthiest way to handle your anger is through assertive expression and then letting it go. According to the American Psychological Association, to express your anger assertively "you have to learn how to make clear what your needs are, and how to get them met, without hurting others. Being assertive doesn't mean being pushy or demanding; it means being respectful of yourself and others."[2]

Contrasting Styles of Behavioral Expression of Anger – Examples*			
Behavior	**Non-Assertive**	**Aggressive**	**Assertive**
Eye Contact	Minimal, eyes downcast	Glaring, stare-down	Direct, steady, attentive
Facial Expression	Timid, apologetic	Glowering, menacing	Unflinching, serious
Body Posture	Head and shoulders slumped	Upright, leaning, harassing	Upright, relaxed
Gestures	None, or helpless	Threatening, bullying, violent	Expressive, non-threatening
Distance, physical contact	Stays distant, no contact	"In your face", too close	Conversationally appropriate
Voice tone, inflection, volume	Whiny, flat, quiet	Bellicose, shouting down, loud	Strong, firm, conversational
Fluency	Hesitant, awkward	Rapid, cocksure	Consistent, confident
Timing	Waits, avoids	Immediate, inappropriate	Chosen, appropriate
Listening	Listens more than talks	Doesn't listen or interrupts	Attentive, listens, responds
Content (choice of words)	Apologetic, ineffective, denying	Arrogant, contradicting, cursing	Confident, persistent, articulate

* N.B. Cultural differences are a significant variable in defining and determining the appropriateness of these behaviors.

Robert E. Alberti, Ph.D. (c) 2004. Adapted from *Your Perfect Right: Assertiveness and Equality in Your Life and Relationships*, 9th Edition © 2008 by Robert E. Alberti and Michael Emmons. Reproduced by permission of Impact Publishers, Inc., P.O. Box 6016, Atascadero CA 93423, USA. Further reproduction prohibited.

The Roots of Anger

Before you can learn to express your anger in a healthy way and be released from the chains of anger, it's helpful to understand what is at the root of your anger. This requires us to stop long enough to examine our anger before we react. If you will, picture a plant with *four roots. Each root represents a core trigger for anger.* Sometimes our anger is triggered by our *need to control, or have control* in our life. When our children misbehave, our anger can be triggered if our goal is to control their behavior. Control is an illusion because we can't control other people. We can, however, control our response to our anger.

The second root represents our *feelings of insecurity.* When someone criticizes us, our insecurity can cause us to feel angry. The core issue is really about whether or not we feel "good enough." We can learn to evaluate what we want to believe about ourselves. Sometimes the criticism may be valid, but others times it is not. Another person's opinion does not need to shake our self worth.

Another anger trigger is *self-absorption.* We are born selfish. Think of a two year old. What is her favorite word? You guessed it: Mine! As we mature, we hopefully learn that the world does not revolve around us, and it's important to think of other people. Sometimes, however, it's easy to slip back into our old patterns. We want time for ourselves, and our anger gets triggered because our child will not go to sleep. Or perhaps you've planned a night out with the girls, and your husband calls to inform you that he has to stay late at work and cannot be home for the kids. You are angry because he has (or his boss) interfered with <u>your</u> plans. Does this mean we don't have a right to feel angry? The answer is no, but we do have to step outside ourselves and consider the needs of those around us. It is possible to balance our needs with the needs of others.

Lastly, the fourth root symbolizes our *fear.* Anger is often triggered by fear. What are you afraid of? The pile of bills may mean you will be in debt forever, or you'll never have enough money to retire. Conflict might mean someone is going to leave you. Fear is your imagination running wild. Acknowledge your fear and then reframe your thoughts to diminish your fear. Reassure yourself that everything will be okay, or that you can handle whatever life has to offer.

An Anger Journal

Healthy expression of your anger and being free from the traps of anger will require you to take some action. For the next month, keep an anger journal. Each time you feel angry, irritated, impatient or frustrated, write the situation down in your journal. Answer the following questions about your anger.

- How did you handle your anger?
- What do you think the root cause of your anger is?
- What would be an assertive and appropriate response to this situation?
- How can you change your thoughts to let go of the anger?

At the end of the month, look for patterns. Do you consistently deal with your anger in the same manner or does it vary? Review the four roots and identify any consistencies in your own anger. Now that you have a good understanding of your anger, you can make different choices. Stop now before you react to your anger. Make a mental note of what's driving your anger. Then you can choose a healthy response to your anger.

Anger, while a normal part of life, does not need to
hurt your relationships or spoil your mood.

TAKE ACTION ASSIGNMENT

Follow the instructions in the section on keeping an anger journal. How can you use this information to respond to your anger in the way you would want to?

SPIRITUALITY

CHAPTER 12
✳
A Spiritual Approach to Motherhood

"I feel that the essence of spiritual practice is your attitude toward others. When you have a pure, sincere motivation, then you have right attitude toward others based on kindness, compassion, love and respect."
—Dalai Lama

✳

It was breakfast time at Janet's house. The baby was in the high chair watching her brother and sister fight over who gets the Mickey Mouse plate. The kids didn't want cereal for breakfast, nor did they want eggs and toast. Not having much left in the house to fix, Janet was beginning to feel crabby. Why did the morning have to start like this? Janet took a deep breath, and vowed to remain patient.

Breakfast was done, and it was time to get the chores started. Still trying to remain cheery, Janet assigned a small chore to her five year old, and another one to her eight year old. The kids were not in the mood for chores, and they dragged their feet, begging to be motivated. "If we can get our chores done, we can go play miniature golf," Janet announces to her son and daughter. "This is going to take forever," her daughter counters. Just then the baby starts to cry. Janet has to tend to her little one, and this gives the older ones the perfect outlet for abandoning their chores. Not having the energy or the patience to deal with her children's noncompliance, Janet wonders why she feels so out of sorts. Then suddenly, she remembers. Opting to sleep in a little this morning, Janet had skipped her morning meditation.

Is motherhood possible without a spiritual perspective? Sure, I suppose it is, but regular spiritual practice sure makes life as a mom much easier. There are many ways to engage in spiritual rituals, and each has its benefits. What works for one person may not be the answer for someone else. But if you find the right outlet or combination of practices, life as a mom will be more fulfilling and peaceful.

Meditation

For Janet, meditation was the answer. By spending 30 minutes every morning in a quiet space listening to her meditation program, she is able to center herself and find the *peace, patience and positive energy* she needs to get through her day. The purpose of meditation is to clear your mind and body of negative energy, and center your soul so you are one with the Universe. Meditation is an excellent way to *relax and unwind* at the end of a busy day as well. The state of deep rest that is achieved through meditation *counteracts the stress* that our body experiences throughout the day.

Prayer

There is *power* in prayer. Have you ever had a parenting problem you couldn't solve on your own? When my older son was in middle school, he was hanging out with a group of boys in the neighborhood who were unhealthy for him. Every day these boys would get together, and they were always yelling and arguing over something. I tried to encourage my son to find some new friends, explaining to him what a healthy friendship looks like. I talked myself blue in the face, and the fighting continued. Exasperated, I turned to prayer. I started praying for these boys to be removed from his life. I prayed for awhile, and then forgot about the situation. One day, I woke up and realized that this group of boys who were once in my son's life, were now gone. They hadn't moved, or even had a big blowout. Divine intervention took place and my prayer was answered. Today my son hangs with a good group of kids in high school. Prayer gives you the *strength* to face life's challenges, and the Universe gives you the *wisdom* to make the best choices. Prayer enables you to *let go* and allow a Greater Power than yourself to take over.

Journaling

The other night I was talking to a friend. She was telling me about her recent spa getaway and the wonderful experiences she had pampering herself. There was one incident, during her massage, that her soul opened up and feelings of sadness tried to engulf her. Waiting until after her massage, she went back to her resort room and pulled out her journal. All the feelings of grief and sorrow poured out of her onto the piece of paper. Journaling is a *release*, a way to *purge your mind and spirit* of the thoughts and feelings that are weighing you down. The result of a good journaling experience is often *clarity, resolve and refreshment.*

Nature

Yesterday I went out for a walk in the morning. It was a cool day, with a perfect breeze for walking. The night before it had stormed, so the clouds were still thick and actively moving across the sky. As I made my way around the ecosystem, I made eye contact with a beautiful Saint Bernard dog sitting peacefully in his yard. I noticed a big bird playing in the water. The wild flowers and grasses were swaying gently in the wind. Looking around, I was reminded of the beauty and wonder of Creation. Spending quiet time in nature *grounds you* and *helps you appreciate the gifts* you have been given. Nature *simplifies our life*, if only for a few moments.

The Arts

I define the arts as anything that is created by another individual for the purpose of inspiring others. Any work of art can speak to us. Whether it's a good book, inspirational song, or a beautiful painting, art has a way of *touching our soul*. By listening to, reading or admiring other works of art, we can *heal, rejuvenate, and be encouraged*. I can't tell you how many times I have been tired, emotionally drained, and had to push myself to go downstairs for a good workout. After putting on my iPod, I begin to walk on the treadmill or ride my stationary bike, listening to my favorite music. Before I realize it, the beautiful music and the words in a song begin to fill my heart. Sometimes I purge my emotions; other times my spirit is lifted and I begin to sing. The Universe speaks to us through other people. Just like others move us through their creations, we can return the same gift with our works of art. The process of creating *connects us to our soul, and puts us in touch with the Master Creator*. So the next time you need to be lifted up, consider engaging in a creative activity.

Community Fellowship and Service

Every year our church organizes an event called Operation Helping Hands. The purpose of this event is to bring the hands and feet of God into the community, and be of service to the many people that need our help. This year our family was assigned to Eastwood, low income housing units, in the city of Aurora. Our job was to paint a room inside one of the resident's homes. Although the resident didn't get a choice, she was blessed with a beautiful and sunny yellow paint. As we began to transform her living room, our *hearts were being changed* forever. There is nothing that gives greater *joy* than to know you are making life a little better for another individual. And an even bigger gift for me was hearing my teenager tell me how good he felt about helping this grateful family. Being a part of a community group like church, or any organization that serves mankind, reminds you that *you are not alone in this world*. By *serving* other individuals and *receiving support* when you need it, life becomes a little easier. We were created to be in fellowship with other people so that we can *learn and grow together in love*.

Regular spiritual practice is essential for one's total emotional and physical health. By staying connected to a spiritual Source, we are reminded we are not alone in this world. When we can transcend our ego and connect to our soul, we can be transformed and renewed. *Where else can you get an abundant supply of unconditional love, joy, peace, and patience that is required for motherhood?*

TAKE ACTION ASSIGNMENT

What form(s) of spiritual practice works best for you? What benefits do you receive from regular spiritual practice? What gets in the way of you engaging in regular spiritual practice? Use the information gathered in your answers to set up a plan for spiritual renewal.

CHAPTER 13

✳

Why on Earth Am I Here?

"I don't know what your destiny will be, but one thing I do know: the only ones among you who will be really happy are those who have sought and found how to serve." –Albert Schweitzer

✳

Have you ever asked yourself, "Why on Earth am I here?" Maybe you've never asked yourself this exact question, but perhaps you've wondered, "What is the purpose of life?" For me, about 10 years ago, I started questioning my life. It's not that I didn't have a good life. I was married and had a beautiful boy, and another one on the way. I guess the real issue was that I did not feel deeply fulfilled in my life. I kept wondering if there was more to life than what I was currently experiencing.

The deep longing that kept coming up for me was a desire to be making a difference in the world. At the time, I worked as an operations manager for a small food brokerage company. In a nutshell, I worked in business for a sales and marketing company. I suppose I could have said that I was contributing to the process of bringing great food to our community. For someone who loves food, I guess that would be a very rewarding career, but I am someone who doesn't much care about food, unless I am hungry.

I wanted to be making a difference in a way that was meaningful to me. Some people would say that I was making a difference by raising my children and loving my husband, family and friends. No doubt raising a family is significant and meaningful, but for some moms, it's not enough. For others, it is absolutely everything they could ever want in life and they believe their sole purpose in life is to be a loving mom. Wherever you are on that spectrum, it's perfectly okay.

What is most important is that you feel fulfilled and have a deep connection to your life purpose. Without purpose in life, we wander around aimlessly with no direction. Figuring out and honoring your life purpose will help you live a fulfilling and passionate life. It will connect you to who you truly are at the core. When I speak of your core, I am referring to your soul – your true being. Your ego, on the other hand, is concerned with making you feel good and protecting you from pain. Your ego will drive you toward things like making money, being happy all the time, and gaining love and respect from others. Your soul is concerned with being, not doing. It has a long-term view on life and sees your life as a journey – a path in which you learn and grow. Your soul is connected to other souls so that all of life can be a learning and growing experience for everyone. When you understand your life purpose, you understand who you are in relation to the bigger world.

"What is my life purpose?" can be a rather complicated question if you ask people. Some individuals might give you a blank stare, while others may attempt to answer the question, not knowing though if they are "correct." It's a rather subjective question, to which you will get many different answers.

But I like to simplify the question by defining life purpose like this:

Your life purpose is using your gifts/talents and your passions to make a positive difference in the lives of other people.

Your purpose is your true essence. It's who you were created to be in this world. If we use this definition of life purpose, it becomes a whole lot easier to identify our purpose in life. There are two main components you need to figure out if you want to be in touch with your life purpose. What are your gifts and talents? What are your passions? Simple, right? Unfortunately, not always, but I will help simplify the process for you.

Identifying Your Gifts and Talents

Identifying your gifts and talents enables you to answer the question, "<u>What</u> will you do or who will you be to make a difference in the lives of other people?" Your gifts and talents consist of such qualities as your personality characteristics, your life experiences, your strengths or talents, and any acquired skills you've learned in life.

Personality Characteristics

Personality is something each of us is born with, and we are all unique in our own way. Understanding your personality helps you know how you respond to the world. Do you receive your energy from people, or do you reenergize by being alone? Do you tend to think things through carefully, or are you impulsive in your decision making? Do you tackle problems with heart

solutions or head solutions? When you understand and accept your personality for what it is, you know what you have to give to other people just by
being who you are. Take a look at this list of personality characteristics and
put a check mark by the traits that seem to match who you are.

Abstract	Flexible	Possessive
Active	Focused	Practical
Affectionate	Follower	Private
Aggressive	Friendly	Quiet
Agreeable	Funny	Reactive
Aloof	Gentle	Relaxed
Ambitious	Giving	Reliable
Analytical	Gullible	Reserved
Apprehensive	Humble	Responsible
Argumentative	Imaginative	Rigid
Assertive	Impatient	Rule-conscious
Caretaker	Impulsive	Scattered
Charming	Individualistic	Selective
Competitive	Inspirational	Self-assured
Complex	Introspective	Self-reliant
Concrete	Introverted	Sensitive
Confident	Intuitive	Serious
Consistent	Judgmental	Shy
Constant	Leader	Silly
Controlling	Lively	Simple
Creative	Logical	Socially bold
Critical	Loving	Spontaneous
Curious	Loyal	Stern
Decisive	Melancholy	Submissive
Detail-oriented	Methodical	Talkative
Disorganized	Open	Team Player
Dominant	Optimistic	Tense
Easy going	Organized	Traditional
Emotionally stable	Outspoken	Trusting
Empathetic	Patient	Trustworthy
Encouraging	Perceptive	Value-driven
Extroverted	Perfectionist	Warm
Factual	Performer	Watchful
Feeling	Pessimistic	

This list is by no means exhaustive of all the personality characteristics that are used to describe people. If you still have a hard time identifying your personality, ask your loved ones for their input. In addition, there are many types of personality tests including the Holland Codes, the Rorschach test, the Minnesota Multiphasic Personality Inventory (MMPI), the Myers-Briggs Type Indicator, NEO PI-R, and the Thematic Apperception Test. Seek a professional who can administer the test to you.

Life Experiences

There is always something to be learned from everything that happens in life. Every relationship teaches us more about ourselves. Unfortunately, some of the most painful events in our lives are our greatest teachers. Without those lessons, we would not be who we are today.

When my older son's father told me he wanted a divorce, I thought I would fall apart. I'll never forget the day he walked out the door. We struggled for years, and I knew this time was the end. I slid down the wall and burst into tears. My marriage and my family, as I knew it, were over. I was alone, once and for all, with my five year old son. Within that same 24 hour period, I felt liberated and blessed to be free from the pain our marriage caused me. As much as I wanted our marriage to work, I knew I would live again and be happy. I do not regret the years I spent with my ex-husband. He taught me so much about myself and life. I learned what was important to me by not having the things I needed. I learned more about what love is and isn't. Through venturing out, I learned I can take care of myself and create my own happiness.

Even the joyful events in life remind us about who we are. The day of my college graduation stands out very clear in my mind. It was the greatest feeling to walk across that stage to receive my diploma. I had worked extremely hard, as a single mom and full-time employee, to earn a 4.0 GPA. I didn't go through college the way most people do — directly after high school. I labored for 10 years part-time to receive my education. What did I learn about myself? I have amazing discipline and incredible strength. I never give up when something is important to me. I am intelligent and I give 100% to everything I do. I learned my hard work pays off. Most of all, I learned I can be proud of myself, and still be humble.

Your life experiences are meant to be shared with other people. What we learn can be passed on to help others. Our life experiences may make us a better teacher for our children. Perhaps we will use our life lessons to inspire people we don't know. Look at all the public speakers and authors that help change the world by disclosing their life stories. Numerous recovering drug addicts and sexual abuse victims go on to help others with the same challenges. Use the questions below to reflect on what life has taught you about yourself.

- When you think back to your childhood, what did you learn about who you are from the significant people in your life?
- What beliefs are true and which beliefs do you want to discard?
- What painful events have you experienced as an adult, and what did you learn from them?
- What joyful events have you experienced that taught you positive things about yourself?
- Which of these life experiences could help other people if you shared them?

Strengths, Talents and Skills

I believe that everyone has strengths and talents. People don't always use them, but they are there. Whenever I work with clients who struggle with identifying their strengths and talents, I ask them to list 50 of their strengths, talents and skills. This assignment is always met with resistance because most people believe in their heart this task is impossible. Sometimes we are so programmed to focus on our shortcomings that we forget we have positive qualities.

What were you good at as a child? Did you excel in math or was reading and writing your strength? Were you athletic or musical? Maybe you had artistic tendencies or maybe you excelled in home economics. Did you gravitate toward technical skills or were you good at fixing things? Were you a leader in school or did you like working behind the scenes? Your talents and skills as a child are probably very similar to what you have now as an adult.

What have you learned over the years that have made a positive contribution to your life? Are you good at typing or are you a natural on the computer? Have you learned how to sell products or services? Maybe you have developed planning skills or the ability to teach people. Perhaps you are excellent with children or maybe you have a knack for working with special needs people or the elderly.

More than likely, you have several talents and skills that you bring to the table. Appreciate what you have to offer this world. I know sometimes it can look like more fun to have someone else's set of talents and skills, but remember it takes all kinds of people to operate this world. You have a unique place in life and you are just as valuable as anyone else. It is our culture that places varying levels of importance on certain people. Get out a piece of paper and make three columns. Label the columns "Strengths," "Natural Talents" and "Acquired Skills." Fill in as much as you can about what strengths, talents and skills you have to give to other people.

Identifying Your Passions

Identifying your passions enables you to answer the question "<u>Where</u> will you make a difference in this world?" In what area do you have a lot of passion? What lights your heart on fire? Getting in touch with our passions and interests helps us get in touch with our heart. When we are passionate about something, we become very excited and animated. We love to talk about our passions and interests. My husband is a huge Rolling Stones fan. Every day he talks about Mick Jagger or Keith Richards. He spends time on the Rolling Stones website every night. When giving him gifts, I know I can never go wrong with something from the Rolling Stones store. His face will light up from the simplest little Rolling Stones keychain.

My younger son, however, is passionate about transportation. From the time he was 10 months old, he loved cars. This is not just a passing phase for him. His passion for cars, trucks, trains and planes has been with him for years, and I don't see things changing. He collects Matchbox and Hot Wheels cars and the majority of his books contain some type of vehicle. He loves racing car video games, Tonka movies and board games with little cars.

When you can serve the world from your area of passion, your life will be so fulfilling. Your passions and interests help refuel you and connect you to who you are. Giving to other people, when you are passionate about what you are doing, is a blessing to yourself and others. You are at your best when you are connected to your true essence and other people will benefit. You will have a smile on your face, and giving will feel effortless. If you are unsure about what you're passionate about, think about your answers to the following questions.

- What would you like to do if time or money were not an obstacle?
- What new activities would you like to try if fear didn't stop you?
- If you had a whole week to yourself to just PLAY, what would you do?
- Think back to times in your life when you were having a blast. What were you doing?
- What are you excited to talk about?
- If you had $1000 to spend on a hobby, what would you spend it on?
- What do you have a secret desire to do?
- When you play with children, what do you love to do?
- When you were a child, what were your favorite activities?
- What types of gifts do you love to receive?
- If you could pick any three books in the bookstore, what would they be about?

Putting it All Together

Defining your life purpose takes some time to process. It doesn't always happen overnight. It requires honesty and soul searching, but its well worth the wait and effort. Here is an example of my life purpose.

"Using my wisdom and authenticity, my purpose is to coach and inspire busy moms to be the role model they want to be and leave a legacy their children can pass on to future generations."

If you break apart my life purpose, you can see how all these components work together to define my purpose. Wisdom is a characteristic I have developed from my life experiences. Authenticity is one of my natural personality characteristics. Coaching is a skill I have acquired through hours and hours of training and coaching. My passion lies in personal growth and my love for moms. Because of the life I have lived, it is important to me to help strengthen families all over the world. I want to leave this world knowing I made a positive difference in the lives of moms, children and their families, including my own. Everything I do is related to my life purpose, and when I am fully connected to who I am at my core, I am completely fulfilled.

Perhaps now it will be easier for you to answer the question, "Why on Earth are *you* here?"

THE *Momnificent!* LIFE

TAKE ACTION ASSIGNMENT

Work through the exercises outlined in this chapter. Identify your gifts and passions. What do you want to do or who do you want to be to make a difference in this world? Where will you make a difference in this world? Write out five attempts at identifying your life purpose. Pick the best one and try it on for a few months. Does it feel authentic? If not, repeat the process until it feels right for you.

CHAPTER 14
✴
Seeing Life through Gratitude Glasses

"Let us rise and be thankful, for if we didn't learn a lot today, at least we learned a little, and if we didn't learn a little, at least we didn't get sick, and if we got sick, at least we didn't die; so, let us all be thankful." —Buddha

✴

When my older son was diagnosed with Attention Deficit Hyperactivity Disorder, my first reaction was relief – I finally knew the reason for his behavior. However, I was also overwhelmed with sadness, fear and anger. I felt sorry for my son and for myself. Like many others in similar circumstances, my question was, "Why me?"

Today, I am now able to focus on my gratitude. I believe I was chosen to raise my son because I would give him the best I have. Through Divine wisdom, I will learn to love and understand him for who he is. I am grateful for my son and his challenges. He has taught me how to be an amazing mother.

There is power and healing in gratitude.

How can gratitude help us in our everyday lives as moms? Think about the difference you can make in your family's life just by noticing and being thankful for all the great things they do. When you express gratitude, you show your love and appreciation. Everyone needs to feel loved and appreciated – it's a basic human need. Sometimes as moms we feel that no one appreciates us – and it is true that moms are usually last on the list to be thanked. One way you can teach gratitude is by example. Even on the days when it seems your children or husband are doing everything wrong, find a reason to thank them. Take the time and energy to look for the good. Think about what your family members do on an everyday basis. Instead of taking these thoughtful acts for granted, give them a big thank you instead. You might say to your husband, "Thank you for working so hard for our family," or, to your child, "I really appreciate your sense of humor – it feels good to laugh." Expressing your gratitude helps family members to understand how it feels to be appreciated. By being an example of gratitude to our loved ones, we encourage gratitude in them. When they do notice and thank you for your efforts, let your family members know how good it feels to receive their gratitude.

Gratitude is a wonderful motivator when you need cooperation. When enlisting the help of your children, praise them often and with enthusiasm. When my children help out, I let them know how much I value their help. Sometimes we get so busy and caught up in daily life that we forget to be grateful. We expect everyone to do their share without being asked. The only time anyone hears from Mom is when a chore has not been completed. This attitude, over the long haul, will develop very resentful and uncooperative family members.

When life is good, gratitude is easy. It becomes more challenging to be grateful when we are experiencing hard times. Financial hardship, long-term illness, the death of a loved one and marital strife can all be trying and difficult. It is not easy to be thankful when we're sitting in the valley. When life seems to be handing us a bunch of lemons, we usually feel bitter or victimized.

But what if I told you there is a new product out on the market? You can pick up a pair of "gratitude glasses" at Target for $19.99. These glasses enable you to see life in a whole different way. Here are some of the benefits you can expect from these "gratitude glasses."

There are no problems.
With these glasses, you have no problems in your life. Everything in your life is an opportunity. When we perceive life through our fears, unpaid bills and conflict, for instance, become problems or challenges. However, these glasses enable us to see life with loving eyes. The unpaid bills are an opportunity to learn more about financial responsibility. Conflict is an opportunity to learn how to love more deeply.

Sometimes when my children are acting out, I am thankful they are alive, healthy and independent. I see their strong will as a behavior that will help them in their lives. As their mother, I have an opportunity to channel this personality characteristic in a positive and constructive way.

There are no mistakes.
With the gratitude glasses, mistakes disappear. These glasses help us understand that we are doing the best we can at any given moment, and so is everyone else. We all make decisions based on who we are at the time.

Instead of viewing choices as "mistakes," why not look at them as an opportunity to learn more about ourselves and other people?

As a recovering perfectionist, I used to beat myself up for every "mistake" I made. Today I accept my humanness, which enables me to embrace my limitations. I recently attended a wedding for my husband's cousin. This was his second marriage and during the toast by the best man, his best man accidentally called his new wife by his ex wife's name. The whole crowd gasped at the "mistake." For days, the family talked about what happened. I am absolutely positive the best man was doing the best he could at that moment. This episode was an opportunity for people to embrace him with love and forgiveness.

There are no annoying people.

Put on the gratitude glasses and suddenly all the annoying people in your life become your friends. You've heard the saying, "Mean people need love." More often than not, the people we are most annoyed by are mirrors to what we despise in ourselves. The faults in others remind us that we have faults too, often the same ones. The next time someone acts in a way that makes you angry, ask yourself when was the last time you acted like that? With your new gratitude glasses, you now have the ability to release your anger and understand the annoying people on a much deeper level. You begin to appreciate your differences and the judgments disappear. Your love begins to transform not only you, but others as well.

Change is good.

You pick up your gratitude glasses and put them on, and suddenly you embrace change. You are thankful that life does not always happen as planned. You stop trying to control life, and instead let life unfold. Change is exciting, fear of the unknown is gone, and you can't wait to see what happens next. Your faith is strong and unstoppable.

As a business owner, one of the greatest insights I have had is the importance of letting go. I learned that the more I tried to control the outcome of my business goals, the more frustrated I would get. By practicing being grateful everyday for every little success, amazing doors have opened up for me. Writing this book was one of them.

Pain has a purpose.

Whether it is physical or emotional pain, it's hard to go through life without experiencing it. But with your gratitude glasses, you see that your pain has a purpose. Your physical pain tells you that something in your mind or body is not working well. Your emotional pain is a wake up call to the transformation that is possible. Without the valleys, we cannot appreciate the mountain-tops.

When I look back at all the painful moments and periods in my life, I am so grateful. Without this pain, I would not be who I am today. I would not be able to empathize with my clients when they are experiencing pain. The pain in my life has shaped my character, making me a woman of strength and perseverance.

These inexpensive "gratitude glasses" offer so many more benefits, but what if you only received these five advantages? Would you purchase the glasses? Would you wear your gratitude glasses all the time? What if I told you the glasses were yours for free? All you have to do is shift your energy by changing your thoughts.

When we allow ourselves to wallow in victim and fighting thoughts, our brains release catabolic hormones that are destructive to our entire physical system, and ultimately, our success. By wearing your "gratitude glasses" you shift your thoughts to positive and constructive ones. Thinking thoughts of thankfulness and love makes an energetic shift in your mind and body, and the results will be astonishing.

So have an attitude of gratitude. Look at everyone with grateful eyes. Listen to your heart and the heart of your loved ones. Speak words of affirmation every day of your life. Be grateful for your life with all its lessons and bless-ings. The more grateful thoughts and feelings you experience and express, the more instrumental you will be in healing the world. And your outlook on life will improve in the process.

TAKE ACTION ASSIGNMENT

Keep a gratitude journal. At the end of every day, before you go to sleep, run through your day and record everything that you are grateful for. It can be something as simple as "I had a nice hot shower," or something as major as "I got a raise today." Focus on even the challenging situations and look for things to be grateful for. This exercise will help you to focus on the positive, and put you in a healthy state of mind before retiring for the evening.

CHAPTER 15
✳
Finding Peace in Letting Go

"God grant me the serenity to accept the things I cannot change, the courage to change the things I can, and the wisdom to know the difference."
—Reinhold Niebuhr

✳

When I was in my twenties, one might say I was a control freak. I wanted to be in control of everything. The problem was I tried to control things I could not control – other people and circumstances beyond my control. If I didn't like something, I would try and change it, even if it meant changing someone else. If I felt scared or unsure of the future, I would do my best to control the future. I lived in fear of what might happen if I lost control. Then I read a life changing book for me called *Compelled to Control* by J. Keith Miller. In his book Miller says this:

"We are a nation of people who fear we are not 'enough.' Deep in the recesses of our hearts, in places we rarely reveal even to ourselves, we feel shameful and inadequate – and we're terrified someone will find out. We live in constant fear that our shortcomings will be exposed to family, to friends, to the world. We wake up at night reliving a mistake and feeling overwhelmed with shame.

"We worry. Our personal relationships don't satisfy nor do other aspects of our lives. We are lonely and frustrated, our marriages often end in separation or divorce, our children are estranged. In an effort to 'fit in' we may turn to compulsive or addictive behaviors only to find that our unconscious attempts to cover the pain are unsuccessful too, and bring only more loneliness and fear.

"We look everywhere for someone or something outside of ourselves to blame or complain about, for something to kill the pain and bring us peace. But when we increase our efforts to find happiness, we come face to face with the uncomfortable feeling that we are 'not doing it right.'

"Our answer is to try frantically to 'get control' of our work, our schedule and our relationships. Our control attempts leave in their wake some very unhappy mates, lovers, children and parents who make up our nuclear families. Even our friends and co-workers are affected. There are few truly happy campers in the world of a controller.

"There are millions of controllers – and we are burning out at an incredible rate. Our relationships are hollow, ragged, distant. We're exhausted and feel totally alone inside though we may be surrounded by people. Instead of achieving that serene and happy life that our frantic, controlling activity was supposed to produce, we have tense stomachs and bruised or broken relationships."[3]

So what is the answer? For me, it was learning to accept the things I could not control and building my self-image so I felt strong enough to walk away from the things I was unwilling to accept. I learned to believe that God is the one in ultimate control, and surrendering my life to Him brought me peace.

Understand What is within Your Control
How do you know what you can control and what you can't? It's very simple – you can only control yourself. The more you try to control other people, the stronger they will resist. Besides, if you try to control other people, they don't have to take responsibility for themselves. You become an enabler. Circumstances in your life cannot be controlled. You can control your part and your reaction to them, but you can't change the circumstance. To help you better understand the issue of control, let's look at the following scenarios.

Scenario #1 - You are unhappy because you need to lose 40 pounds.
In scenario #1, you have complete control. This situation only involves you and you have complete responsibility to lose 40 pounds or decide to be happy regardless of the weight loss.

Scenario #2 - Your son has some behavior problems due to his recent diagnosis of ADHD.
In scenario #2, you have partial control. You can put into practice a discipline program to address your son's behavior. You can explore the possibility of medication for his ADHD. You can be the best mom you can be in this situation. You cannot change the fact that he has ADHD. You cannot ultimately control his behavior – that is his job.

Scenario #3 - Your husband is driving you crazy because he can't hold down a job. In scenario #3, you have no control. This situation is the complete responsibility of your husband. He has to figure out how he's going to maintain a job. He has to change any of his behaviors that may be affecting his ability to hold a job. You have two choices: to accept this situation and take care of your own financial situation, or walk away from the marriage if you can't accept it. You need to know what your limits are – what you can and can't tolerate.

Acknowledge and Process your Feelings

What causes us to hold on tight and try to control in the first place? Normally, it's fear. What might happen if we lose control? Might we have to deal with life on different terms – terms that were not part of <u>our</u> plan?

Cheryl had a situation with her husband. He was required to pass two licensing exams for his job. The problem was his lack of commitment to studying. Cheryl was frantic and doing everything she could to make him study because she was afraid if he failed the exams, he would lose his job. She was taking control of a situation that was not within her control, and she was miserable. Her husband did fail the exams. As a matter of fact, he failed them twice, and had to take them a third time. For Cheryl to move forward and let go of this situation, she had to process her fear that her husband will lose his job and they may have to sell their house. She needed to acknowledge her fear and anger that she may have to be the breadwinner of the family.

Examine your Options

You cannot let go of something you can't control until you process your fears. Once you deal with your fear, you can decide how you will deal with the situation. You can either choose to be at peace with the situation and accept it, or you can decide you can't live with the circumstances the way they are.

When my son Kai was on the sophomore baseball team in high school, he sat on the bench a lot. In the beginning of the baseball season, I would have said it was because he wasn't performing. However, as the season progressed, when he did receive a rare opportunity to play, he performed well. One particular Saturday his batting average was .500. He had 3 runs, 2 RBI's and 1 stolen base. Although his statistics were good, he still remained on the bench.

As his mom, I was frustrated. I knew how important baseball was to my son and I didn't believe he was receiving a fair chance to show what he could do.

As my frustration mounted, I needed to examine my options. I could sit back and say nothing. I could encourage my son to talk with his coach. I could talk to the coach myself. I could ask God to work His will in this situation. We usually have options when life hands us situations that are difficult, painful, or at best, different than what we expect. Exercise your right to choose.

Look for the Lesson

Have you ever felt like you were beating your head against the wall and getting nowhere, or talking yourself blue in the face but being heard by no one? I have. One time I had a friend who was grieving the loss of a loved one. I tried everything I could to reach out and love and support her. All of my efforts were met with silence and distance. In one final attempt to connect, she slammed the door on my love. At that time of her life, she was not able to receive my love. It was a wake up call for me. I had to stand back and ask myself what the lesson was I needed to be learning.

For me, the lesson with my friend was that in the future, if ever I am hurting, and someone reaches out to love me, I never want to reject his or her love. I want to learn to embrace love as a gift to me, and a blessing to the person who loves me. The Universe delivers powerful lessons and messages. The question becomes can we see them, hear them, and learn from them? If not, I believe, we will keep receiving the same lesson in a different situation.

Focus on the Gift

The gift of letting go is peace. When we finally decide to stop controlling, a huge burden is lifted from our shoulders. Life is much easier when we let go and let life unfold naturally. When we have faith that life is exactly the way it is supposed to be in any given moment, our fears are minimized and the need to control diminishes. By trusting in Divine wisdom, you can let go of needing to solve all your problems. As a solo entrepreneur, it can sometimes be scary when you don't know where your next dollar is going to come from. I have learned that when I let go of controlling my financial and business growth, the Universe steps in and opens doors for me. The process of controlling blocks our energy and the natural course that is planned for us. So let go and trust the flow.

TAKE ACTION ASSIGNMENT

List the circumstances you are currently unhappy about in your life. Decipher which circumstances you have the power to change and which ones you don't by placing them in one of the following categories:

- Unhappy Circumstances I Can Change
- Unhappy Circumstances I Can Partially Change
- Unhappy Circumstances I Cannot Change

Work on changing the circumstances you can and accepting the ones you can't change.

CHAPTER 16

✳

Gifts that Never Go Out of Style

"You give but little when you give of your possessions. It is when you give of yourself that you truly give." –Kahlil Gibran, The Prophet

✳

Holidays and special occasions are always a time for giving. And when most of us think of giving, we think of gifts. We search the stores or the worldwide web looking for the perfect gift. For those hard-to-buy-for people, we give gift certificates. Sometimes we make it easy on ourselves and give money. Some creative people make homemade presents or give some sort of food they have made especially for their loved ones.

Although it may be traditional to give gifts for special occasions, gifts of "you" can be given every day of your life. I was thinking how wonderful it would be to make a conscious effort to give one or all of the following nine gifts. These gifts can be given to anyone and everyone, they cost you nothing but your heart, and they never go out of style.

Love
What is love? So many people think of love as a strong feeling we have. We love our kids, our spouse, and our friends, especially when they are nice to us. But do we love people when they are unlovable, or do we love people who have hurt us deeply? Love is a matter of choice, and love is an action, not a feeling. How can we stretch ourselves and offer love in the most difficult situations? One of the most challenging individuals I have had to love is my own teenage son. When he is self-absorbed and thinks about no one but himself, he is difficult to love. I am not proud of him during these times; I don't even like who he is. But as his mother, I choose to give him the gift of unconditional love. Give the gift of forgiveness to someone you've been holding a grudge against. Think loving thoughts of people when they are aggravating you. Act lovingly to someone you do not like, and pray for people who mistreat you.

Joy
What would it be like for you to experience joy, not just on special occasions, but all the time? Most of us try, but often fall short. We equate joy with

happiness, but the two are not the same. Your happiness depends on your circumstances — whether you're having a good day or bad day. Joy, on the other hand, is an attitude we can choose to have. Regardless of our situation, we can choose to be joyful. Consider changing your perspective and chucking self-pity. A victim attitude will rob you of the joy that is possible. Focus on Divine love and how the valleys you may be walking through today prepare you for the mountaintops you will experience in the future. Give the gift of gratitude, cheerful giving, and service. Every year our church organizes a program for needy children in our community. It's called Adopt-a-Child. This year I volunteered to help with that awesome event. On the church's holiday tree hung ornaments for each and every child who needed to be adopted. People would pick an ornament from the tree and sign up to purchase gifts for these children. Being a part of a program that gave 460 children a blessed holiday helped cultivate joy in my heart. It was a great feeling to know that our church could pull together to serve our community and put a smile on the faces of hundreds of children.

Peace
Most moms long for peace in their lives. The day-to-day activities of a busy family offer anything but peace. More often than not, we feel stressed and at war with the demands on our time. So how can you offer peace to the people around you when they most need it? Spend time in prayer or meditation so that you can receive the spiritual and emotional peace that comes from being centered. Then you can give relational peace to others by having an internal sense of peace and turning away from conflict. Meet criticism with a calm and listening ear, instead of defensiveness. Offer compassion and understanding instead of anger and fighting words. Manage your own stress so you can be an example to everyone around you.

Patience
Rick Warren says you can test your patience in four ways. How do you deal with interruptions? How do you handle inconveniences? How do you respond to the irritations in your life? What is your reaction when you have to wait?[4] Let's face it. There are opportunities every day for us to practice patience. Your children interrupt you while you're on the telephone, or they push all your buttons on the days you have the least amount to give. The other day I was trying to pay a $26.49 bill over the telephone. I called the number on the statement that I received. What was I met with? A series of automated voices, of course. When I finally did receive a live person, I was told I called the wrong number. So I called the new number and went through the same automated process again. Once again, I reached a person

I could talk to, only to be told he couldn't handle my account. As my frustration mounted, I listened to the man tell me to hang up and call the number again. As I slammed the phone down, I wondered to myself if these people even wanted to be paid. After closing my eyes and taking a deep breath, a solution came to me. I would write a check and mail it to the company. You might be wondering why I didn't do that in the first place. Who knows? Maybe I needed a chance to see I still have work to do in the area of patience. Give the gift of patience by developing a deeper love for people, changing how you view situations, learning to laugh at the craziness, and taking some time for yourself during stressful times.

Kindness
Do you ever stop and ask yourself how you can be kind to someone today? Acts of kindness require thoughtful effort. Smiling at people who are having a bad day is an act of kindness. Kindness can be expressed by taking the time to listen to someone who is hurting. Giving people genuine compliments and seeing the best in people is a way to show kindness. Go out of your way to do something nice for someone, and don't wait until it's convenient for you because that time often does not come. In this busy world, everyone can benefit from a little kindness.

Goodness
Goodness is simply the act of doing good or being good. Giving our best every day is a gift of goodness. When we fall into the patterns of the norm, we are just like everyone else. Why not set yourself apart and hold yourself to the highest standards of moral excellence? When other people are lying, tell the truth. In a heated exchange of angry or demeaning words, rise above and be silent or speak words of love. Act in ways that are worthy of respect. Be honorable in your character. This world can always benefit from more people practicing goodness.

Faithfulness
Giving the gift of faithfulness means you are reliable, trustworthy, dependable and consistent. If you say you're going to do something, do it. If you make plans to meet a friend, follow through with the plans, and do not cancel. Keep your promises and be a woman of integrity. Let people know you can be depended on for help. Avoid gossiping and instead be a trustworthy friend. Be a faithful servant by giving of your time, talent, and financial resources. We all need faithful people in our lives – don't underestimate the power of this gift.

Gentleness

Everyone loves a gentle spirit. Gentle people are well liked and offer the gift of love and healing to wounded souls. There are so many ways to be gentle to people. Consider having compassion and understanding by setting aside your own needs and seeing things from someone else's point of view, instead of demanding your own way. One of the greatest gifts you can give to someone is that of being non-judgmental. Have you ever wanted to share something that was really important to you, but you feared how people might judge you? How good it would feel to open your heart to someone that was totally non-judgmental. A gentle-spirited woman is easy to talk to. She listens deeply and empathizes with your feelings. Her spirit is strong, and her ability to comfort and support lifts people up. Gentleness involves talking to people with respect and disagreeing peacefully.

Self-Control

Give yourself the gift of self-control. Many of the problems we face in our life develop from a lack of self-control. Whether we face weight loss issues, financial debt, bad habits, or disorganization, the root of the problem usually starts with us. So how can you give yourself the gift of self-control? It starts with taking responsibility and committing to change. Think positive, believe in yourself, and do not let your past failures dictate your future success. Ask someone in your life or hire a life coach to hold you accountable to the change you'd like to make. Stay away from anything that tempts you to backslide on your goal, and rely on Divine power to see you through to the end. While most of the time you give to other people, you too deserve a gift.

Giving the gift of "you" never goes out of style, and is always appreciated by all who receive it. You don't have to wait for special occasions to give gifts. You can give your family, friends, neighbors, strangers, and yourself the gifts of love, joy, peace, patience, kindness, goodness, faithfulness, gentleness and self-control. Give these gifts today and every day.

TAKE ACTION ASSIGNMENT

Which of these nine gifts is easiest for you to give? Which one is the hardest for you to give? Stretch your spirit by practicing giving the most difficult gift for you to give. Give this gift as many times as you can over the next week. Give yourself a sticker on your calendar each and every time you give this gift so you can see the great effort you are making to bless another person's soul.

CHAPTER 17

＊

Forgiveness – Breaking the Cycle of Resentment

"When you hold resentment toward another, you are bound to that person or condition by an emotional link that is stronger than steel. Forgiveness is the only way to dissolve that link and get free." —Catherine Ponder

＊

When Lisa was 21, her mother disowned her for a period of 10 years. It wasn't something she could ever imagine doing to one of her children, but it happened. It was one of the most painful times of her life. She was angry at her mother and she cried a lot. Lisa got married and gave birth to her first child and her mother wasn't there. She missed her and longed for a mother-daughter relationship. Today Lisa and her mother have a beautiful relationship and she is so grateful for their reconciliation. Did this relationship they have today happen overnight? The answer is no. At the core of their relationship today is forgiveness.

What is forgiveness?

Forgiveness is something virtually all Americans aspire to – 94% surveyed in a nationwide Gallup poll said it was important to forgive—in the same survey; only 48% said they usually tried to forgive others.

I don't think a single person can escape life without experiencing hurt by another person. Maybe the hurt is angry words spoken during an argument or a friend who surprises you with betrayal. Perhaps the pain comes from emotional neglect, infidelity, divorce or even sexual and physical abuse. Sometimes the hurt is a one-time event. Other times the pain continues for a long time.

Forgiveness is a necessary step to healing from pain. It is a choice to extend mercy to the person who hurt you. Sometimes forgiveness allows you to move forward with the other person and experience a new relationship. Other times, reconciliation is not possible. In this case, forgiveness is more for you and your own personal growth.

Why forgive?

Anger and resentment drains your energy, and keeps you imprisoned by your past. By choosing to let go of your hurt and anger, you give yourself the freedom to fully experience joy in life. Anger builds inside us, so by letting go, you improve your ability to control your anger. We've all seen the person who blows up at the smallest incident. It is the accumulation of built up anger that is unreleased that causes this explosion. So many diseases, like heart disease and cancer, can be triggered by unresolved resentment. By choosing to forgive, you can dramatically improve your emotional and physical health.

You might be saying, "But you don't understand what's been done to me." And you're right; I don't know all the hurts you've endured. However, I know from experience that it pays to forgive. Forgiveness is a sign of strength – not weakness. It is the strong who can put aside the past and let go of anger and resentment. Relationships and families everywhere are estranged or strained because of the inability to forgive one another.

Without forgiveness, you cannot move forward in your own personal and relational growth. As an accredited Energy Leadership' coach, I have learned something very important about forgiveness. Bruce D Schneider, the founder of iPEC Coaching and the author of Energy Leadership' describes forgiveness in terms of energy. In his Energetic Self-Perception Chart', he states that forgiveness is a level of energy you experience when "you are prepared to take responsibility for what you think and feel, knowing no one can *make* you feel anything. You start to *forgive* others when you begin to let the 'blame game' subside."[5] Until you forgive, you will remain stuck in blaming other people for your unhappiness.

What forgiveness is not?

Forgiveness does not mean you allow people to treat you badly. It does not mean you ignore the wrongdoings. It means you accept that the person has made a mistake, and you choose to grant them mercy. When you forgive someone, you won't necessarily forget the hurt. Lisa will always remember the pain she felt when her mom disowned her, but she does not dwell on it, and she does not let it interfere with the quality of their relationship today. She has allowed herself to heal and move on. Forgiveness does not mean you are condoning or excusing the person's behavior. And it doesn't mean you have to trust that person again. Some acts, like physical and sexual abuse, require that you limit your trust or at least test the trust with the person who hurt you. Remember, forgiveness is more for you than the other person.

The process of forgiving

So you've thought about it and you're ready to forgive. You're tired of holding on to old pain and you've decided it's time to let go and move on. What do you do? First of all, you need to stop seeing yourself as a victim. When we view ourselves as victims, we don't empower ourselves to take responsibility for our lives. Life feels hopeless; we remain stuck in this belief that we have no power. To release yourself from feeling like a victim, you must face and release any anger that you feel. On the surface of the hurt is anger, and you need to break away that layer first. Underneath the anger is the pain and hurt that you must grieve. There are many ways to release anger and hurt. You can talk about it with trusted people. You can spend time journaling. You can pray about it and ask for your pain and resentment to be taken away. You can express your feelings to the person who hurt you, provided that it's possible to have a healthy conversation where both you and the other person speak and listen in respectful ways.

One of the best and most cleansing ways to release your negative feelings is to write a letter to your perpetrator. In this letter, you pour out every emotion you feel. You tell them everything that hurt you and everything they did to make you angry. Do not hold anything back. Allow yourself to deeply feel the anger and cry the tears by reading it out loud to yourself. When you are done, burn or bury the letter as a symbol that you are ready to move on. Do not give the letter to the person. This letter is for you and you only.

After processing all your emotions, you are ready to make the choice to forgive. It is a choice that requires compassion, understanding and an open and loving heart. By choosing to forgive, you are taking responsibility for your own personal happiness. When Lisa and her mother first reconciled, they talked about their feelings. Sometimes they even fought because the pain was still fresh. But they listened to one another and they tried to get inside each other's shoes. It wasn't easy, but today, even though Lisa doesn't agree with some of her mother's beliefs, she has compassion and understanding for who she is and why she made the choices she did. Lisa loves her mother regardless of their differences.

Each of us makes mistakes in life. At one time or another (probably more than one time), we will hurt another person. Maybe it will be an accident, or perhaps it will be a purposeful reaction to someone hurting you. When this does happen, do you want to be forgiven? Do you want another chance to make amends? Most people don't mean to hurt us – they are dealing with their own pain and unresolved resentment. It's unfortunate that we take it out on our loved ones, but until we break the cycle, it will continue to happen.

Are you ready to break the cycle and do your part to forgive?

TAKE ACTION ASSIGNMENT

Make a list of the people you need to forgive to free yourself from resentment and sadness. Who might you need to seek forgiveness from so you can release the guilt or shame you feel? Seek whatever help you need to process forgiveness in your life so you can experience freedom from the past.

FUN AND ENJOYMENT

CHAPTER 18
✳
Cultivating Joy in Everyday Living

"Joy is the feeling of grinning inside." —Melba Colgrove

✳

The smell of homemade apple pie fills the room. You open the cabinets over and over because you are so proud of your newly organized kitchen. You read a familiar story to your child and mess up all the words just so you can hear him giggle. You lie down next to a fire and listen to your favorite music. Do any of these things make you smile? If you had a list of things that made you smile or laugh, what would be on your "joy list"?

Cultivating joy in everyday living is not something we often think of. We are too busy getting things "done" or tackling the day-to-day demands and needs of those around us to think about having fun. Real fun is something we save for vacations, right? Well, what if we made a decision that we were going to enjoy life every day, all day? What would need to change in our lives?

The first step toward living an enjoyable life is the **belief** that it is possible. Last night I spoke to a group of moms that were members of an organization called Parent and Child Educational Services (PACES). I asked them, "What if I were to give you permission to take a half day off from being a mom? What would you do?" Two moms answered me. "I would read for four hours," said one mom. Another mom said, "I would use Mapquest to map out all the things I needed to get done." That is not exactly the answer I was looking for. I was wondering what fun and nurturing activities moms would choose to do. Most of the moms just looked at me with a blank stare. So I asked a different question, "Does the thought of doing something fun for yourself excite you?" A few more responses came. A very honest mom said all she thinks about doing is running errands without the kids. Another mom said, "I just don't think about it; it doesn't happen." Well, of course it's not going to happen if we don't plan to have fun.

Just think how much more enjoyable life would be if you were **intentional** about creating a joyful life. Most of the time, we don't stop long enough to think that it is within our power to create something different. The truth of the matter is we can be the author of our own life storybook. One of my clients, a doctor, came to me in search of a more balanced life. Angela was working and living life at a very frantic pace. During one of her sessions, we began talking about her vision for her life. When I asked her what she wanted, she replied, "a lake house where I can go to get away from everything and enjoy some peace and much needed down time." Angela was being intentional about creating her life the way she envisioned. I am happy to say she found the perfect lake house for her family. With some planning and focus on her need to create peace and joy in her life, I am positive she will enjoy many days in her new getaway home. Maybe a lake house is not your idea of fun and joy, but surely something is.

You were created uniquely different than anyone else, with different passions, likes, and dislikes. **What makes you tick?** Think back to the times in your life when you felt totally blissful. What were you doing? Who were you with? Where were you? Dig deep and make a list of as many activities, people and places in life that make you smile and feel wonderful. Be as detailed as possible. This is your "joy list." Here is an example of a joy list.

· Enjoying hot chocolate on a cold winter day
· A Saturday afternoon lunch with my best friend
· Two hours reading a romance novel while lying in a hammock
  in the back yard
· Listening to worship music while I take a walk in nature
· Sending the kids to grandma's house so I can make love to my husband
· Hosting a party for some neighborhood friends
· Playing Marco Polo with the kids in the pool
· Going to see a "chick flick" by myself
· Getting my hands dirty in the garden
· Baking cookies and having the pleasure of eating that first warm
  one that comes out of the oven

Now, think of things in your life that drain your energy and put you in a grumpy mood. For me, my "energy drain list" consists of things like cold weather, negative people, clutter, loud noises, and overeating. Make a list of people, places and things in your life that deplete your energy. Here are some examples of energy drains:

- Cat food on the kitchen table because it's the only surface the dog won't get to
- Cleaning supplies that won't fit under the sink
- Throwing away money on things I don't really need or use
- A child that constantly interrupts me when I am on the phone
- A long commute to work
- A bedroom closet that you can't stand looking at
- A friend that constantly calls you up to complain
- An ugly bedspread
- Socks and underwear with holes in them
- A struggle with being on time

Now that you have your two lists, start saying yes to your "joy list" and no to your "energy drain list." **Saying yes to more joy** means you will create opportunities to experience joy on a regular basis. You will spend time with people you love, hang out in places that fill you up and do things you love to do. Maybe it means you will journal under a tree with a tall glass of lemonade. Perhaps you'll go for a run with your best friend or have a snowball fight with your family. Creating joy can be as simple as watching a good movie, taking a cat nap in the sun, or making ice cream sundaes for dessert.

Saying no to the energy drains will require that you set some boundaries in your life to protect your energy. What personal standards do you need to set to take care of yourself? What agreements do you need to make and keep with yourself and others in order to be at your best? Saying no to your energy drains might mean you plan ahead so you can be on time and better organized, or go to bed early so you have plenty of sleep. Maybe there will be conversations or people you need to politely excuse yourself from. Give yourself permission to decline the activities that take too much from your energy supply. Saying no to the energy drains may mean you have to ask for help.

Sometimes in life we have to do things we don't particularly care for. At times, we can rectify the problem by changing our situation. We can find a new job or hire someone to do the housecleaning. Other times, we don't have a choice about our life circumstances. Life hands us matters we have no control over. This is when our *attitude* must prevail. Remember, you are the author of your story and you can choose how you are going to respond to the

unpleasantness of life. Find ways to make the mundane exciting. Relieve the stress and tension with humor. Soften the sadness and pain with sweetness.

And to help us with our attitude and our ability to cultivate joy at all times during life, *God is available*. We can choose to connect to His love, His strength, His joy and His peace at any time during the day. By *staying conscious* of our moods and feelings, we can tell very quickly when we fall off the path of joyful living. Immediately make a choice to say yes to the belief that joy is possible, intentionally create joy, eliminate any energy drains, and reconnect with the one and only Source for infinite joy.

TAKE ACTION ASSIGNMENT

Make your "joy list" and your "energy drain" list. Hang them on the refriger-ator so you can see them. This week, and every week, schedule and participate in one activity from your "joy list" and eliminate one energy drain.

CHAPTER 19
✳
Selling Laughter in a Bottle

"Always laugh when you can. It is cheap medicine." —Lord Byron

✳

With all the physical and emotional benefits we receive from laughter, I wish I could package it in a bottle and sell it. Wouldn't that be great? Take a laughter pill and suddenly you are laughing hysterically and having the time of your life. Maybe then we could get rid of all the other medications and drugs. Blood pressure medicine, antidepressants, and anxiety drugs would be replaced by laughter pills. It's too bad we can't sell laughter – I might be laughing myself to the bank.

Not too long ago I attended a conference on developing a healthy money mindset. I participated in a rather effective exercise involving laughter. We were asked to close our eyes and repeat an old money belief that we wanted to get rid of. I chose to release the belief that "you have to work really hard to be rich." As I was repeating the belief in my mind, suddenly laughter was filling the room. It wasn't that people could read my mind and they were responding with laughter. The trainers of the conference were playing a laughter track. Instead of hearing music coming through the speakers, we were listening to a group of people who were laughing hysterically. The more the people laughed, the funnier my belief became. Within a few minutes, I was laughing. Laughter is contagious. Not only was I getting drawn into the group of laughing people, but I was also reprogramming the hilarious belief I had hung on to for years.

The Benefits of Laughter

Laughter really is a drug, but a healthy one. Laughter *lowers our blood pressure*, and recent studies have show that it may protect our heart by *helping to prevent heart disease*. Laughter *changes our biochemical state* and *improves brain function* by stimulating both sides of the brain. It *relieves stress* by allowing us to release tension and anxiety in our bodies. And believe it or not, laughter actually gives your body a little *internal workout*. According to HelpGuide.org, "it is estimated that hearty laughter can burn calories equivalent to several minutes on the rowing machine or the exercise bike."

Laughter does more than improve our physical well-being. There are emotional and social benefits as well. Laughter helps us *connect with people*. Recently, I had a phone call with another coach I was speaking to for the first time. She was asking me how I balanced everything in life with my business. I thought it was a perfect time to make light of just how difficult it can be sometimes to balance our lives. I proceeded to tell her I had recently taken on four new clients at one time, and there were times I was afraid I was going to forget who my clients were. I pretended I was talking to a client and I said, "Now who are you, and what are you working on?" Before you knew it, we were both hysterically laughing together on the phone. Now, of course, I would not forget my clients in real life, but laughter enabled us to release the real fear that might happen if we became too overwhelmed. But more importantly, those few moments of laughter we shared bonded us together on an emotional level. I felt closer to her. There was no doubt I was talking to another human being and she understood what I was feeling.

Laughter helps us *replace distressing emotions*. Annie is one of my clients and she is working on making some hard changes. Annie is learning to take better care of her self by setting boundaries in her life. I know deep down she is experiencing a lot of fear and stress because her body is reacting with panic attacks. Annie has always struggled with telling people no, and she is now being forced to make some hard decisions and practice self-care. But I appreciate my calls with Annie because I know I can count on her to have a great sense of humor about all that is going on in her life. Annie uses laughter to release the fear she feels when we talk about hard stuff.

The other day my six year old was having a "hissy fit" over not getting his way. In other words, he was throwing a little tantrum. As he was stomping his feet and screaming in anger, his shorts fell down. My husband and I couldn't help it; we started cracking up laughing. I guess my son realized just how ridiculous he was acting because then he started laughing. In the big scheme of things, laughter sure beats getting stressed out and angry at our children's tantrums.

Laughter increases the oxygen level in our blood, *giving us more energy*. What mom can't use more energy? So instead of drinking energy drinks or eating energy bars, we can just start laughing more. But don't laugh too much or you might be up all night.

Life can get too serious sometimes. Laughter is a great way to *keep things in perspective*. I admit some things are not a laughing matter, but there are a

THE *Momnificent!* LIFE

whole lot of situations that we take far too seriously. About six months ago, my teenager blew out two tires on our car because he ran into a curb on the side of the road. One of the wheels was bent and the car had to be towed to the shop. Now some parents might be upset that they had to spend $800 to fix the car. I took this opportunity to keep things in perspective; my son was not injured and that was most important. One day while driving down the same road the accident happened, my son showed me the curb he ran into. Not understanding how on Earth he managed to run into that curb, I teased him about his driving. He knew I was using humor to give him a hard time and we laughed about the accident.

Laughter *makes us feel good* because it releases endorphins in our brains, and endorphins are the "feel good" hormone. If you are laughing, it is almost impossible to feel sad or mad. A sad person is uplifted by laughter. Tension is broken with laughter. Laughter helps to *lighten our load*. We can carry around heavy burdens with all the responsibilities that come with raising a family. Laughter reminds us that we can relax and enjoy life, even when we are experiencing a lot of stress. Julie Ann Barnhill, a popular author for mothers, always takes the lighter approach to being a mom. She has the ability to talk about tough subjects with an added sense of humor that makes mothers laugh.

Ways to Add More Laughter to Your Life

Hang out with funny or lighthearted people. My sister-in-law and her family are funny. They are a blast to hang out with. I'm not sure I've ever seen my sister-in-law act seriously. She takes the lighter approach to life. Very little bothers her. Much of life to her is hilariously funny. My sister-in-law is a prankster at heart, and she has taught her daughters her little antics as well. One time she and her daughter played a little prank on one of her daughter's boyfriends. They invited him to a party at the house. When he asked what he should wear, they told him it was a formal party. I'm not sure if he thought it was very funny when he was the only one that showed up in a suit, but all three of the girls thought it was hilarious. Even when they told the story later, you couldn't help but laugh and be affected by their infectious and playful spirit. Funny and lighthearted people can teach us very valuable lessons about how to take life less seriously. And if you hang out with them all the time, you will laugh a lot more.

Smile. Smiling is the beginning of laughter. When someone gives you a big smile, it's hard not to return the smile. If you are feeling down, force your-self to smile. Try to smile at everyone you see. Stand in the mirror and smile at yourself. Before you know it, you might just start laughing.

Actively look for the funny side of life. Looking for the funny side of life is much like looking for things to be grateful for. If it doesn't come naturally for you to see humor, you will have to be proactive about it. Look at all the times we have laughed later about a situation that at the time we deemed serious. If we practice, we can begin to see the more serious situations as funny in the moment. What would you rather do? Laugh, or cry?

Stop taking yourself and other people so seriously. Have you learned to laugh at your mistakes? I used to be so hard on myself. It was not acceptable for me to make a mistake. Then I got real. Everyone makes mistakes. How does it serve you to beat yourself up? You can laugh at your mistakes and still take responsibility for learning from them. When you lighten up and treat your-self and others with grace, you and other people will more likely succeed. The negative emotions of guilt, anger and embarrassment will attract more negative events into your life. The positive energy of laughter will bring you more good feelings and situations.

Watch funny movies and television shows or read funny books. My teenager hates to go to funny movies with me. I embarrass him because I don't hold back my laughter. If something is funny to me, I am going to passionately express my sense of humor. There is nothing that feels better than to laugh out loud. So rent a funny movie, watch your favorite comedy show, or pick up a joke book. Put some humor into your life.

Learn from children. Children know how to have fun. They can show us how to laugh and giggle. Get into the minds of children. Start seeing life from their perspective. I guarantee you will be less serious. As adults, we some-times make the mistake of stripping our children from the playfulness that is inherent in them. Instead we should allow them to teach us a thing or two about life.

Do you remember being a child and trying to catch fireflies in a jar? Wouldn't it be great if we could walk around and catch laughter in a jar? Then when we felt sad or stressed, we could take the lid off the jar and be infected with laughter. We could give a jar of laughter to every serious person. The world would be a much happier place if we all laughed a little more.

TAKE ACTION ASSIGNMENT

Put more laughter into your life. If you're too serious, lighten up. If you feel sad, smile. If you already laugh a lot, laugh even more. Have fun today and every day.

CHAPTER 20
✸
The Best Time is Right Now

"It is difficult to live in the present, ridiculous to live in the future, and impossible to live in the past. Nothing is as far away as one minute ago."
—Jim Bishop

✸

It was a beautiful autumn morning, but I'm not sure I really noticed. In a spur of a moment before church, I found myself outside with Ian. Bored with kicking the soccer ball around, I suggested we work on his kindergarten homework assignment. We moved from tree to tree, picking off the leaves and gathering them in a Ziploc plastic bag. Some leaves were big and others were small. A few leaves were still green, but most were rich colors of orange, red and yellow, but I wasn't really paying much attention. I was just focused on getting as many different leaves into the bag. That was the assignment, so I just wanted to get it done. For whatever reason that morning, I was distracted, slightly crabby, and stuck in my own head. Until, my son's words jolted me into reality. He said, "Mommy, this is so much fun."

Oh my gosh, I was missing this fun with my son because I was not in the moment. The simplicity of his words and the tenderness of his heart reminded me of the joy I was missing because I was somewhere other than right there in the present. We can learn from children about living in the moment. Children aren't thinking about yesterday, what they should be doing, or fantasizing about some future point in time. They are concerned with what is going on right now.

Benefits of Being in the Moment

I admit; it's not easy to be in the moment. As a matter of fact, I actually had to do a little research on this topic before I felt totally comfortable writing about it. Even though it can be challenging to stay in the moment, the benefits make it worth trying.

Being in the moment enables us to **enjoy the task we are engaged in**. How many times do you just go through the motions of a task or activity without really concentrating on what you are doing? Consider the task of eating a delicious dessert. Do you really stop to savor every bite or do you just wolf it down? An ice cream sundae is much more enjoyable if you slow down and concentrate on the sweetness, coolness and texture of the ice cream. When I was a teenager, my mom and I use to go jogging around the neighborhood high school track. Our reward for working out was a trip to Swensen's ice cream shop. This ice cream shop had every combination of ice cream sundaes that you could think of. Each time we would try a different kind. The memories of enjoying our special time together eating delicious ice cream sundaes will stay with me forever.

Being in the moment **allows you to be a better communicator**. When most people are having a conversation with another person, instead of listening while the other person is talking, they are thinking about what they want to say or something else completely different. By practicing being in the moment, we suspend our thoughts and give the other person all of our attention. Have you ever talked with a person that gave you 100% of their attention? How did it make you feel? Chances are you felt totally nurtured and heard. One of the greatest gifts you can give your friends and family members is the ability to be in the moment when you are spending time with them.

Another benefit of being in the moment is that it **increases your work efforts**. When we are totally in the moment, we are completely focused on what we are doing. This increase in focus helps us to be more productive. We can work more efficiently, leaving us time for pleasure.

Sometimes when I write, the words just flow onto the paper. I can knock out an article in a very short period of time. Other times, I sit and stare at the computer screen, my thoughts everywhere other than where they are supposed to be. When I can stop my mind chatter and be in the moment, I get into the "flow" and the result is **abundant creativity**.

Being in the moment gives us **peace of mind** and helps us **embrace and love life**. If you're constantly reliving the past or worried about the future, how can you truly relax and enjoy life? Being in the moment allows us to let go of everything that is clouding our mind and get lost in the bliss of timeless living. By paying attention to the now, we are able to truly see all the beauty that is around us.

How to Be in the Moment

You're probably saying, "That all sounds really nice, but can it truly be a reality?" I think if we work at it, it can be a reality more often than it is now. Like anything we try for the first time, it will seem foreign in the beginning. But the more you experience being in the moment, the more you will desire to return to that state of mind. So let's look at the keys to achieving an "in the moment" state of being.

AWARENESS

Having awareness means that you have the ability to direct and control your thinking in a manner that produces the best results. So often we operate on autopilot without giving much thought to what we are thinking about. Whenever I conduct a discovery session, I ask clients how aware they are of the various thoughts that go through their mind. The question always makes people stop for a moment. It's almost as if they need to think about whether or not they know what their thoughts are. The reason is because so many of our thoughts are automatic. We've been thinking the same type of thoughts for so long that we don't pay attention anymore. By developing awareness, you now move from operating in life from your automatic thoughts to choosing your thoughts more carefully before you take action.

RESPOND VS. REACT

Once you become aware of how your thoughts control your emotions and your behavior, you can choose to respond to people and life's situations instead of reacting. The other day I went to pick up my son from kindergarten. Our elementary school has a big circle drive that cars line up in to pick up their children. I arrived later than normal so my car was far away from the school. Concerned that my son, who is only 5, wouldn't see me, I put my car in park and got out of my car to go get him. As I passed a big SUV in line, I realized the woman was honking at me. Trying to understand what she wanted, I walked back to her vehicle. Much to my surprise, she started yelling at me, "How are people supposed to get around you when you get out of your car? The sign says 'NO PARKING FROM 3:15 TO 3:45'." I'm not sure what else she screamed at me; I was kind of taken aback by her anger. Instead of reacting to her obvious reaction to me, I responded by saying "I'm very sorry ma'am." Once again she reacted, "Can't you read the sign?" Now I can't help but wonder: if this woman would have stopped long enough to pay attention to her thoughts, would she have responded the same way to me? Responding instead of reacting gives you the space in your mind to generate solutions, pick the best one, and stay calm and centered under pressure. When you choose to respond to people and life, I can guarantee you will be happier with your choices.

USE THOUGHTS OF PAST AND FUTURE APPROPRIATELY

How many times do you catch yourself running an event from the past over and over in your mind? Maybe you relive the hurt and anger you felt. Perhaps you beat yourself up for what you didn't say or what you should have done. Reliving the past, especially if it conjures up negative emotions, does nothing for maintaining a healthy and peaceful state of mind. You cannot change anything about the past. It is done; it is over. The only and most constructive use of the past is to learn from it and move on. If you're holding on to hurts, forgive and let it go. The inability to forgive is only holding you prisoner in your own mind.

In addition, you can't be in the moment if you're living in the future. Human beings have a tendency to fantasize about how much better life would be if only things were different. When I lose those 20 pounds, I'll feel much better about myself. As soon as we get out of debt, I can relax and be happy. After I get a new job, I'll be able to spend more time at home with the family. Why wait for some future occurrence to be happy, peaceful or successful when you can choose those states right now in the moment? Use your thoughts of the future to plan and realize your vision, but then return to the present moment and appreciate all you have today.

SUSPEND ALL JUDGMENTS

To experience the peace and calm that comes from being in the moment, you need to be able to have no judgments about what should be happening. What happens is we get caught up in how we think others should act or how life should unfold. The fact is we don't have control over anything other than ourselves. People around us make choices; situations in life take place unexpectedly. Life is what it is. People are who they are. About two weeks ago, a friend of mine called me with some unexpected news. With three children under the age of 6, she announced that she was pregnant again. Another child was not part of her plan, or was it? She certainly wasn't trying to get pregnant; she wasn't even really thinking of having another baby. When I asked her how she was feeling about this surprising news, she told me she was choosing to feel joy. My friend is wise enough to make the choice to make this new baby a part of her plan. A failure to integrate her present reality, by entertaining thoughts of why this happened, would interfere with her ability to maintain a peaceful state of mind.

Pay attention to your thoughts. Direct them in a positive and constructive way. Notice all the blessings in your life. Each and every moment, open your eyes and mind wide to all the possibilities that are waiting for you. This morning, as my pregnant friend was losing her breakfast in the toilet, her one year old was using sign language to communicate her need to nurse, and her four and six year old girls were screaming for her to settle their differences, she began to laugh. Another baby is on the way and laughter at the sometimes craziness of life was her choice.

TAKE ACTION ASSIGNMENT

Pick one day this week to focus completely on being in the moment. Every time your thoughts wander away from the present moment, ask yourself "What does this have to do with right now?" Then return to the moment. For this day, concentrate on every task you do and every conversation you have. Choose to respond to your life instead of reacting. Notice things you wouldn't normally notice. Appreciate everything and everyone around you. Make no judgments about your life on this day. Notice how you feel at the end of the day.

CHAPTER 21
✳
The Value of Spending Time Alone

"Grace decided she also needed to spend time just being quiet. She did not use the time to run errands, shop, or even get together with a friend. She sketched, she read, she painted, she simply sat and noticed the beauty of the marsh, the woods, the birds. She embraced solitude and silence in a way she never had. She knew she was onto something, because she felt a deep peace and joy in her heart."

(Excerpt from Breathe – Creating Space for God in a Hectic Life *by Keri Wyatt Kent)*

✳

At the end of summer 2005, I went to Door County, Wisconsin by myself. The sole purpose of the mini vacation was to spend some time alone. It had been a long summer with the children and I needed some time to refuel and regain my identity as a woman. It was a weekend I will always remember. The resort I stayed in was located in the woods overlooking the waters of Sister Bay. It was a quaint and quiet place, with the romance and charm of a country inn, but the luxurious amenities of an elegant resort. Each morning, I started with a peaceful walk in the woods. My days were spent shopping in all the unique stores, exploring the landscape with my camera, and tantalizing my tongue with different cuisines. I ended each day with an entertaining movie in the quiet of my room.

It might seem somewhat strange to you to consider taking a mini retreat to spend time alone. Spending time alone, however, is necessary for developing a healthy relationship with yourself and nourishing who you are. Time alone can involve quiet time in which you are doing nothing, or it can involve activities that you engage in by yourself.

Spend Quiet Time Alone for Self-Reflection

Getting to know yourself requires a lot of self-reflection. Self-reflection is best done in a quiet space. By being alone in quiet, you think more and are forced to pay attention to your feelings. So often, people drown out any opportunity to hear themselves by flipping on the television, listening to distracting music, or engaging in some other activity that requires concentration. When your focus is shifted to other things, there is no chance to just "be" with yourself and experience whatever comes up.

Self-reflection helps you figure out who you are. You can begin to appreciate how you feel about certain things. It allows you the time to process and sort out your emotions. You can use this time to work on building your character. It is not a time to criticize your weaknesses, but instead to focus on healing and learning from life's lessons. It gives you the opportunity to brainstorm solutions to challenges and ask yourself how things should best be handled. All of this brings you closer to knowing and embracing your truest self.

When you are quiet and still, you can more clearly hear the voice of God and your own intuition speaking to you. You need to quiet your mind's chatter and the background noise of your day to make room for the still, small voice to speak to you. It may be the voice of God giving you an answer to your prayer. That little voice could be your intuition nagging you to make a different choice in your life. It is through quiet and solitude that the truth speaks the loudest.

Spending time in quiet solitude nourishes your soul. Why do you think you feel so refreshed after a good night's sleep? When your body and mind have completely shut down, they are refueled for a new day. By spending time in quiet solitude, you recharge your battery. You only have so much energy to function on before you start running out. When you start running out, you become short-tempered, irritable, impatient, tired, or even spacey. Regular time for yourself will do wonders for keeping you refueled, emotionally available, relaxed, and happy.

Spend Time Alone Engaged in Activities You Love

During your alone time, give yourself the gift of engaging in activities you love but seldom get the opportunity to participate in. Engaging in activities that bring you joy is another way to nurture you soul. Every night before bed, I escape to my bedroom for my nightly ritual of reading. I love books! I spend some time reading spiritual material that feeds and grows my soul. Or I increase my learning with whatever non-fiction book interests me. Then I indulge in whatever fiction book I happen to be reading at the time. My husband, on the other hand, stays up late at night watching his Rolling Stones DVDs or listening to his favorite music. This alone time for each of us is extremely important. We protect it like a mother bear protects her cub because it's what we need to wind down and refuel for the next day.

Spend Time Alone Engaging in New Activities

Engaging in new activities during your time alone can help you explore more about yourself and learn things you didn't know before. When I took my trip to Door County, I brought with me an open mind and a desire to try new things. My favorite activity I participated in was a trip to a local art studio. It was a two-story house set up for all kinds of art activities —ceramics, glass painting, metal, woodworks, etc. I chose something I had never tried before — creating a mosaic piece of art. There were jars upon jars filled with porcelain and glass tiles of every color, shape and texture you can imagine. There were endless possibilities for creating mosaics on wooden boards. I chose a board in the shape of a big coffee cup that I could hang on my kitchen wall. I had so much fun creating it; plus I learned something about myself. I really enjoyed doing mosaics. Had I not ventured into something new, I would have never known this about myself.

Create Time to Be Alone

For some people spending time alone is something they wrestle with. It may be scary for those who fear being alone. Initially it may feel boring. It is easy to become distracted and lose your alone time. It may be difficult to make time for being alone, especially if you live with other people or you're a mother of small children.

To begin, you will have to acknowledge the sacrifices you may have to make in other areas of your life to create time for yourself. Perhaps you'll have to leave the house or escape to a private section of your home. You may have to unplug the phone.

You will need to choose a block of time that feels comfortable and ask other family members to respect this time and assume responsibilities, if needed, to help you out. You might consider going to your local coffee shop and having a cup of coffee with yourself. Consider a personal retreat. Find a corner in your local library. Spend time in nature by going for a walk in the park. Shoot for a block of at least 30 minutes several times per week.

During your time alone, spend time reflecting on your life. Think about areas in which you would like to grow. Write your thoughts and feelings for the day in a special journal. Participate in activities you love or experiment with new activities. Enjoy being with yourself as much as you would enjoy being with someone else you loved. If you do this regularly, I can guarantee you will be a better mom, a more loving wife, and attentive friend. Try it and reap the amazing benefits of spending time alone.

TAKE ACTION ASSIGNMENT

Look at your calendar and figure out a time for you to spend 2-3 hours by yourself. Arrange for a babysitter for your children. Create a plan that includes one or two activities that will allow you to experience quiet reflection, refueling of your spirit, and simple pleasure. Go home, after spending time alone, and pay close attention to how you feel. Put aside any guilt and notice the positive feelings that are coming up. Record your experience so you can remember the value of spending time alone.

CHAPTER 22

❋

4 Beliefs that Block Fun from Our Lives

"Might as well remove those doubts. Fun is what it's all about." —from Purported Utterances of The Oaqui

❋

Bonnie was a 40 year old, successful businesswoman and single mother of a teenage boy. She came to me because her life was falling apart. On the outside, she seemed to be holding everything together, but on the inside, she was slowly unraveling. Bonnie was recently diagnosed with chronic fatigue syndrome and was beginning to experience anxiety attacks. All her life, she was conditioned to take care of everyone else and pay very little attention to her own needs. As a result, the stress was mounting and she did not have the tools to cope.

Bonnie was a doer. She didn't sit still for long because there was always something to be done. She worked 60 hours a week, and in her spare time, she was taking care of everyone else in her life. As we began to explore the idea of having fun in her life, she nervously laughed at me. Having fun was a foreign concept to Bonnie. Trying to understand her resistance to using fun as a means to release stress, I uncovered the belief that was keeping her stuck in her world of "all work and no play."

Having Fun is a Waste of Time

A lot of moms put "fun" on the back burner. Of all the things that need to be done, having fun is a frivolous activity that interferes with real accomplishment. It is not uncommon for moms to be focused on the unending "to do" list, sacrificing fun until the tasks are completed. Did I mention that the mom "to do" list is never completed and never goes away?

There is a greater perceived value in completing tasks and meeting everyone's needs than there is in meeting our own need for fun. Many moms have blocked that need so they don't even recognize it anymore. They feel the stress and irritability that is the result of blocking fun.

So how do we change this belief that having fun is a waste of time? When we can recognize and experience the benefits of having fun, we can begin to change the perceived value. After taking some time to have fun, how did you feel afterwards? Were you more relaxed and patient? Did you have more energy to give back to your family? How productive were you after you took some time to cut loose and unwind? Did anything fall apart while you were out having fun? After several fun outings with herself, Bonnie reported that having fun could become a habit in her life. I was glad to hear her think like that. Sometimes we need to be reminded that having fun is an excellent use of our time.

But I Feel So Guilty When I Take Time for Me

Not every mom struggles with feeling guilt when they decide to leave their children with a babysitter to engage in a little fun, but a lot do. The single most determining factor of whether or not moms feel entitled to have fun is how much time they spend playing with their children. If a mother spends a lot of quality time with her children, she is not as likely to feel guilty about taking time for herself. However, if a mom struggles to balance work, family, marriage and household responsibilities, taking time for herself falls to the bottom of her priority list.

Another issue that can cause guilt for moms is who they have to care for their children while they are gone. Christine decided to go out on a date with her husband one evening, and her in-laws were in charge of watching her baby boy. Although she knows grandma and grandpa love their grandson, she was not completely comfortable with their parenting style. To relieve her anxiety, she decided to call home to check on her son. After speaking with her mother-in-law, her guilt about leaving Ben increased. Ben was screaming and her mother-in-law did not know what to do to settle him down. It was very clear to Christine that the home environment was not what she planned for Ben. She had a sudden urge to go home.

It's difficult to relax enough to have fun if we're not comfortable with who is taking care of our children. In addition, if our children are not receiving enough time with us, we feel guilty about having fun. Creating a life that includes regular time to have fun as a mom requires a balanced approach. We have to make choices about how best to use our time so our time is distributed between our various responsibilities in a way that feels authentic to us. We have to know what is important to us so we can make decisions about who is best equipped to take care of our children. When we feel comfortable about how much time we spend with our children, and we have created a list of people we truly trust with our children, much of the guilt can be alleviated.

Having Fun Diminishes the "Good Mom" Image

How do you define a "good mom"? Does a "good mom" pour her life into the lives of her children? Many moms believe that to be a good mom you have to be in constant service to your children. Society rewards the mom that sacrifices her life for the lives of her children. The mom who works endlessly to keep a clean home, provide for her family, cook healthy meals, support all the children's activities, and nurture her children is an image many moms strive for.

The problem with this "good mom" image is there is no time for mom. While she may do all these great acts of service, there is a price that is paid. Normally this "good mom" is stressed out, irritable and often resentful. To suggest that she take some time for herself to have fun would go against the "good mom" image she is trying to maintain. In her mind, there is something wrong with her because she can't cope with the image, but the real issue lies in the image itself.

A new "good mom" image needs to be created; an image that allows mom to have fun too, and still be considered a good mom. To be really good moms, we have to take time to refuel, and we refuel when we're engaged in fun activities. It's okay to take a break from our children; as a matter of fact, it's healthy. When we take time to have fun, we are telling our children that we value fun, and we are worthy of having fun as well.

Mom's Fun Takes a Backseat

When planning a fun family activity, how many times have you put your needs for fun in the backseat? You let your children or your husband decide what you're going to do. They pick their favorite restaurant or recreational activity, and you quietly go along with whatever they choose. It's not a bad choice, but it may not be exactly your idea of having fun. You just want your kids to have fun; your time to have fun will come later. The problem is that most of the time it never comes.

I'll never forget my most recent Mother's Day. First of all, it took a special holiday dedicated to moms for me to plan a fun day for myself. When my husband asked me what I wanted to do, I struggled to answer him. My natural tendency was to take the emphasis off of me, and minimize the celebration. At first, I started to think about what would be fun for everyone. Isn't this what moms do?

Weird feelings came up as I focused my attention on what I wanted to do.

However, it's important to me that my children learn to take the focus off themselves once in a while and think about the needs of others. So I decided we would have lunch at the Egg Harbor Café – one of my favorite restaurants. This choice didn't make either one of my boys very happy. Even my husband made a comment that the place was kind of feminine. You think that's why I might like it. Next we made a trip to the local bike shop to pick out a new bicycle for me. Bike riding is fun for me. Keeping my boys interested in the bike shop lasted for about five minutes. I tried on different bikes and went through the purchase process, while answering the same question over and over, "Are you ready yet?" It's no wonder we put our fun on the backseat. But I think its okay for us to take the front seat on fun once in a while.

Our needs for fun are just as important as anyone else's. When we begin to believe this, we start breaking down the old beliefs that block us from having fun. We find ways to make time for our fun, without feeling guilty. We redefine our "good mom" image to include being carefree, spontaneous and full of life. Isn't that what having fun is all about?

TAKE ACTION ASSIGNMENT

What currently stands in your way of having fun on a regular basis? Make a list of the beliefs you hang on to that interfere with you being carefree, spontaneous and full of life. What new beliefs would you like to replace the old ones with?

CHAPTER 23
*
Developing a Family Recreation Plan

"The bond that links your true family is not one of blood, but of respect and joy in each other's life." —Richard Bach

*

With more and more structured activities taking up our children's time, this leaves little time for family recreation. Linda has two girls; one is eight years old and the other is ten. Each girl can be involved in up to three different extracurricular activities during the school year. Whether it is music lessons, gymnastics or swimming, there is hardly time to do anything together as a family. Sure, mom and dad juggle the responsibilities of getting each child to their respective activities and they stay to watch the practices or meets, but they are not truly interacting with their girls. Competitive activities such as these have replaced family recreation.

Family recreation would be defined as a pleasurable or relaxing activity done together as a family. Examples would be having a picnic together at a local park, going on a hike together in the woods, or exploring a fun museum together on a Saturday afternoon. You don't have to leave the house to enjoy family recreation. You can play board games together, kick the soccer ball around in the back yard, or blow bubbles on the front porch.

The Benefits of Family Recreation

Family recreation teaches life skills. Children learn a number of life skills from hanging together as a family. They learn how to solve problems and coop- erate with one another. Any time you have two or more people together, each with their own personalities and ideas, compromise must be practiced. We have to learn to take turns and consider the needs of other people. Children learn to cope with their frustration when they don't get their way or they are learning something new. And family recreation allows us to teach our chil- dren about having a positive attitude. When we play a game together as a family, we don't allow our children to be poor sports. We use the opportunity to teach them how to lose gracefully and congratulate the winners. We show them that playing a game is not always about winning and losing, but more about having fun.

Family recreation builds positive character. When we spend time together as a family, children learn a number of positive character traits. They learn to respect everyone in the family. If you're playing a game together, they are learning to be honest. Cheating is not allowed. Children have the opportunity to develop their creativity, especially during imaginative play. And they learn to be flexible because everyone is different. When Donna decided to start a family night in her family, she gave each member of the family an opportunity to pick a fun family activity. Mom, Dad and the two children took turns choosing something fun to do. When it wasn't your turn, you were not allowed to complain about the activity because they were trying to teach fairness.

Family recreation promotes physical, emotional, mental and social development. We all need recreation in our lives. Active activities exercise our bodies. Games that require us to think or activities that encourage learning promote healthy mental development. Spending time together as a family and interacting in relationship with one another develops our children socially. Emotionally, we receive love, companionship and the release of stressful feelings when we engage in recreational activities.

Family recreation strengthens family bonds. Spending time together builds intimacy in our lives. For children to feel loved, we need to spend quality time with them. This helps them feel valued and worthy of attention. The more time we spend together, the more we get to know one another. This helps us feel closer as a family. When we play together, we laugh and enjoy life together. These emotional feelings strengthen our family bonds.

Family recreation relieves stress. We all know adults need to release stress, but so do children. Believe it or not, children are stressed by school work, peer relationships and other normal childhood stressors. Playing and engaging in relaxing activities is a great way to blow off steam. Run around and play hide and seek, plunge into cool water at your local pool, or play a silly game of charades. Laugh and have fun.

Family recreation builds family memories. What are some of the best memories you have from your childhood? When I divorced my older son's father, my son lost some of his favorite memories with his dad. He and his dad used to play basketball on a little basketball hoop in the house. They would run around in a small area of his bedroom, acting crazy and shooting baskets. My ex-husband instilled some great memories with his son by engaging in family recreation with him. Fun times always stick in a person's mind, so enjoy life with your children.

Make a List of Fun Activities to Do

To put together a family recreation plan, you must first have an idea of what everyone in the family enjoys. With paper and pen, sit down together as a family. Give each member of the family an opportunity to talk about his or her idea of fun and relaxation. Family members as young as three can give input. Think about activities you like to do, outings you'd like to go on, people and places you'd like to see, etc. Make a separate list for each member of the family. Mom and Dad should include activities they like to do as adults as well. You will use your "Fun Activities Lists" when planning your family recreation schedule.

The Many Faces of Family Recreation

Family recreation is about meeting the fun and relaxation needs for the whole family. While it is important that the family engages in recreational activities together, it is equally important to recognize all the many faces of family recreation:

Family Recreation Activity – an activity shared by all members of the family at the same time.

Individual Recreation Activity – an activity to meet the needs of an individual by himself/herself. It is important that members of the family have some time to engage in fun and relaxation without other members of the family. Dad might enjoy golf with his buddies. Mom may go for a walk by herself. Little Joey might play with his friend outside.

Partner Recreation Activity – an activity to foster the need for fun and relaxation in a marriage or partnership. Mom and Dad need to get out without the children so the marriage/partnership can be nurtured.

Parent/Child Activity – an activity that enables one parent to foster a relationship with one child at a time. Sometimes Mom or Dad need to spend individual time with each of their children, without the other children being involved.

Sibling Activity – an activity that allows siblings to spend time together as playmates. This helps to build healthy sibling relationships.

Put a Systematic Plan in Place

The more systematic you can be about planning the various family recreation activities, the more likely they will actually take place. Putting a plan in place not only helps the family establish a routine, but also gives the family members something to look forward to.

There are no set rules about how often you should engage in each of the different activities. Based on your current work/home schedule, you will need to decide what works best for your family. Below is a sample schedule for a hypothetical family of four.

Recreation Plan for...	Frequency/Schedule
Family Time	Weekly / Sunday afternoons
Mommy Time	Weekly / Wednesday evenings
Daddy Time	Weekly / Saturday mornings
Mom and Dad Time	Bi-monthly / 1st and 3rd Friday evenings
Mommy and Joey Time	Monthly / 1st Saturday evening
Mommy and Becky Time	Monthly / 2nd Saturday evening
Daddy and Joey Time	Monthly / 3rd Saturday evening
Daddy and Becky Time	Monthly / 4th Saturday evening
Becky and Joey Time	Bi-monthly / 1st and 3rd Friday evenings
Family Vacation	Yearly / 1 week vacation Bi-yearly / 3 day weekend

Use your lists of fun activities you created to plan your special times together. Remember, when more than one person is involved, you will need to share ideas and compromise about what to do together.

Family vacations and/or individual vacations are also part of your family recreation plan, but should never substitute for regular time spent together. Making time to relax and have fun in life is an integral part of a healthy and happy family. By being proactive about scheduling this time, you are helping to develop your children, build family bonds, and create memories that will last a lifetime.

TAKE ACTION ASSIGNMENT

Schedule a family meeting to talk about your family's need for fun and relaxation. Use the guidelines in this chapter to put together a family recreation plan that fits the lifestyle your family wishes to enjoy.

RELATIONSHIPS

CHAPTER 24

✳

C.O.N.N.E.C.T

"The most basic and powerful way to connect to another person is to listen. Just listen. Perhaps the most important thing we ever give each other is our attention.... A loving silence often has far more power to heal and to connect than the most well-intentioned words." —Rachel Naomi Remen

✳

From the moment we are brought into this world, communication is a part of our life. We are communicating our needs and feelings to our caregivers through the use of cries, smiles, goos and other primitive forms of communication. People in the world around us are communicating to us as well. They are holding us, ignoring us, using their words, sighing, laughing or using some other method of telling us how they feel. Communication is our primary means of connecting with other human beings.

If communication were just about learning the language of our origin, it might be easy, but it is so much more than words. That is why communicating in relationships can be so complex and sometimes so difficult to master. Communicating effectively takes a lot of practice, but fortunately, it's something that can be learned if you understand the key ingredients.

I like to use the acronym C.O.N.N.E.C.T. to highlight the seven keys to effective communication because one of the main purposes of communicating is to connect with another individual. If you aren't communicating effectively, the conversation and the relationship will disconnect. If you use the following key ingredients, your success in communication will greatly improve.

C is for Clarity

One day I received an email from a potential speaking client. She wanted me to speak to a group of administrative professionals. In her email she asked me if I had a book for sale, and if I did, would I offer a discount. I replied to her email and told her I did have a book that I sell and I offered her a $10 discount per book. Boy was I surprised when she placed an order for 50 books.

Now on the surface, it seems the communication was clear, but in reality, we were on two different wave lengths. When my client asked for a discount, I assumed she wanted a discount off my speaking services if a few of the audience members purchased a book. With an audience of 30 women, I estimated that maybe six women would purchase a book. Therefore, I would give her a $60 discount off my speaking fee.

That's not what my client wanted. She wanted a discount off the book, so you can imagine the predicament I was in when I realized I just offered her a $500 discount (50 books x $10.00/book). We were both unclear in our communications. She asked for a discount and did not clarify what she wanted a discount on. I assumed she wanted a discount off my speaking services and did not clarify with her whether my assumption was correct. The result was a big mess.

How many times have your communications gone awry because of a lack of clarity? It is a good idea to be crystal clear when you communicate with someone. It is also helpful to ask the person to interpret what they heard. Everyone has a filter in their brain through which all information passes. What you intend to communicate can in truth be received in a completely different way. What someone communicates to you can also be misunderstood by you. Everyone thinks differently and attaches different meanings to words so be absolutely positive that you understand one another.

Pay close attention to important details when communicating. Sometimes little details are omitted and they can make a world of difference in what you intend to communicate. "Meet me at the library" is very different than "meet me at the Batavia library, downstairs in the children's section." Watch for possible details that may be missing from the communications and ask for clarity. Assuming can cause all kinds of communication snags.

O is for Openness

I am a firm believer in being lovingly direct, open and honest with people because it develops trust in a relationship. Sometimes people think they are being kind by being dishonest or indirect, but people can sense dishonesty. As long as you communicate with kindness, openness is always the healthier alternative.

Recently, we took steps to refinance our house with a mortgage company that we thought we could trust. We were referred by a friend of ours, who also referred many of her other friends and family members. When she heard that one of her family member's refinances took a bad turn, she quickly communicated her concerns with all her friends. As a precaution, my husband and I decided to back out of the refinance. My husband called the mortgage broker and told her that we were not interested in refinancing our house anymore. Confused, she asked why and my husband gave her a vague answer.

Several days later, the woman called me and wanted to better understand why we changed our mind. I was upfront and honest with her. I explained that we had heard about the refinance deal that went bad at closing, and that we were not comfortable moving forward. In a very nice way, I let this woman know exactly where we stood. Even though she may not have liked what I had to say, I communicated to her that I can be counted on to be open and honest.

Being indirect with people is confusing. The person you are trying to communicate with is left to try and figure out what you mean and exactly what you are trying to say. There should be no guessing games in communication because people can and will guess wrong. Sometimes it can be scary to be honest and direct with people. But with practice, it gets much easier.

I've had moms ask me how to handle a negative friend or family member who is dragging them down. They are usually hesitant and unsure when I tell them to communicate honestly with their friend about the effects of her negative behavior. I then proceed to demonstrate to moms how to communicate their feelings in a loving way. Moms usually say, "That sounds really good coming from you, but I don't think my friend could handle that." Our goal in communicating is not always to communicate easy things to hear. Sometimes we have to give constructive criticism or express our negative feelings. It may not be easy for the receiver to hear, but it's necessary if you want to continue to connect with your friend or family member. Keeping the lines of communication open is critical to connecting.

N is for Non-Verbal Communication

How do you feel when people cross their arms in front of their body or roll their eyes when you are talking to them? What are you thinking when someone can't keep her eyes focused on you while you are speaking? We communicate in more ways than just our words. We use our tone, our bodies, silence, gestures and other ways to communicate messages, consciously or not.

More often than not, we are unaware of how we communicate non-verbally. But I can assure you, the person you are talking to is totally aware of your non-verbal language. The other day I was speaking to a group of business owners about procrastination. Being that I was the only one speaking, no one else was making a sound. However, I could tell a lot about people by the way they communicated non-verbally. One gentleman sat in the back of the room, slouched down, with a big frown on his face during the whole presentation. Another gentleman smiled and nodded his head continually. He was relating to what I was saying, and he was engaged. Who would I choose to focus on or speak to? Of course I would choose the smiling individual.

People can express anger, happiness, interest, lack of interest, boredom, confusion and other feelings without using a single word. It's important to watch other people's non-verbal communication when you are talking because it tells you something about where the other person is. If they are communicating something negative to you, ask yourself why. Are you boring them or are they frustrated with you? If you don't know, ask them what they are feeling.

In the same way, pay attention to your own non-verbal communication. You can use words communicated in a fun and playful tone, and it will be received in one way. The same words, spoken with an angry or irritated tone will send a completely different message. Check your body language. Make eye contact with the person who is speaking to you so you convey interest and concern. Nod your head in agreement. Watch your arms and your posture. The non-verbal is often more powerful than the actual words we use.

N is for iNtuitive Listening

Listening is probably the hardest aspect of communication to master. We are good at talking and sharing our feelings, ideas and thoughts. And then when it comes time to listening to the other person, we get distracted because we are thinking about what we want to say next. Some people are better than others at listening, but truly listening is something we all struggle with at times.

When someone is speaking to us, they want to feel heard. They want to know you understand what they are saying and that you care about their feelings. In my Core Energy Coaching training with iPEC Coaching, I learned the best way to demonstrate this understanding and concern is through two skills called acknowledging and validating.[6]

For instance, if your friend is telling you that she is stressed out because her boss yelled at her today, you could demonstrate that you are listening by saying something like, "Wow, it sounds like you've had a rough day. It makes sense you would feel stressed knowing that your boss is upset with you." You are acknowledging that you understand what her day was like and you are validating her state of mind.

Acknowledging and validating is not about turning the subject back to you. "Well, let me tell you about my day." In addition, you do not have to agree with the other person to acknowledge and validate. Your child may come home from a bad day at school and tell you, "My teacher is so dumb." You don't have to agree with your child to say, "You seem really upset with your teacher." Acknowledging and validating another person lets them know you care and you are listening.

Another important component of listening is learning to listen on a deep level to what another person is saying. I can't tell you how many times I talk to my husband when he is barely listening to me. He hears my words and he may give me an occasional "uh huh." But he is not truly listening to me. Intuitive listening, or what iPEC Coaching would call Level 3 listening, is about hearing more than just the words another person is saying. It's about tapping into the deeper meaning underneath the words. Listening deeply is about sensing the emotions the person is feeling and even hearing what is not necessarily being expressed.[7] When we take the time to deeply listen to another human being, we can connect to their heart and soul. And connecting to someone on a heart level is an amazing gift you can offer another individual.

E is for Energy

Imagine that your friend comes to you in a melancholy mood. Maybe she's had a bad day and she's feeling somewhat sad and hopeless. How might she feel if you meet her mood with an energetic response like "Cheer up, you'll be fine. Let's go out and have a good time!" There will be a serious disconnect between the two of you because there is a difference between your two energy levels.

There is energy in our words, in our tone, and in our body language. Take for instance a motivational speaker. A motivational speaker usually has dynamic energy, uses empowering words and is normally quite animated in his body language. What is the effect of a motivational speaker on the average person?

They normally leave the presentation in a good mood, feeling positive and on top of the world. That is because the speaker's ` high energy was transferred to the audience members.

Pay attention to the energy of other people when they are communicating to you. How do they make you feel? Are you excited about listening or do you want to get away from them? According to iPEC Coaching, "conversations take place at all levels of energy. The energy behind your message and the core thoughts which drive what you say are felt by the recipient."[8] If you are thinking positively, you will emanate positive energy. If you are having victim or angry thoughts, that energy will be communicated as well.

Yesterday my six year old was challenged by his fear of asking neighborhood children to play with him. He wanted to call his friend Megan or go to her house to see if she could play, but he could not muster the courage. He wanted Mom or Dad to do it for him. My husband and I decided that we wanted him to learn how to overcome his fear and practice effective social skills. For 30 minutes my son whined, cried and begged us to help him.

Consider what energy I might communicate if I had any of the following thoughts about my son:

· There is something wrong with him. It's not normal for him to be so afraid.
· My poor child. I want to rescue him from his pain.
· His whining is getting on my nerves – he's so irritating right now.
· I know this is hard for him, but I have faith he can do this.

What feelings do you think each of these thoughts would produce in you? How might your energy be different depending on how you are feeling? When we communicate, people can feel our energy and sometimes this energy speaks louder than our words. So pay attention to what you are thinking and feeling before you communicate your message.

C is for Confidence

It takes hard work to be a confident communicator, but the rewards are well worth the effort. A confident communicator is respected and listened to. She speaks with self-assurance and carries herself with dignity. A confident communicator feels good about the choice of words she uses and the way in which she presents herself to others. She respects her listeners because she respects herself.

Confidence comes from believing in you. You must believe that your ideas, thoughts and feelings are just as important as anyone else's. One of my clients, Margie, has a difficult time communicating with confidence because for 25 years her husband did not value anything she had to say. She came to believe that what she had to say was not worthy of being heard. It can be difficult to erase years of negative programming that might have been passed on by loved ones, but it is definitely doable.

Fear is the number one obstacle that gets in the way of communicating with confidence. You may have a fear of disapproval — maybe you believe your listener will disapprove of what you have to say. You could have a fear of making a mistake; perhaps you're afraid of saying the wrong thing or using a poor choice of words. It's possible you have a fear of rejection; maybe your listener will have a negative reaction to what you communicate.

One overcomes fear by stepping out with courage and testing the waters of communication. Prepare yourself by practicing what you want to say. Think about all the possible responses the other individual might have and know what you would say in return. Role play with a friend if you have a difficult conversation you need to plan for. The more you practice effective communication, the better you will become, and the more confident you will feel.

T is for Timing

The best time to communicate is not always the moment you have a thought or feeling. The best communicators are reflective before they speak. They evaluate their own mood and the other person's mood before they decide when to communicate. A good communicator looks at how much time it will take to effectively communicate their message and she plans for the appropriate amount of time. To evaluate the timing, you must look at when is the best time for all parties to talk. Everyone's schedule and priorities are different and we should respect that what may be a good time for us may not be a good time for someone else.

When my best friend calls me, she always says to me "Is this a good time to talk?" She is respectful of my time and I am honest with her. If I can give her my time, I gladly do it and I give her 100% of me. If I am busy or preoccupied, I tell her I will talk to her at another time that works for both of us. By choosing the right timing for a conversation, you have a much greater chance of having a successful interaction. Both parties should be willing and able to be available to one another.

Silence is another aspect of effective timing in communication. Sometimes *never* is the best time to communicate. Some things are better left unsaid. If, for example, your child makes a mistake and you see the effects it has on him, sometimes saying nothing at all is the best way to handle the situation. By choosing not to lecture him, you allow your child to feel and suffer the natural consequences that come from making this mistake. Oftentimes, we want to rescue our children and save them from feeling pain, but this does not teach them valuable lessons they sometimes need to learn. And more often than not, we don't need to add insult to injury.

Silence is always the best option if our words or other non-verbal communication are going to hurt another person. Take the time to cool down and think clearly about what you want to communicate. It's okay to sleep on it and make your decision in the morning. Time always heals and gives us a clearer perspective.

The purpose of communication is to C.O.N.N.E.C.T. with another individual or a group of people. If you don't connect, your listeners will not hear you or respect you. They will not be motivated to respond positively to your message. Human beings need connection and how we communicate greatly affects our ability to connect and feel like our listeners are connected to us.

TAKE ACTION ASSIGNMENT

Which of the seven keys of communication is the most challenging for you? This week commit to practicing this particular aspect of communication with your friends, colleagues and family members. Evaluate how your conversations might have improved.

CHAPTER 25
✳
Growing and Connecting with your Spouse

"I'm certain that most couples expect to find intimacy in marriage, but it somehow eludes them." –James C. Dobson

✳

Do you remember when there were no children in your life? Hanging out with your spouse was your first priority. You had fun going on dates. You had time to talk and share with each other your day's events. And sex was something you looked forward to. And then along came Ryan or Megan, and then maybe Benjamin or Kaylee. Suddenly, life became centered on your children. Time spent together as a couple became rare.

If you and your spouse plan to be a happy couple after the children have left, it's important to grow and connect with each other today. While there are no guarantees that you and your spouse will be one of those cute, old couples in "When Harry Met Sally," there are things you can do to increase your odds.

Foster Unity
When I think of the marriage ceremony, the unity candle is an excellent symbol for what should happen in marriage. Two candles (two people) come together to light one big candle (one team). A healthy marriage has unity. Always think of your spouse as a teammate. The minute you decide to enter into a committed relationship, the moment self-centeredness becomes an idea of the past. Intimacy requires a balance between self, the other person and the relationship. It's not about just you anymore. You have to take the feelings and needs of the other person and the relationship into consideration. Decisions about money, routines, time, children, etc. need to include your partner's input.

There cannot be one person in a relationship who sees him or herself as more important than his or her partner. A relationship consists of two people with perceived equality. That doesn't mean one person isn't smarter, more knowledgeable about certain topics, or has greater strengths in certain areas. It means the difference is not highlighted, flaunted or disrespected. Having a balance of power requires each person to have equal say in a discussion. It means the needs and feelings of each person are equally important. Working together allows you to create a marriage with a shared vision and shared goals.

Nurture Your Friendship
So many couples, after time, begin to live separate lives. Either their differences separate them or lack of awareness or intention cause them to drift apart. Intimacy requires people to spend time together and share in each other's lives. A relationship is like a garden. You need to take the time to pull the weeds, fertilize and water the flowers. In other words, it requires time, love, and a commitment to keep the negative to a minimum.

Your husband should be one of your better friends, and you should be his. Your marriage is a place for intimacy, and being intimate means sharing completely and honestly who you are – your feelings, likes and dislikes, your dreams, and what is important to you. Intimacy happens when both people can share anything and feel safe in doing so. You and your spouse will always be growing, so take the time to understand each other in every way – socially, emotionally, mentally, physically and spiritually. Intimacy is only achieved by spending time together regularly.

Create Emotional Safety
Safety in marriage comes from knowing you can trust your partner completely. Being trustworthy means you love and respect your spouse. To respect means you hold a high opinion and highly value yourself or another person. You appreciate and show consideration for people. The closeness of intimacy needs a general feeling of respect for self and your partner. It also means you need to behave in a way that deserves respect. You cannot expect your partner to respect you if your actions do not warrant respect.

Intimacy requires honesty and openness. It only takes one lie to destroy the trust in a relationship. To be close to someone, we need to be able to share what is true and real about us. And we must be willing to hear someone else's truth. Sometimes we may think it is best to not say anything at all if it means our words will hurt our partner. So we silently hang on to our truth or share our truth with the wrong people. When we do this, there is no opportunity to create an honest relationship.

Creating emotional safety requires us to keep our commitments and strive to treat each other with compassion and understanding. Your spouse needs to know without a doubt that you are not going anywhere, even when the going gets tough.

Resolve Your Conflicts

Every marriage has conflict and every couple has differences. In my marriage, we fight over disciplining the children, among other things. If you are going to grow and connect with your spouse, you have to learn to work through your disagreements. Angry words, unresolved arguments, and inflicting emotional and physical pain will destroy intimacy.

Make every effort to understand each other. Communication is a two-way street. Many of us have no problem talking, but listening poses more of a challenge. Listening requires us to hear our partners with our *heart*. An added step to listening is acknowledging what we have heard. Are you really hearing your partner's feelings and needs? Or are you busy blaming your partner or jumping in to defend yourself? If your partner is constantly communicating the same need or feeling to you over and over, chances are you are not hearing your partner with your heart.

On the flip side of listening to our partner, we need to express our own needs and feelings. Unfortunately we, as humans, do not have the power to read minds. It is each person's responsibility to express their needs and feelings. By sharing who we are and what's important to us, we significantly increase our chances of having our needs met. On the other hand, if we repress our needs and feelings, we shut the other person out of our world, and make intimacy impossible. It's so much easier to brainstorm win-win solutions when there is a clear understanding of what is important to each partner.

Appreciate Your Differences

Speaking of differences, the healthy couple accepts and embraces each other's strengths and weaknesses. If you think about it, there is an up side and a down side to every quality. I have a lot of compassion, but sometimes I am too sensitive. My husband provides structure in our family, but sometimes he is too rigid. When one spouse has a perceived weakness, often times the other balances it with a perceived strength. For instance, my flexibility and my husband's structure often conflict. However, our family needs both.

True intimacy necessitates acceptance. Having acceptance of yourself and your partner is a powerful indicator of love. It doesn't mean you have to like everything, but you need to let go of the need to change another person. When we lack acceptance of another person's qualities, our tendency is to control. That control manifests itself in disapproving feelings, and sometimes even pressuring people to change. To feel close to another person, you must feel unconditionally accepted for who you are. Encourage the development of your spouse's strengths and be patient with his weaknesses.

Maintain Physical Closeness

When you spend time getting to know each other and sharing yourself, you will naturally feel affectionate. Sexual intimacy is an important element in marriage. In order for women to desire sex, there needs to be healthy emotional intimacy. And men, unfortunately, achieve emotional closeness through physical intimacy. It is important for each partner to work to satisfy the other's needs. Make the time to ignite the passion. Hug and kiss your spouse. Touch each other; remember what created the romance when you were dating.

It is important for a couple to grow together, but it is also important for each person in the marriage to grow individually. It takes a lot of hard work and maintenance to make your marriage thrive, but it is well worth it. Your children need a model for a healthy marriage. And, when the children have left to start their own lives, won't it be nice to look at your spouse and say, "I want to spend the rest of my years with you, my friend"?

TAKE ACTION ASSIGNMENT

Schedule a date with your husband this week. Concentrate on having fun and nurturing your friendship. Put any differences aside and focus on what you like about your spouse. Establish a regular date night (weekly, semi-monthly, or monthly) so you always stay in touch with one another.

CHAPTER 26

✳

Friendship – A Gift to be Cherished

"Piglet sidled up to Pooh from behind. "Pooh," he whispered.
"Yes, Piglet?"
"Nothing", said Piglet, taking Pooh's paw. "I just wanted to be sure of you."

✳

When I think back over the course of my life, I've had a lot of friends. I remember my childhood friend Lisa Catalano. In the lower level of her home, her parents had a real live jukebox and a set of drums. We used to go down in the basement, punch in the numbers to play "Proud Mary," and pretend we were rock stars. Lisa would play the drums and I would sing. If we weren't doing that, you might catch us riding around the neighborhood on an adult sized three-wheeled tricycle. Lisa was bigger and stronger than me so she would pedal as I relaxed in the big wire basket in the back of the bike.

When I was in high school, I would hang out with my friend Denise all the time. She was a cheerleader like me, and the two of us were inseparable. Denise lived with her mom in a three-level townhouse, and I spent a great deal of time there. Denise had a dog that must have been having some issues with potty training because I remember one hilarious episode vividly. As I was walking barefoot through her house, minding my own business, I just so happened to step into a big pile of fresh dog poo. As we screamed and laughed, I hopped on one foot to the bathroom. Four feet from the bathroom door, I gracefully hopped right into yet another big pile of dog poo. You can only imagine the squeals coming from our mouths. Could something more gross happen to a teenage girl?

Although some of us still have some of the same friends we had in elementary and high school, many of us have moved on to form friendships with other adults in our lives. Some of your friends may be lifetime friends, while others may move in and out of your life. We make friends with co-workers, moms we meet at a playgroup, or through a shared hobby or interest. Sometimes these friends turn out to be great friends; other times we outgrow one another. Life circumstances often change and friends can drift apart. There was one friend I met while I worked at Pella Windows and Doors. Her name was Liz; I called her Lizzy. Liz was one of the most caring women I ever met. She always had lots of hugs and love to give to me. We accepted each other for who we were, and our time together was incredibly special to me. She saw me through my entire first pregnancy, and was even present for the birth of my first son. Lizzy moved on to take a job in California, many miles from where we lived. As she struggled to leave behind her life in Illinois, she withdrew and slipped out of my life. I will never forget Lizzy because her spirit remains in my heart today.

Friendship is much like a garden. You have to water it, weed it, protect it from bugs and give it lots of love so it can blossom into the gift that it was designed to be.

Watering your Friendships

At the very basic level, flowers and plants need to be watered or they cannot survive. However, not all flowers and plants need the same amount of water. Some need to be watered daily, while others might only need water once per week. The only way to know how to water your garden according to its needs is to understand each flower and plant. It requires a little research on your part.

You need to do the same research with your friendships. There are two parts to understanding your friends on a deeper level. You must understand what your friend's needs are and you need to be clear about what needs your friends fill for you. Every one of your friends is different, and each of them has different needs. Do you know what your friends need from you? Don't assume they need the same thing that you do. Ask each of your friends what they need from you as their friend. This gives you the opportunity to better understand your friends and be clear about how you can meet their needs. As part of an exercise I did to better understand myself, I asked each of my friends "What do you count on me for?" These were some of the responses I got.

· I count on you to tell me the truth about what you see that I may be blinded to.

· I need you to support me as I grow as a person.

· I count on you to be my friend through the great stuff, the not so great stuff and everything in between.

· I count on you to be honest and give me an unbiased opinion.

· I need you to help me look at a situation from different perspectives.

· I count on you to be on time because I cannot tolerate people that are late.

· I count on you to be an understanding conversationalist.

By asking this question, you are able to understand what is most important to your friends. Listen to what your friends tell you. I will never forget what my friend Donna told me one day. She shared a story about one of her friends that almost forgot to call her on her birthday. She expressed how important it was to her to receive a birthday phone call from her friends. With this information, you can bet I will do everything in my power to always call my friend Donna to wish her a happy birthday. If I don't, I know that I will seriously disappoint her.

Friendship is a two-way street. Not too many friendships will survive very long if only one party is doing all the giving. You have needs too, and your friendships are one resource for getting your needs met. Think about each of your friends and what needs they fill for you. You might have a friend who is a lot of fun to be around. You may have a friend who loves and accepts you unconditionally; you can share anything with this friend. Some friends fill intellectual needs, while others fill emotional or spiritual needs. You may even have friends who don't meet any of your needs. By understanding your needs and your friends' needs, you are tending to your friendship, according to each and every person's uniqueness.

Weeding your Friendships

Every garden grows weeds, and if you don't remove them, they will take over. Your garden will lose its beauty, and you will no longer be able to sit outside and appreciate your garden. Some friends are like weeds too. A friend is a weed when you cannot trust her or when she drains every bit of emotional energy you have. Weedy friends have very little to give or they rob you of your self-esteem. If you don't feel good when you are around your friend, she may be a weed. If your friend does not lift you up and help you be your best, she might have characteristics of a weed. Consider which of your friends might be weeds. To fully appreciate your garden of friendship, you must remove the weeds or at the very least, minimize them.

Tina struggled with a particular friend she had. When they first met, they were on the same page emotionally. They would get together and complain about everything they didn't like about their lives. However, as Tina grew and began to change her thinking and her life, this friend became a drain. Every conversation and encounter was smothered by negativity. There was no room for any positive experiences. Tina eventually distanced herself from this friend because of the effect she was having on her life.

Protect your Friendships from Bugs

Every relationship, if it lasts long enough, will have some issues. Some of the issues may be small, while others might be big. Just like bugs will eat away at your plants and flowers, unresolved issues will eat away your friendship. Talk with your friends about what's "bugging" you. My friend Michelle and I don't have too many problems, but every once in awhile, there will be hurt feelings. One time Michelle made a comment to me that shook up my confidence. For a long time, I tried to ignore it because I knew she didn't mean to hurt me. However, I noticed it was starting to affect what I would share with her, and I knew that was grounds for distancing. Not wanting the issue to eat away at me any longer, I decided to talk with her about it. She was so remorseful and sincerely expressed her desire to build me up. We agreed that we would always try to be sensitive to one another's feelings and speak our truth with grace. By having this type of conversation or any others that help heal our differences, we are building a friendship based on true intimacy. Don't let the little bugs or the big bugs destroy your friendship. Get rid of the bugs by talking about your feelings, what's important to you, and how you can help your friendship grow.

Nurturing your Friendships with Love

What kind of friend are you? If you were to rate yourself on a scale of 1 to 10, a ten being an awesome friend, what score would you give yourself? An awesome friend loves you and accepts you for whom you are, but also helps you to continually grow so you can be your best. You know you have a great friend if she gives honest and loving feedback when she sees you heading down a bad path. A true friend does not tell you everything is okay when it's not. My good friends have challenged me to look at the ugly parts of myself, and they've done so with grace and compassion.

An awesome friend is the one who comes in when everyone else goes out. Authentic friendships stay around in spite of the fireworks. It's easy to be a friend when everything is going smoothly. When your life is challenging and you need someone to lean on, your true friends are there to hold you up. Do you back away when a friend is experiencing difficulties or do you hang in there with her? Do you make it safe for your friend to share her pain, as well as her joys?

Awesome friends don't seek the spotlight. Their focus is not on themselves, but on their friend. It's not about what can I get from this friendship, but what can I give to this friendship? It is through giving that we are blessed. A great friend calls to check in, makes time to listen, and gives of herself in a way that is life changing. My friends inspire me and fill up my soul, and I strive to give the very same gift in return. Your garden of friendships will be a gift to your life if only you water, weed, debug and love your beautiful flowers (friends).

TAKE ACTION ASSIGNMENT

Make a list of all your friends. Find out what each one of your friends needs from you. Eliminate the weeds and remove any of the bugs in your current friendships. Then focus on loving your beautiful friends and creating a garden of friends that will give all of you a gift that you can hold in your heart forever.

CHAPTER 27

✷

Sibling Rivalry – Lose the Fighting, Not the Love

"Siblings are the people we practice on, the people who teach us about fairness and cooperation and kindness and caring – quite often the hard way"
—Pamela Dugdale

✷

Are you tired of listening to your children bicker? Do you long for them to get along and love each other? Sibling rivalry can be exasperating, often interfering with our ability to enjoy our children. It may be helpful to know that sibling rivalry has been going on forever. Some degree of fighting is perfectly normal. It exists in every family that has two or more children, so take comfort in knowing you are not alone. Some siblings get along fairly well, while others fight constantly.

Having awareness about what causes sibling rivalry can help you begin to understand this dynamic. When you can get to the root of an issue, it is easier to brainstorm solutions. Just like adults, children have their own *personalities and temperaments.* As a matter of fact, Dr. Phil, in his book *Family First,* identifies three child types: Rebellious, Cooperative and Passive.[9] Sometimes it is the differences in children that cause them to clash, but other times it can be their similarities. I have two strong willed boys, and even though they are ten and a half years apart, they regularly antagonize each other.

Age is another factor involved in sibling rivalry. An older child may feel burdened by more responsibility or a younger child may be caught up in trying to compete with his older sibling. In addition, differences in interests change as a child ages. What is fun for a five and seven year old may be considered immature for a 10 year old. One wise father quickly diminished the sibling rivalry that was taking place in his home by creating a game. His four and six year old girls were building houses with magnetic tiles. They were quite proud of their creations, so you can imagine their extreme frustration when their 10-month-old sister crawled over to knock them down. So the game was to see who could build the coolest structure – the winner was determined by the baby. If your house got knocked down, you were the winner. The screams of anger were transformed into squeals of delight.

A *child's sex* can cause resentment as well and fuel the sibling rivalry. It's a fact. Boys and girls are treated differently. A boy could be jealous of how his sister's emotions are pampered. A girl could envy the time her brother spends wrestling with his father. One time my little boy went over to my friend's house for the evening. Her husband loves car video games and so does my son. My friend's little girl became intensely jealous of the fun times her daddy was having with my son doing "boy" activities.

A *child's position* in the family can also play a role in sibling rivalry. We often expect more from our first-born children. By the time the 2nd and 3rd come along, the rules loosen somewhat. And sometimes the baby of the family receives very special treatment. Everyone tries to make her happy when she is mad or sad. At times the youngest will be overly assertive to gain her equal place in the family. The eldest is often expected to be the example for the younger siblings.

All of these issues can play a part, but the most significant factor that affects sibling rivalry is parental attitude. As parents, we know we should treat our children equally and fairly. And most of us probably try very hard to do that, however inconsistencies will still exist. Your personality may blend better with one child's personality, while you may experience personality clashes with another. Perhaps one or more of your children are easier to handle so they have a tendency to receive more loving treatment from you, and less discipline. Children pick up on every bit of inconsistency and they don't always understand why things are different for each child. Older age children have more responsibilities, but more independence. A younger child thinks it is unfair that she has to go to bed earlier than her older sibling. How many times do you hear the words, "It's not fair!" or "You love her more than you love me!"

I know you're waiting for the magical secret to eliminate sibling rivalry in your home. Sorry – there are no magical secrets, but here are ten practical suggestions to help minimize the tension between siblings.

Avoid making comparisons of any kind.
Do not compare your children to each other; not directly or in any conversation they may be privy to. Help your children understand they each are unique in their own way, and no one child is better or worse because of who they are as individuals. Teach your children to stop comparing themselves to other siblings because the treatment can be and will be different according to each child's needs. Remind them that your love for each child is always the same.

Encourage your children to express their resentment or angry feelings.
This does not mean you allow them to scream at or hurt each other. Teach
your children to handle their anger constructively, not destructively.
Acknowledge and validate your children's feelings so they feel understood.
Help each child see things from the other child's perspective. If necessary,
encourage them to take a break from each other until they can speak and play
respectively with one another.

**Have very clear boundaries about personal belongings and personal
space.**
Make it a rule that no one is allowed to use another person's belongings
without permission. Teach your children to respect each other's personal
space – bedrooms, their bodies, etc. A child needs to feel like there are at
least some things that belong to him.

Avoid situations that promote guilt in siblings.
Don't allow your children to do something they will regret later. Teach them
self-control. When my younger son was small, he helped himself to my
older son's room. In there he found a snow globe that was extremely important to his brother. Being the mischievous child that he was at the time, he
threw the glass snow globe over the banister of the stairs. As it landed downstairs, on the ceramic tiled floor, it shattered. Glass, water and artificial
snow (glitter) went everywhere. My older son was screaming at his brother
to buy him a new snow globe. At two years old, I'm not sure his brother
understood. As parents, we need to do our best to remind our children to
think about the consequences of their behavior.

Teach your children to settle their own differences.
Learning the art of resolving conflict is an extremely valuable skill for life.
This doesn't mean you allow your children to have a knock down drag out
fight. It means you teach them what respectful behavior looks like and how
to compromise and work together. Have them practice these behaviors until
they become the norm. Don't expect perfection, however, because even
adults struggle in this area.

Help your children live a balanced and healthy life.
Stress can play a big role in children's moods and ability to handle everyday
situations. Many emotional disasters occur when children are tired or
hungry. Monitor the amount of activities your children participate in. Make
sure they get plenty of sleep, eat well, exercise, and take time for quiet relaxation.

Introduce a "value" of the month program.

Teach and reinforce family values like respect, cooperation, peace, and kindness – focus on one value per month. Use family devotionals, games, books, and movies that help the children understand and practice these values.

Spend one on one time with each child.

Children are always fighting for individual attention from their parents. They don't want to share the one or two most important people of their life. Make a point to give each child your undivided attention and quality time with you on a regular basis. Create a family ritual. On Tuesday nights, Joey gets special "mommy time" and on Thursday Sally gets the same.

Have family fun nights.

Encourage family togetherness by instituting a family fun night. Sit down and play games together or go play miniature golf. Give each child an opportunity to pick the activity for the week. Rotate so all siblings get a chance; encourage all family members to support each other's choice. One rule: No fighting, or family time is over. Make this time sacred for everyone in the family.

Hold weekly family meetings.

This is a time when the family comes together to talk about their concerns and brainstorm solutions. To keep the meeting productive, all complaints must be spoken with at least one answer to the problem. All family members are encouraged to listen and share their ideas. Communication should be healthy and respectful by avoiding blaming one another.

Sibling rivalry adds stress to family life, but if you actively implement some of these strategies, you will begin to see improvements. Keep working at it. The reward of having healthy and loving adult sibling relationships is well worth the effort you make today.

TAKE ACTION ASSIGNMENT

Purchase the book *Keep the Siblings, Lose the Rivalry* by Dr. Todd Cartmell. Educate yourself on this topic and begin to implement some new ideas to improve sibling relationships. Praise your children when they are getting along.

CHAPTER 28

✳

The Roots of Conflict

"Conflict is the beginning of consciousness." —M. Esther Harding

✳

Whether it's with a spouse, a parent, a child, or a friend, occasional conflicts are bound to happen. It is quite normal to disagree at times. However, when conflict becomes the norm, your relationships will be dissatisfying. No one can live with continual conflict for very long before it begins to affect your emotional energy levels and your happiness. At the root of most conflict is a core issue. Oftentimes what we fight about is not really reflective of what is actually going on. Sometimes it can be helpful to dig a little deeper to uncover what's at the root of the conflict.

Value Conflicts

Are you having a value conflict with your loved one when you fight? Everyone has a set of values they live by, conscious or not. Sometimes what is important to one person is not so important to another. I know a couple who struggles with a particular issue in their lives. Bob keeps everything he owns for years and never gets rid of anything. He is afraid to throw things away for fear of needing that item at a later time. He values *security*. His wife Janice, on the other hand, wants a clutter free home, and has a need to get rid of things that aren't wanted or needed anymore. She values *order* or *organization*, much more so than she values security.

Get to the heart of your arguments and try to identify what values you may be trying to protect. Even if you think you share the same values, it's still possible to place a different level of importance on that value. Susie and Ted have an excellent system for resolving value conflicts. If they disagree on something and can't seem to make a decision, each person rates how important the issue is to them. Whoever places the highest level of importance on the issue gets their way.

So for instance, let's say you are arguing with your spouse on whether or not to send your child to a private school. You want your child to go to a private school and he wants your child to go to a public school. You would ask yourself how important it is that your child goes to a private school. He would ask himself how important it is that your child goes to a public school. If he rates his level of importance at a 5 and you rate yours at a 9, then your child goes to a private school. It is obviously more important to you that your child goes to a private school than it is for your husband that your child goes to a public school. What do you do if the issue is equal for both of you? Both parties have to give and reach a compromise that is acceptable for both of you.

Part of resolving conflict is knowing when to back off if you are deadlocked. I can remember my husband and me arguing over the severity of a consequence for one of my son's misbehaviors. My husband was dead set on grounding him for three weeks and I thought the punishment was too severe. Every compromise I suggested was unacceptable to him. In order to honor the marriage, I allowed my husband to decide the punishment. The only way this type of compromise can work is if there is not unresolved resentment that results from either party feeling like they have lost. The ideal solution to a conflict is a win-win scenario. Both individuals should feel like they are being heard and valued and an effort should be made to find a solution in which everyone feels like they are winning.

Unmet Needs

Our emotional needs are another component that can result in conflict. We all have needs — basic needs like food and shelter — and complex needs like security, love, friendship, fun, etc. Sometimes when we argue with our loved ones, we are fighting for an unmet need of ours.

Consider a wife who constantly argues with her husband because he works too much and is never home. It could be she has an unmet need for intimacy with her husband, or a need to feel loved. This example is easy, but it can be tricky at times to identify what needs we're fighting for. In the beginning of our relationship, my husband and I argued about alcohol. I didn't like it if he drank, and he didn't want any restrictions put on his alcohol consumption. He didn't see any harm in drinking alcohol. We had this same argument for years. On the surface, it seemed like we were arguing about alcohol and freedom. It took a professional to help us identify what our needs were. I had a need for *security*, and he had a need to be seen as *responsible and trustworthy*. Because I came from a family that broke up because of my father's drinking, I associated alcohol with pain and divorce. I needed to know that my past would not be repeated in my own family. My husband needed to feel trusted. He wanted me to acknowledge that he was not my father and that he could be responsible with alcohol. If you are experiencing continual conflict with someone, ask yourself what might be missing in your relationship. What emotional need of yours is not being met?

Unresolved Issues from Your Past

We all come into a relationship with a history – good, bad, or indifferent. Our life experiences have shaped so much of who we are – our perceptions, our beliefs, our values, our needs, our behaviors and our personalities. Underneath some of our repeated conflicts are unresolved issues from our past. Maybe you have some hurts that have not healed from your parents. Perhaps you experienced a very traumatic event in your life that has changed you forever. Or it could be that a friend from school really burned you and you have never forgotten it.

If we don't take the time to heal from life's injuries, other similar situations will reopen the wounds. We store a lot of memories in our brain – some that we don't consciously remember. Have you ever had an argument with someone and your reaction was way beyond what a normal reaction would be? Chances are something from your past was triggered and your reaction was not only to the current issue, but also to the unhealed issue.

I have a dear friend who experienced an extremely traumatic event when he was three years old. For years he buried the fear, pain and anger. Eventually these feelings leaked out in all his relationships. He would find himself unusually angry or fearful – not proportional to the situation at hand. It wasn't until he did some major healing work that he was able to bring his emotions in check. Past issues can stir up all kinds of feelings – fear and anger are the most common. A neglected child will have a fear of abandonment. An abused woman will develop a fear of conflict. Look for any recurring themes in your arguments and analyze whether there could be past issues dictating your present life.

Look at all the recurring arguments in your life right now. Ask yourself these questions:

· What values are you fighting for?
· What unmet emotional needs do you have?
· What situations from your past remind you of this argument?

By looking at the roots of your conflict, you have the opportunity to resolve them once and for all.

TAKE ACTION ASSIGNMENT

Keep a diary of all your conflicts with everyone important in your life for a period of two months. Using the three questions above, try and determine the root issue of the conflict. Look for patterns of value conflicts, unmet needs or unresolved issues from your past. Work with your loved ones to put an end to your continual conflicts.

CHAPTER 29

✳

4 Ways to Create Emotionally Healthy Relationships

"A loving relationship is one in which the loved one is free to be himself — to laugh with me, but never at me; to cry with me, but never because of me; to love life, to love himself, to love being loved. Such a relationship is based upon freedom and can never grow in a jealous heart."   —Leo F. Buscaglia

✳

What is a relationship? A relationship occurs when two or more people are connected to one another on a physical, intellectual, spiritual or emotional level. In a relationship, you relate to another person. We have relationships with many people in our lives: our spouse, children, parents, friends, boss, co-workers, sisters, brothers, aunts, uncles, grandmothers, grandfathers, cousins, and other significant people. When a relationship is working well, it can be satisfying and nurturing. A healthy relationship…

- Provides love and encouragement
- Gives us an opportunity to give love
- Enables sharing of resources
- Nurtures our heart and soul
- Is an outlet for getting some of our needs met
- Provides companionship
- Encourages fun and laughter
- Teaches us how to work together
- Gives us positive energy
- Provides loyalty and support

Unhealthy relationships, on the other hand, have a negative impact on our overall well-being and self-esteem. It's no secret that relationships require work. Think about a time when you argued with your spouse, your children or one of your parents. Depending on how the conflict was handled, you can either feel resolved and relieved, or drained and frustrated. Your success in creating emotionally healthy relationships depends largely on how well you manage relationship draining behaviors. By learning to substitute productive and uplifting relationship behaviors, you can encourage growth and peace in your relationships.

As we review each relationship draining behavior, I want you to think about all the relationships in your life. Do any of these behaviors create problems in your relationships? It will be quite easy to recognize these behaviors in other people, but it's equally important to see these behaviors in you. Although all of us can experience these behaviors, at times, what's most important is the frequency in which they occur.

Stop Complaining and Seek Solutions
Everyone knows what it is like to be around someone who constantly complains. I don't know about you, but when I see that person coming, I want to run fast and far away. I am not referring to a friend that calls me up needing to vent about her bad day. I am talking about the person that has a bad day every day, all day. This person whines about everything. Instead of finding something positive to talk about, he or she always sees the negative side of life.

Complaining may help you release negative feelings, but it does nothing towards resolving your problem. Every problem has a solution. It may not be readily seen, but there is one. Take the time to think about how you can resolve a problem before you complain about it. For instance, I absolutely hate the cabinet in my kitchen that holds all my plastic containers. I could go on and on about how messy it is, the injuries I could experience from falling plastic containers, my husband's lack of organization and all the frustration it causes me. Instead, I should focus on a solution that will enable me to have an organized system for storing my plastic containers.

Complaining is dead weight in a relationship; a lot of people learn to tune it out. There have been times when I was complaining to my husband about this, that and the other. He literally looked at me and said, "I can't listen to you." Why? Because I was bringing him down. Complaining is like asking someone to hold a suitcase full of weights. It exhausts you very quickly because there is transference of negative energy.

Sometimes people complain because they need to be heard. Oftentimes letting the person know you are truly listening and you understand is enough to make the person feel better. Try acknowledging and validating the person's feelings, and then help them to move toward a solution. Point out the positive so you can help them shift their energy.

Avoid Blaming and Accept Responsibility
If you ask a child how they got a detention in school, you might hear some-

thing like "The teacher is stupid. She said I was talking when I wasn't." Blaming usually occurs when a person doesn't want to take responsibility for his or her own behavior. Blaming is easy to pick out in a relationship with a child, but can be a little trickier with an adult. The person who blames is usually upset about something. Let's suppose you are running late because your child can't find her shoes. In your moment of frustration you say, "If you would have put your shoes in the closet like I asked you to, we wouldn't be in this mess." And maybe that is true. However, how does that statement help the situation? And how does it make your child feel?

Blaming immediately puts a person on defense and puts a stop to resolving the situation. If you use the word "You," you'll notice the problem shifts to the other person and a need to defend is created. Many times a person will defend by disagreeing with you or making some accusations about you, and the cycle continues. Focus on yourself and not the other person. Do your best to stay focused on your feelings and your behaviors. Let the other person focus on himself. Use "I" statements to communicate your needs and allow ample time for each party to share. Be a good listener when you are not speaking.

Blaming people doesn't help them to feel better about themselves. It puts people in a position of feeling bad. And when a person feels like he has failed, he is more likely to give up because he doesn't feel capable of doing good. What difference does it really make who's at fault in a given situation? What matters most is how you can resolve the situation. Blaming will not help you resolve an argument, nor will it fix anything. A productive solution is to focus on how you can make things different. Instead of getting caught up in the problem, discuss how your relationship can grow and change to make both people happy. Look for solutions that help each person feel comfortable. Talk about what is important to both of you and brainstorm ideas. Be flexible and willing to compromise. Your relationship will be stronger as a result of working together.

Take Care of You and Let Others Take Care of Themselves

You might remember when codependency was a hot topic in the self-improvement arena in the 1980s. Although the word codependency is not used so much anymore, the issue still exists in relationships. Codependency occurs when we take responsibility for another person's feelings and behaviors and try to fix another person. As hard as we sometimes try, I think we all know it doesn't work to change someone else. Change has to come from within. This area can be my own personal struggle at times. My husband will come to me with negative feelings about something relating to our family. If I am not careful, I will absorb these feelings and immediately take responsibility for something that, in reality, is about him. Sometimes I have to laugh at myself. I will be in a perfectly good mood, and my husband will be in a bad mood. After unloading his feelings on me, he feels much better and I become the one in a bad mood. Negative energy was transferred and I allowed it.

When you take on other people's problems and solve them on your own, you deny them the opportunity to work through the solution for themselves. This is one of the hardest skills to practice, especially when it involves our children. We always want to tell our children how to handle situations, but sometimes it is better to let them learn to do their own problem solving. The same concept applies to protecting others from feeling pain. Sometimes it is necessary to let loved ones experience uncomfortable feelings in order to learn more about themselves and adapt to their given situation.

No one likes to be fixed — it implies something is wrong with them. Each person is responsible for making changes in himself, and it is the only way it actually works. Just because you don't like something about someone doesn't mean they will think anything needs to be changed. My husband doesn't always agree with or even like my style of parenting. Although I can certainly understand and empathize with his views, the traits he doesn't like are the ones I think make me a good parent. You have complete control over how you choose to respond to life's circumstances and other people. So focus on who you want to be and let others focus on them.

Understand Your Words Can Lift Up or Tear Down

Anyone who lives with someone who makes critical or demeaning remarks will tell you just how damaging and draining these comments can be. We are all human beings, and we can all have a tendency to be critical of our loved ones at times. However, when judgmental remarks are part of your everyday interactions, your relationships will deteriorate quickly. Your words have the power to lift another person up or tear them down. Remember, also, the words that are said are only a small part of what is being communicated. Tone and body language play a much bigger part in communication. An angry and demeaning tone or rolling the eyes and disgusted looks speak much louder than words. It is said that it takes nine positive and affirming comments to counteract one negative or critical comment.

Underneath an individual's critical remarks is often anger or an issue with poor self-esteem. Perhaps there is healing from our past that needs to take place. If a child has been raised with an overly critical parent, the result is often an adult who carries around a lot of anger and feelings of insecurity. Until this pain is healed, the victimized adult often shows the same tendencies to be critical.

Before we judge another human being and make a hurtful comment, we must realize that we aren't always going to like everything about everybody in our lives. Our job is not to change other people so we can be happy, but figure out how we can be happy despite our differences. Sometimes we learn to tolerate minor differences, or set boundaries when our limits are being compromised. Grace allows us to see in other people what is also present or possible in us. Our "judgments" can act as a mirror for us to see ourselves more clearly. Whenever I begin to judge another person, I ask myself "When was the last time I acted like this?" More times than not, I can truthfully say I, too, am guilty of the very behavior I am judging.

When we are critical with ourselves, it naturally follows that we will be critical of others. By learning to love and accept those things about you that you don't like, you learn to be more tolerant of other people. You realize that we are all imperfect human beings doing our best with what we have. "The Judge" in us blocks opportunities to see the best in ourselves and others. When you can make "the judge" sit down, you will have the ability to harmoniously walk, side by side, in your relationships, and grow in the process. So stop and think before you speak. Ask yourself, "Will these words lift my loved one up or tear her down?"

You have the power to create the healthy relationships you deserve. Seek solutions to your problems; accept responsibility for your own behavior and give your loved ones the emotional safety and space that is required for their own personal growth. In turn, you will be blessed with relationships that will naturally grow and thrive.

TAKE ACTION ASSIGNMENT

Take an honest look at all your relationships. Using the signs of a healthy relationship outlined in the beginning of this chapter, rate the emotional health of each of your relationships on a scale of 1 to 10 (10 being healthiest). Identify two changes you can make to increase the overall emotional health of your relationships.

CHAPTER 30

✳

The Two B's – Boundaries and Button Pushing

"If we don't deal with our baggage that we bring to any given situation, then those hurts and issues will interfere with whatever new situation we find ourselves in. In a very real sense, our past will become our present." —From Cloud-Townsend — Solutions for Life website

✳

Just this morning I was challenged with the two B's – boundaries and button pushing. I woke up after having a restless night of sleep and proceeded to help my six year old get ready for school. His backpack was overly stuffed with valentines for his classmates and a valentine shoebox to hold all the valentines he would be receiving at school. I needed to find a way to add his lunch box to his bag without smashing the 23 valentine cookies that filled his bag. My son was insisting that he could fit the lunch box in the same space as the rest of his stuff. He kept saying to me, "I can do it. I can do it." I was trying to tell him that it would not fit in that section of his bag. As his frustration and mine mounted, he screamed at me. That's it – my buttons were pushed. I was triggered because my six year old was yelling at me in what I perceived as a disrespectful tone of voice. At the same time, I needed to set a boundary to let him know how I wanted to be treated. I sent him to time out while letting him know that he is not allowed to get sassy with me.

Managing our buttons and setting healthy boundaries in relationships are perhaps the hardest skills we are faced with. However, they are so important if we want to have peaceful and healthy relationships with the various people in our lives.

Boundaries

Boundaries define the limits we need to set in our lives to protect what is most important to us. I look at boundaries as part of the foundation that holds our lives in place. Without boundaries, everything can – and will – happen. Our lives can slowly unravel, and before we know it, our lives are nothing like what we envisioned them to be. Boundaries establish clear lines and they keep life from becoming blurry or fuzzy.

I think it can be helpful to establish boundaries in terms of minimums and/or maximums. For instance, you may have a boundary that states you will work out three times per week at a minimum. The minimum is the boundary that defines what is considered "good enough" for your life. You can also set a maximum boundary around working out. This boundary might say that you will not work out more than five times per week – you will allow two days for rest. The minimum and maximum boundaries protect you from patterns of perfectionism and procrastination. If you go below your standard, you are not honoring what is important to you. If you go above your standard, it might mean you are placing unrealistic expectations on yourself.

Boundaries are designed to protect you and the life that you want to live, and there are seven types of boundaries to consider:

Self-Esteem Boundaries
Self-esteem boundaries protect your sense of worth. These boundaries help you feel good about you. What is the minimum you need to do to maintain self-respect? Perhaps you need to follow through on your promises, or maintain honesty in your life. What are the limits you need to set with yourself and other people to make sure your self-esteem is not compromised?

Body Boundaries
What do you need to do to protect your body? What physical limitations might you need to recognize? What standards need to be in place for you to protect your physical health? It could be that a certain minimum amount of exercise or a maximum amount of food or drink is required. It might mean you always honor regular health and dental appointments.

Energy Boundaries
Energy boundaries obviously protect the amount of physical and emotional energy you have to operate from. What energy drains in your life need to be eliminated or minimized? Which energy refuelers must be present to help you maintain the energy you need for your life?

Time Boundaries
Time is a precious commodity. Without the proper time boundaries, we lose something we can never get back. What non-negotiable boundaries must be in place to protect your time? What is the maximum amount of time you will spend on a particular activity, at a specific event, or engaging in work? Time management is all about having clear boundaries.

Space Boundaries

Our space includes any environment we spend time in. We need to protect our spaces so they nourish us and enable us to live our lives optimally. Pay attention to your needs for organization or beauty in your environments. How do you know when your housecleaning is "good enough"? What does the minimum and maximum state of your environments need to look like?

Money Boundaries

Just like time, we need money to survive in this life. Your money boundaries protect your finances. What are the limits you need to set on spending and saving? What is the minimum salary you are willing to work for? Consumer debt, for instance, is the result of unidentified or compromised boundaries.

Relationship Boundaries

What boundaries need to be in place to protect your relationships? Our relationships are truly our greatest gift in life. How much time do we need to spend to nurture our relationships? What limits do we need to set on our behavior in relationships? Boundaries help ensure our relationships remain healthy.

Boundaries are essential to helping us identify who we are, what's important to us and how we want to live our lives. Without them, other people will decide these things for us.

In our life, we will have people who will both respect and disrespect our boundaries. Another person's reaction to our boundaries should not derail us from setting healthy boundaries. Part of being healthy in our relationships is being able to communicate to our relationship partners what our boundaries are. A telltale sign that a boundary needs to be communicated is when you are frustrated by another person's behavior. That is a signal that you have reached your limit.

Dora is a natural people pleaser. She will do everything she can to make sure everyone else is happy, sometimes to the detriment of herself. The other day she was having a particularly stressful day. Her morning started off with a hot shower that turned cold halfway through her bathing routine. With a large list of things that needed to be accomplished before she picked her daughter up from school, she was feeling a bit frazzled. After her daughter was home from school, Dora asked her to help clear the table for dinner. Instead, she went to her mom's bedroom to eat her food and watch television. Feeling frustrated that she was cleaning the table by herself and that her daughter did not listen to her, she continued to take care of things without expressing her anger. Wanting some alone time to rejuvenate, she went to a room that would enable her to be by herself. The problem was that her daughter decided to infringe upon her alone time, and in the process of entering her mother's space, she knocked over a glass vase that shattered all over the floor. At her wit's end, Dora exploded and yelled at her daughter. Dora's limits had been reached long before the vase incident, but she did not communicate her need for alone time.

Sometimes we struggle and have difficulty setting healthy boundaries in our lives. Perhaps you fear the other person's reaction, or maybe you never learned how to set appropriate boundaries. If you grew up in a dysfunctional environment, chances are setting boundaries was never taught. It can be hard when you first start practicing this new concept. People in your life may react negatively to this new change in you. Setting boundaries can rock the boat a little in a relationship. Sometimes you may be challenged with feeling selfish when you set a boundary. Maybe you were raised to feel guilty if you put your needs ahead of other people's needs. Or perhaps there are people in your life who are skilled in using guilt to manipulate you. It is not selfish to set limits in your life. It is absolutely okay, and necessary, to take care of yourself. There is nothing wrong with saying no. Setting boundaries is healthy and necessary to maintain your emotional and physical energy.

If you're unsure how to begin setting boundaries, practice with someone you trust. Write out a boundary setting scenario, imagining how you think the scene will take place. Role play with a friend until you are comfortable setting your boundary. Below is an example of a boundary setting scenario.

Example of a Boundary Setting Scenario

The phone rings and it is 9:30 PM. It is your mother and she is upset about your brother again. This is nothing new – an ongoing saga. You have had a long day, and you are tired. The last thing you feel like doing is listening to your mother complain about your brother.

Mom: You are never going to believe what your brother did today.

You: Mom, it is 9:30 at night, and I am tired.

Mom: You're always tired. I'm tired too…your brother exhausts me.

You: Mom, I have told you in the past that I do not want to talk on the phone after 9:00 PM.

Mom: Why, you need your beauty rest?

You: After 9:00 PM, this is my time for me.

Mom: Oh, it must be nice.

You: I need you to call me back tomorrow during the day.

Mom: You're never home.

You: Then leave me a message...I'll call you back.

Mom: Give me a break. Can't you just talk to me for 15 minutes?

You: No Mom, I can't. Call me tomorrow.

Mom: Fine. (she hangs up in a huff)

You: (you sigh but remind yourself it is okay to take time for yourself and set a boundary with your mom)

In this particular scenario, you are setting a boundary that protects your body (need for rest and sleep), your energy, your time and your relationship.

Button Pushing

A stay-at-mom has been working all day taking care of her small children and trying to keep her sanity. The house is a mess when her husband comes home from work. He walks in, gives her a kiss, and looks around. Then he says, "So what did you do all day?" Whoa! Mom feels a rise of anger inside and she begins rattling off her day's events. Mom's button got pushed. Take your corners – she's ready for a boxing match.

We all have internal buttons, or triggers (conscious or not), that inadvertently get pushed by people in our lives. These triggers, more often than not, stem from old beliefs or experiences that have yet to be healed. One woman shared with me that she became infuriated when she discovered her husband had accidentally locked her out of the house. Even though it was a complete accident, and her husband profusely apologized, she was still angry. After doing some journaling, she discovered the anger actually came from the many years of disrespect she received from her ex-husband. Her old experiences with her ex-husband were dictating how she felt today when something similar happened to her.

We all get our buttons pushed from time to time, and it can be helpful to know how to respond when this happens, so we are not reacting in a way we later regret. So here's a process you can use to manage your buttons, or triggers.

When you first feel the trigger, you will feel an emotional charge. Instead of letting your body take over and reacting to the situation, stop for a moment and breathe. Ask yourself what you are feeling. What are you telling yourself about the other person and the situation? In our example with the stay-at-home mom, she might have believed that her husband didn't appreciate her. She could have been telling herself that her husband thought she was lazy or unproductive. These beliefs may or may not have been true. It would be important for her to check out her beliefs with her husband before she responds.

When managing your triggers, it's important to look back at your history and identify your earliest memory of feeling this way. When someone gets angry at me, I often feel triggered. The reason I feel triggered is because I was once physically abused by an ex-husband when his anger got out of control. As a result of this situation, I formed a belief in my mind that says, "When people get angry, someone gets hurt." In order for me to manage my buttons, I have to realize that not all anger looks the same. Although one person hurt me when he got angry, not everyone is going to be the same. I must change the belief in my mind to something that works for me today. A new belief could be, "When people get angry, they are feeling hurt, and they need to be heard." This belief will help me manage my own triggers and instead of reacting by backing away from anger, I can stay and listen to another person's anger.

Remember, when someone pushes your buttons, the triggers are about you and your interpretation of the event. Dig down deep and be honest with yourself about what is at the core of your feelings. What can you learn about yourself and what do you need to change about your beliefs to manage your buttons? Managing your buttons means you are responding to situations instead of reacting.

We learn a lot about ourselves by being in relationship with other people. We learn what our limits are, and how to communicate those limits with the use of boundaries. We also learn that other people can trigger old baggage in us. Our buttons can be used to get to know ourselves on a deeper level. As we begin to heal from our old beliefs and experiences, our responses to our relationships are healthier. The result of setting healthy boundaries and managing our buttons is more peaceful and harmonious relationships.

TAKE ACTION ASSIGNMENT

Make a list of all the people you are in relationship with on a regular basis. As you look more closely at each of these relationships, identify the buttons and boundary issues that show up. Pick one relationship that you will actively work on to set boundaries and manage your buttons. Transfer these skills you've practiced to all your other relationships.

CHAPTER 31
✳
8 Ways to Deal with the Negative People in your Life

"It is easier to avoid the effects of others' negativity when we question if an action or attitude is appropriately directed at us. If it isn't, we can choose to sidestep it and let it pass." —Sue Patton Theole

✳

Have you ever been faced with trying to stay positive when others around you are negative? Negative people can be a challenge to be around. They will bring you down and drain your energy. A negative person can throw your best laid plans to be positive right out the window. Whether your child or spouse has an occasional negative day or you deal with a family member, friend or co-worker that is chronically negative, there are things you can do to remain positive in the face of negativity.

Let the Negativity Pass
Whatever you do, do not argue with a negative person. Arguing only adds fuel to the fire. A negative person will feed off any negativity that will strengthen his mood or attitude. I have noticed when my children are in a crabby mood, it is best to avoid trying to convince them to analyze and adjust their attitude. As soon as I take the approach of being in opposition with them, they seize the opportunity to prove to me that life stinks. Their negativity intensifies and the situation gets worse before it gets better. Sometimes the best approach is to remain silent and let the negativity pass.

Negative People Need Love
You know how difficult it can be to give love and positive attention to negative people. Unfortunately, that is often exactly what they need. Deep inside that mean and critical person is a person that is usually afraid he or she is unlovable. It is our challenge to rise above the negative attitude and love the injured person inside. How do you show love when someone is negative? You must listen to what she is trying to tell you. Acknowledge the feelings she has by saying something like, "You sound very angry right now." Even if you don't quite understand the person's feelings, know that your reality is different than someone else's. Ask how you might help the negative person.

This shows legitimate interest in her happiness. Offer a hug even if you get rejected. Remember not to take a rejection of your love personally. A negative person often has difficulty receiving love from others.

If you've ever lived with a teenager, you know it can be an emotional roller coaster. My teenager is no different. One day he is a loving and happy young man; the next day he acts mean and grumpy. On these days, his self-esteem and confidence is waning. As he searches to feel good about himself, he takes his struggles out on his family. In these moments, my son needs to know he is lovable. When I acknowledge his pain, he is more apt to open up to me and share what's truly in his heart. The negative feelings inside him are released because I am able to listen and love.

Focus on the Positive
If you try really hard, there is always something positive to be found in any situation. Pretend you are on a treasure hunt and search for any gold or jewels you can emphasize. Even a negative person has positive qualities. When a person is drowning in negativity, it can be difficult for them to see the positive. So often my clients focus on the negative aspects of themselves. They forget about all the great qualities they have. I admit that sometimes a negative person doesn't want to see the positive. This might require her to shift her outlook. Negativity can become a habit and habits are hard to break. Be patient and gently remind your grumpy friend or family member to look for the pot of gold at the end of the rainbow. Hopefully, in her down time, she will begin to reflect on what you have said.

Ask Negative People to Elaborate
You may hear a negative person say things like: "Women are fickle." "You can't trust doctors." "My husband makes me miserable." These kinds of statements are a type of cognitive distortion referred to as generalizations. To help a person sort through her distorted thinking, ask for more specifics. Questions like "Which women are fickle?" or "What specifically about your husband is making you miserable?" forces a person to evaluate what he or she is really trying to say. A negative person will either give up because it takes too much effort to explain himself, or he will get to the bottom of the issue.

Detach and Avoid Trying to Change the Negative Person
Learning to detach emotionally from a negative person can greatly benefit you and the other person. A negative person will fight you if you try to change them. If you want, you can try a little reverse psychology and agree

with everything she says. I once read a great article about a mother who was exasperated with her son's negative mood. Everything she tried to soothe him and make him feel better backfired. She finally gave up and started agreeing with everything he said. When her son told her his friends were mean, she agreed with him. When he complained that his teacher didn't know anything, she couldn't agree more. After several minutes of this kind of dialogue with her son, his mood suddenly shifted. He declared that he was tired and he went to bed with a smile on his face.

Set a Time Limit with Negative People
"You have two minutes to complain and then time is up." Negative people need boundaries and giving them a time limit lets them know you will only tolerate a small amount of negativity. Check your watch and allow them to vent for two minutes. At the end of two minutes, tell the person it is time to focus on solutions or stop complaining. Play a game with your negative friend. Take turns coming up with solutions to her problem. Brainstorm together until you have at least 10 solutions. If your friend doesn't like this idea, simply excuse yourself from the conversation.

Stay Away from Negative People
If you have negative people in your life that are critically affecting your mental and physical health, you need to evaluate whether you want these people in your life. Some people are so chronically negative that you have no other choice but to remove them from your life. It's possible to do that with friends. You can find another job if your boss or other co-workers are bringing you down. Other people, such as children and spouses, are more difficult to remove from your life. In this instance, professional counseling may be the answer. To protect your well-being, you need to enforce very strong boundaries with negative people.

Keep Your Own Negative Thoughts and Behaviors in Check
If you do nothing else but focus on managing your own negative thoughts and behavior, you will come a long way toward remaining positive. A negative attitude is contagious, but a positive attitude is infectious as well. Hang out with positive people that encourage you to be your best self. Use positive affirmations to overcome negative self-talk. Express your gratitude for all the positive things in your life. Take the time everyday to watch all the beautiful things going on around you. Read inspirational material and listen to joyful music. Take care of yourself spiritually. Do whatever you have to do to remain positive and happy despite the negativity you face. The world will be a better place because of you and your attitude. And you never know – you

just might help a negative person make a change to a better way of living.

TAKE ACTION ASSIGNMENT

What negative people in your life are draining your energy? The next time you are faced with dealing with this person, try one or more of these ideas to combat the negativity. How did it work? If these ideas don't work, email me at **lori@true2youlifecoaching.com**; we can brainstorm together.

HEALTH AND AGING

CHAPTER 32
＊
It's Not a Diet ~ It's Not Exercise ~ It's a Lifestyle Change

"We all must suffer from one of two pains: the pain of discipline or the pain of regret. The difference is discipline weighs ounces while regret weighs tons." —Jim Rohn

＊

This morning I drove down a suburban street on the way home from dropping off my teenager at school. On this one street alone, there were about a half dozen people out walking. Some had dogs with them; some had a partner; some were alone. These people were different sizes, shapes and ages. I couldn't help but wonder how many of these individuals made walking a regular part of their life.

We are an educated society. We know what a healthy lifestyle looks like. But yet there are more and more new diets popping up all the time. Health clubs make a fortune on cancelled and unfulfilled memberships. The medical and psychological industries are treating more patients with stress related health problems. How we feel about our physical health directly affects our quality of life.

It's not always easy adapting a healthy lifestyle, but by following these tips, you can be on your way to lasting change.

Connect to Your Desire
What do you truly desire when it comes to your physical health? Forget about what your partner wants or what you think you "should" want. If you hear yourself saying, "I should lose 10 pounds," ask yourself if that is what you actually want. *Why do you want to make health changes? Why now?* When I look at my own health choices, exercise is something I truly want to do. Drinking 64 ounces of water, on the other hand, it not a true desire. All my friends tell me I need to drink more water, but until it becomes my own desire, it's probably not going to happen.

What Does Health Mean to You?
In order to adopt a healthy lifestyle, it needs to *fit who you are and your current*

phase in life. For instance, if you perceive exercise as boring, then you will need to incorporate some type of movement in your life that is fun. Consider dancing or walking and talking with a friend. You would be amazed at the number of activities that the average person would not consider exercise, but actually, in reality burns calories. Sometimes a busy lifestyle means you will need to find healthy foods that are convenient. Or you may need to consider a 15 minute workout every day instead of four one-hour workouts every week. Good health does not have to look like what the magazines suggest. Aim for a lifestyle and a physical body that makes you feel good.

What Stops You from Being Healthy?

Deep inside us we store beliefs about health that may or may not be working for us. We use these beliefs, consciously or not, to protect us from change or propel us towards action. *What are your beliefs about food, exercise and other health related matters?* Here are some examples of beliefs that could be hurting you:

· Exercise is boring.
· You can't trust doctors.
· I will never lose these 30 pounds.
· I don't have time to make healthy meals.
· Being overweight will protect me from pain.
· I hate skinny people – they never have to watch what they eat.
· You're going to die of something so why not live it up?
· I need to have my cigarettes.

These types of beliefs keep us hooked in our old patterns. As long as we choose to believe these unhealthy statements, we will remain status quo, and we will never make the lifestyle changes we know are important for us.

Out With the Old Beliefs and In With the New

Positive affirmations are powerful and positive statements that can help you replace the old, self-defeating beliefs you are hanging on to. You need to reprogram your mind to believe something different. *By repeating affirmations over and over every day, you will begin creating new tapes in your mind that will propel you to healthy lifestyle changes.* Choose one to three positive statements that will describe what you want to believe about your health. Write these statements on an index card or other piece of paper and post them where you can see them. Every day, morning, noon and bedtime, repeat these statements with conviction and visualize yourself actually living into these new beliefs. Here are sample affirmations that you can use:

- I am fit and healthy.
- Movement and exercise makes me feel good.
- I choose healthy foods that nourish my body.
- My past health choices do not determine my future choices.
- I am capable of releasing all addictions.
- I can handle stress without turning to food, drugs or alcohol.
- I create the time to take care of myself.
- Rest and relaxation are just as important as getting things done.

Make a Realistic Commitment

Once you've connected to your desire, you have a clear picture of what good health means to you, and you've explored the unhealthy beliefs that may block your success, *make a realistic commitment to adopt a healthy lifestyle*. Take baby steps toward your overall goal. If you currently do not have an exercise plan, but you want to work out five times per week, start small. Shoot for working out two times per week, and do that consistently for several weeks. Then slowly add a day until you reach your goal. So many diets fail because they deprive you of any "yummy foods." Let's get real. Do you honestly think you will go through your entire life never eating pizza or cookies? Isn't it more realistic to allow yourself some non-diet foods in moderation every once in awhile? Remember your goal is to maintain good physical health, not achieve it and then lose it.

Manage Stress in Your Life

So often it's stress in our lives that leads us off the healthy path. *When we are stressed, our defenses get weak.* We seek comfort, and that often means unhealthy and excessive eating, vegetating in front of the television, or other lifestyle choices that do not support good health. Simplify your life. Try slowing down your schedule. Identify your stressors and develop solutions to conquer stress. One of the stressors in my life is sibling rivalry. If I plan to have a peaceful evening, then I need to get very clear with my boys about what is expected of them. There will be no fighting, or they will both go to their rooms. This is an example of taking a proactive approach to controlling stress in life.

Get Support and Celebrate

Success in making lifestyle changes depends on the support of others. Why do you think Weight Watchers is so popular? Weight Watchers is a diet plan just like the rest of them. However, it is helpful to have the accountability and the camaraderie of other individuals who are trying to make changes in their lives. *Join forces with friends and family members that want to develop a healthy lifestyle.* Exercise together. Support each other by sharing healthy recipes. Encourage one another when you're struggling. And most important, celebrate your successes together. The other night I had dinner with a dear friend. A good portion of our dinner conversation focused on our efforts and successes with maintaining a healthy lifestyle. I celebrated her recent commitment to working out daily, and she expressed genuine happiness for my current success with preventing migraine headaches in my life.

While making some of these healthy changes can sometimes be difficult, if you keep at it and don't give up, your new health program will become a way of life. It is then that you know you've adopted a healthy lifestyle. This new lifestyle will become as automatic as tying your shoes.

TAKE ACTION ASSIGNMENT

Design your vision of a healthy lifestyle by answering these questions:

1. What does your heart say about what health changes you want to make?

2. What does it mean to you to be healthy? Describe "good health" in a paragraph.

3. What old beliefs might prevent you from achieving your vision of health?

4. What affirmations will help you make positive health changes?

5. What are your health goals?

6. Who will support you and celebrate with you?

CHAPTER 33

✳

You Don't Have to Like your Body to Love It!

"Each individual woman's body demands to be accepted on its own terms."
—Gloria Steinem

✳

I want you to think about your body as one of your children or someone else you love dearly. When was the last time this person did or said something that really made you mad? In that moment, you might have been thinking "I really don't like this person right now." However, did his behavior cause you to stop loving him? Absolutely not! My teenager regularly acts in a way that I do not like, but I still love him. I will protect him, do what I think is best for him, and give him what he needs.

Now let's return to your body. How often do you look at your body and think, "I do not like my legs, my hips, my butt (or whatever)"? I admit it. I do not like my thicker waist that came from my second child and being over 40. Okay fine, so it also comes from sometimes eating too much of the wrong foods. It's one thing to dislike your body. It's something completely different to have an attitude of hatred or disgust toward your body. This attitude will cause you to mistreat your body instead of loving and honoring your body.

Phyllis hates her body and this hatred is deeply rooted. When she was a young girl, she was sexually abused. Instead of being angry at her perpetrator, she turns her anger inward to her own body. At one time in her life, her pain was so great that she abused her body by making cuts on her arms. Today, she has the scars that remind her of this extreme hatred. Although she has healed in many ways, Phyllis still struggles to lose weight and treat her body with the respect that it deserves.

Your body, with all its imperfections, is sacred. It is the only body you have been given for your entire life. Your body houses all the organs that keep you alive. It gets you around from place to place. Your body pumps oxygen to the brain that enables you to feel, think, create and function. You need to take care of your body like any relationship with a loved one. Loving and respecting your body requires the same ingredients. So what can you give to your body that you would give someone you love?

Daily Attention

To nurture a relationship, you need to pay attention to what it needs. If you ignore your loved one for a long period of time, what happens? The relationship begins to die. In order to grow my relationship with my younger son, he needs daily doses of conversation, playtime with me, and cuddling. In order to thrive, your body needs adequate sleep, proper nutrition, exercise, and plenty of water every day. You wouldn't go for a week without talking to your child or husband, so why would you go for a week giving your body 4-5 hours of sleep a night or regularly feeding your body foods with no nutrition? Love your body by staying conscious about how you treat it on a daily basis.

Get in the habit of paying attention to every healthy choice you make and reward yourself by placing a star sticker on your calendar. Set a goal to get five stars per day or play a game to see how many stars you can get in a month. As you watch your calendar fill up with stars, you will feel a sense of pride and this will motivate you to continue making daily choices that support good health.

Spend Time and Listen

In order to get to know someone you love, you need to spend time together. Your body requires the same thing. It will communicate with you if you only listen. Your body will tell you when it is hungry and when it is full. It will tell you when it is tired and needs to relax. If you are getting sick a lot, your body is screaming at you. It is trying to get your attention. When you exercise, your body will begin to hurt if you push too hard. Or maybe you are short of breath from lack of exercise or being overweight. That is your body's way of communicating that it is working too hard. Pay attention to the cues your body sends you. Respond to them and see them as signs that something needs to change. Someone I know once said, "If you ignore your health, it will leave you." And so will your husband.

Louise Hay, author of *You Can Heal Your Life*, discusses and demonstrates the mind, body, spirit connection. She put together a guide, *Heal Your Body A-Z*, that enables you to look up your particular health challenge and read about probable causes along with instructions on how to overcome it by adopting a new thought pattern. For instance, she says migraine headaches are more likely due to a resistance to being driven, an inability to go with the flow of life, and/or sexual fears. Don't ignore what your body is trying to tell you. Be a good listener.

Special Treats

Sometimes you give your loved ones special treats to show you love them. You don't give them every day because then they wouldn't be special. Your body needs special treats too. Treat yourself to a massage, a facial, or a mocha latte every once in awhile. When I was a teenager, my mom and I used to go running on the local school track. Afterwards, we went to this awesome ice cream shop and treated ourselves to a scrumptious sundae. We didn't overindulge all the time...just once in awhile. Special treats help banish feelings of deprivation.

One of my clients, Nancy, recently decided she was tired of looking frumpy. Even though she has not reached her ideal weight, she is motivated to look and feel good regardless. One commitment she made is to buy some new clothing that she can feel good about wearing. When we treat our bodies in a special way, we are making a bold statement about our commitment to loving ourselves. Acts of love will begin to transform our hearts and minds to believe we are worthy of special attention.

Grace

How many times does your loved one say "I'm sorry"? And how many times do you forgive him or her? We all need grace at times, and so do you when it comes to taking care of your body. Maybe you do well on your diet or exercise plan for two weeks, and then you fall off the wagon. For one whole week, you don't exercise and you don't follow a healthy eating plan. That's okay! Forgive yourself and get back on track. You don't have to completely abandon your plan because you didn't follow it perfectly.

Beating yourself up is self-sabotaging and creates a cycle of guilt that is hard to break. When we self-blame or self-criticize, it lowers our self-esteem. The lower self-esteem results in feelings of anxiety or depression. To cover up our pain, inflicted by us, we sabotage our plans to take good care of ourselves because we don't believe we deserve it. Stop this cycle immediately and instead offer grace and compassion.

Have Fun

Taking care of and loving your body doesn't have to be drudgery. Have fun! Find new low-fat recipes that contain your favorite foods. Adjust your attitude toward your health and your body. Exercise is only boring if you view it that way. Find activities you love that exercise your body. When I was in Las Vegas this past month, I was taking a walk in a local family park. I watched a dad and his two children having the time of their lives. They were riding their bikes and dad was leading the way. He created an obstacle course that required the kids to ride in circles, up and down ramps, over the grass, and around various walkways. They were laughing and having a blast, while exercising their body. This dad knew the value of adding fun to a healthy routine.

When you leave fun out of your relationships, your health, and your life, you lose the passion it requires to keep things interesting. Just like a marriage of 15 years needs a little spice, so does your commitment to being healthy. Adding creativity and fun enables you to remain excited about your health goals. If you're not excited, you will lose interest and fall back into old patterns and routines. It takes effort to nurture our loved ones, and the same effort is needed to nurture our body.

So, here's to good health and loving your body even if you don't like it!

TAKE ACTION ASSIGNMENT

Pick one of the five ways to start loving your body. Love your body in this way for at least one month. Pay attention to any shifts in your attitude about your body.

CHAPTER 34
✳

Take Time to Declutter Your Life

"A house that is cluttered is usually lived in by people whose minds are also cluttered, who need to simplify their lives. This begins with simplifying and clarifying their thinking. Mind and life need to be freed from the 'disorder of the unnecessary.'" —Elisabeth Elliot

✳

When the word clutter is mentioned, people immediately think of all the excess paper, junk and other items lying around their home. That is certainly one definition of clutter, but clutter is so much more than that. Clutter can be unfinished projects that are hanging over your head, or tolerations and irritations that you put up with in life. Clutter is unhealthy relationships, bad habits, negative thoughts and destructive emotional states. Basically, clutter is anything that interferes with living your best life and being your best self.

Why care about the clutter? Clutter is an instant energy drain. Whether it's messy closets, a bad attitude, a job you don't like, or unpaid taxes, they all interfere with living a joyful and fulfilling life. When you get rid of the clutter, you love yourself enough to grow and be your best. You know the old saying, "Out with the old and in with the new." Addressing the clutter in your life opens the door for new and exciting things to happen. Every time I say goodbye to something that is no longer aligned with my best life, a new opportunity magically appears.

There are four major areas of our lives where clutter tends to accumulate. Let's address each of these areas individually.

Physical Environment
Your physical environment consists of your home, office, and automobile. Decluttering your environments includes tossing out the junk and organizing what you wish to keep. When you walk into your space, are you nurtured by it? Is it clean and decorated in a way that brings you peace and happiness? The family room and kitchen accumulate the majority of the clutter in our home. When I wake up in the morning and walk into a clut-

tered kitchen, it saps my energy. The cluttered countertops rob me of the energy I need to be motivated for my day. On the other hand, if I keep the clutter picked up in our family room, the area becomes a stress-free and relaxing place to unwind and enjoy family interactions.

Decluttering your environment also means that everything is in good working order. Right now, my vehicle needs several repairs and it affects me. My air conditioner doesn't work. The driver side's window doesn't open, the electric locks make a loud grinding noise, and the fuel injector pump is going out. Does my car run and get me around? It does, but it's annoying to have these loose ends not taken care of. I don't enjoy driving my car. How are your environments? Do they enable you to live healthily and happily?

Health and Emotional Balance
Your physical and emotional health is all about you. Decluttering yourself physically means you are taking the steps to eat right, exercise regularly and take care of your mind and body. You are addressing any health concerns and keeping regular checks ups with your doctor. Decluttering forces you to address stress in your life and do whatever it takes to live a peaceful existence. Fairly recently, I was battling a lot of migraine headaches. Physical pain in our body is a signal that something is wrong. There is either a physical or emotional component of our lives that needs to be taken care of. To feel our best, we need to experience good physical health.

Maintaining emotional balance includes managing your thought and emotional life – doing your best to keep your mind positive. Decluttering your emotional life requires us to let go of unhealthy choices, attitudes, behaviors and patterns.

· An unhealthy choice is any decision you make that does not support who you truly are and what you truly want in life.

· Unhealthy attitudes are attitudes that are destructive to your life. It could be anger or bitterness that you are holding on to. Perhaps it's a pessimistic attitude toward your future that brings you down.

· Unhealthy behaviors are behaviors that are damaging to you or other people. Engaging in negative self-talk is a great example of unhealthy behavior.

· Unhealthy patterns are habits that you are engaged in that no longer serve you in life. Examples include perfectionism, procrastination and emotional eating.

Nurturing your health and emotional balance means you are intellectually stimulating your brain, fostering creativity, and avoiding the things that are damaging to your mental state, like overworking or watching too much TV. By making a commitment to take better care of our emotional and mental life, we are choosing to respect ourselves on a much deeper level. The result is higher self-esteem and increased happiness.

Money

Decluttering in the area of money requires us to maintain healthy financial habits. What is a healthy money manager? A healthy money manager has addressed all her emotional issues with money. She is comfortable handling money, and uses her money wisely. Decluttering requires you to address overspending or living in the dark when it comes to your financial picture. My friend recently took from her husband the responsibility for paying the family bills. It has given her a much better appreciation and understanding of their financial needs. As a result, she makes different choices about how she spends their money.

Having healthy financial habits means you are saving money for both short term and long term needs. You have a will that addresses all your assets, including your children. People in a healthy financial state understand the value of giving and not holding too tightly to money. Bills are paid on time, and debt is non-existent, with the exception of a mortgage. A healthy money manager is educated in wise investments or has a reliable and trusted financial advisor.

Money issues are one of the leading causes for argument in marriages. It is stressful when your financial life is not in order. Money is a necessary tool for you to live life in the way that is important to you.

Relationships

Relationships in your life include your family, friends, co-workers, and boss. Decluttering in the area of relationships means you are addressing any relationship problems so you get along well with the people in your life. You have removed the relationships from your life that regularly drag you down or damage you. To declutter your relationships, you need to forgive everyone who has hurt you and put full closure to the relationships that are no longer in your life. Keeping healthy relationships requires us to stay in touch regularly with people by face to face visits, through phone calls or email exchanges. Doing your part to maintain healthy relationships requires you to speak truthfully, avoid gossiping, and steer clear of criticizing and judging others. When we've decluttered our relationships, they provide the love and support we need on this journey through life. Healthy relationships give us positive energy and nurture our heart and soul.

Take an honest look at your life. In what areas could you use a little decluttering? What needs to change to help you live your best life and be your best self? Our pastor shared a thought that is worth hanging on to: "If I want my life to change, I must change." I'll take it one step further. "If I want to grow and live my best life, I must grow and be my best self."

TAKE ACTION ASSIGNMENT

Review the four areas mentioned above and make a list of things you need to do to begin decluttering your life. Keep your list with you and regularly work at eliminating each item that keeps your life cluttered. Decluttering is a process, so give your self some time. Every little step you take will make a difference.

CHAPTER 35
✳
Minimize Mommy Stress

"If you ask what is the single most important key to longevity, I would have to say it is avoiding worry, stress and tension. And if you didn't ask me, I'd still have to say it." —George F. Burns

✳

According to Jerome F. Kiffer, a writer for WebMD, stress that continues without relief can lead to a condition called distress — a negative stress reaction. Distress can disturb the body's internal balance or equilibrium — leading to physical symptoms including headaches, upset stomach, elevated blood pressure, chest pain, and problems sleeping. Research suggests that stress also can bring on or worsen certain symptoms or diseases.

There are two kinds of stress. There is stress that occurs from external circumstances. Consider the stress that inevitably shows up when your two year old decides to have a meltdown. You're in a good mood and life is going along smoothly until you tell your child he can't have a cookie. This is the straw that breaks your son's composure. All of a sudden, this once calm and collected little boy turns into a raving maniac, thrashing around on the kitchen floor, his high pitched screams making you cringe. You take a deep breath and try to rationalize with him, hoping this will cease all activity and knock some sense into him. This doesn't work; it only makes matters worse. So you try to ignore him; that's what the books tell you to do. But he wants to blow off steam and get your attention. After 10 to 15 minutes dealing with an uncontrollable and inconsolable child, our nerves are frayed. This is external stress.

The second kind of stress is self-inflicted stress, or internal stress. This is the type of stress we bring on ourselves like worry, poor planning, and unrealistic expectations. Most stress is of the internal kind, especially when you consider stress we feel from external circumstances is often the result of our own internal reaction to it. Stress is bad for your health, and it disrupts the process of enjoying life. Following are six tips for minimizing mommy stress.

Be More Mindful and Plan Accordingly

My husband laughs at my mom and me because we plan early for all the activities in our lives. As funny as it seems to him, it works for us. Waiting until the last minute causes undue stress. If you're organized and use a planning system that works for you, there is more time to relax and actually enjoy your life. Sometimes we have to be mindful about creating our lives the way we want them to be. Otherwise, the busyness of being a mom takes over and we feel overwhelmed with tasks and activities.

One of my clients had great success using little colored stickers on her calendar to plan her life according to her desires. She used five different colors for the five different goals she had. A blue sticker reminded her that she wanted to spend time with her friends. A yellow sticker was the reminder to schedule play time and outside activities with her children. A purple sticker designated her goal to work out three times every week. A red sticker, the color of love, was a reminder to spend time with her husband. A green sticker indicated her desire to read books for pleasure.

Rachel came into her session one afternoon grinning from ear to ear. I looked down at the calendar she brought with her and it was beautifully decorated with all her colored stickers. It was clear to me that she was intentional about planning her life and scheduling her goals. In one month, Rachel went from a stressed out mom to a mom who was feeling happy and in control of her life.

Simplify

The simpler your life, the easier it is, and the less stress you will feel. Look at what is complicating your life and minimize or eliminate it. For some moms, they have too much stuff in their home. Get rid of the clutter and learn to live with the basics. Other moms have too many activities in their lives. Evaluate your social commitments, volunteer duties, children's extracurricular activities and other tasks that fill up your life.

Practically everywhere I turn, I listen to moms express their need to feel balanced and relaxed. And one of the leading causes of a life that is "out of balance" is too many extracurricular activities. While sometimes it is the parent's schedule, more often than not, it is the children's schedule. Why, as moms, do we feel such a need to over-schedule our children in extracurricular activities?

Most of the time, parents have good intentions when they enroll their children in sports activities, church youth groups, scouts or music lessons. They want their children to experience what they feel is a "rich and happy" childhood. There is no doubt that extracurricular activities can be enriching to a child's life. They help children develop skills, enjoy social relationships in a structured environment, and possibly tap into their gifts and talents.

Have we gone overboard and lost perspective on the harmful effects of too many extracurricular activities? According to child psychologists, too many extracurricular activities in a child's life make them prone to stress, anxiety and issues with sleep. According to Alvin Rosenfeld, M.D., the leading expert on overscheduled children, "parents need to relax. Slow down. Activities are fine, but don't go over the top. Focus on building meaningful relationships with your children, not being their chauffeur." My suggestion to moms is to limit a child's activities to one per semester or season. The reason I advise this is because when the schedule is too full, there is no room for the important things that take place in the home. Make sure you are only participating in activities/events that are absolutely important to you.

Let Go of Perfection

Many of us want to be perfect moms. We want to create memories for our children that last a lifetime. We want to make sure we are raising our children in all the "right" ways. If we could go through motherhood and not make any mistakes, that would be just fine with us. But is that reasonable to expect? There is a big difference between being a great mom, and being a perfect mom, and the difference is in the amount of stress you will feel. A perfect mom does not exist so stop trying to be one. The house does not need to be perfectly clean all the time. It's okay if our kids eat junk food once in awhile. It's even normal to lose our tempers when our children are misbehaving. Lighten up! Focus on your strengths and accept your weaknesses. Its okay to work on growing as a mom and doing things better, but don't make perfection your goal. It's impossible to achieve and it causes undue stress in your life. So enjoy your imperfect children, your imperfect husband, and your imperfect self. Life will be much more fun!

Be Wary of Unnecessary People Pleasing

As moms, we often want to make sure everyone around us is happy. We are pulled in all different directions by family and friends expectations, in addition to our own internal expectations. It can become very difficult to please everyone and still take care of ourselves. Remember that self-care is a priority if you want to manage stress. Our needs as moms are just as important as the needs of our family. So find a healthy balance between pleasing other people and pleasing yourself.

Nix the Wonder Woman Costume

It's never a great time to be super mom, and take on the world. Get rid of the attitude that you have to do everything yourself. This attitude will only cause resentment and interfere with the joy that you deserve. Every other Tuesday evening, our house needs to be prepared for our housecleaner to come in and clean. It was the same routine every time. I would start stressing about all the clutter that needed to be picked up and getting the house in the right condition. One night I noticed that I was the only person stressing out. My husband and my younger son were having a great time playing a game. My teenager was talking on the phone to his girlfriend, minding his own business. Now if all the clutter belonged to me, I guess that would be okay, but the clutter belonged to everyone. Why was I the one worried about everyone else's clutter? Because I forgot I am not super mom.

Don't be afraid to ask for help. Instead of getting angry and stressed, I decided I would let everyone know one time what needed to be done before the housecleaner comes. To make it easy on myself, I typed up instructions for everyone on a piece of paper and hung it on the kitchen cabinet. I told my family that I would remind them on Tuesday nights but it would be their responsibility to check their list of tasks and complete them so the preparation didn't all fall on me. I realize some family members are more helpful than others and I am blessed with a family that pitches in when I need it. If you can't get the help you need, then commit to only what you can without causing stress.

Keep a Stress Diary

One way to begin eliminating stress from your life is to keep a stress diary. In this diary, you can keep a record of the minor and major stresses you encounter each day. The essential elements to record are date, time, stressor, a stress rating that tells what level of stress you experienced, and what your reaction was - physically and emotionally. Some of the stressors might include an argument with your spouse, child misbehavior, job stress, traffic, or financial worries. Typical reactions are festering inside, outward expression of anger, crying, worry, and any number of physical reactions.

While some mommy stress is inevitable, certainly much of it can be minimized. By learning to identify our stress triggers and actively working to minimize them, we will experience better health and greater inner peace.

TAKE ACTION ASSIGNMENT

Keep a stress diary for a minimum of one month. Look for ongoing stressors that repeat themselves. Develop a plan to eliminate or minimize these stressors so your health is not negatively affected. Practice stress-relieving techniques like deep breathing, taking breaks, exercise, journaling, meditation, yoga and prayer.

CHAPTER 36

✷

Healing Your Emotional Relationship with Food

"If you use food to run away from feelings; if you eat when you're upset, stressed out, angry, tired, bored, sad, or even just to pass the time; if you eat to feel better, or if you eat to reward yourself, you're an emotional eater."
–Roger Gould, M.D.

✷

One evening in February of 2006, I lay in bed watching Oprah's 20th Anniversary DVD collection – a gift given to me by my best friend. Story after story of incredible people that have touched and changed the life of Oprah opened up my emotional flood gates. There was one particular person I really identified with – the story of Rudine. Rudine suffered severely from anorexia nervosa. She deeply longed to battle and conquer this condition, but Rudine's emotional relationship with food and herself was too damaged.

I can identify with Rudine because at the age of 13, I came face to face with anorexia nervosa. It followed two very painful events in my life. Looking back, I now understand I was unable to cope with all the emotions I encountered. The anger and hatred I felt – because I could not outwardly express it – was turned inward. I began to hate my body and food became the enemy. I exercised like crazy and eventually ate only one small meal per day. After finally breaking that cycle, I swung to the other extreme and began to binge eat late at night. Other destructive habits replaced food until, at the age of 21, I got serious about facing and healing my emotions.

I share this with you because I think it is important to understand the devastating effects our relationship with food can have on our health. Maybe you've never suffered from anorexia nervosa, bulimia or obesity, but your emotional relationship with food is still worth examining. In an ideal relationship with food, you eat when you're hungry, and you eat the healthy foods your body needs. Your body weight is healthy and you aren't experimenting with the latest diet. Healthy eating is your way of life, and your physical well-being reflects that – not just your body, but your energy level, mood and internal health as well. Let's explore some of the common emotions or situations that can trigger unhealthy eating. Pay attention to whether any of these strike home for you. If so, try substituting some of the alternatives I suggest so you can begin healing your emotional relationship with food.

Angry Eater: When you are very angry with yourself or someone else, do you turn to food? Maybe you're mad because you made a mistake and so you beat yourself up with food. Jane forgot to bring an important financial document to an appointment with her accountant. When she realized what she had done, she could not forgive herself for forgetting. She was so upset with herself that she stopped by the drugstore on the way home from the appointment and bought a huge candy bar. In an effort to comfort her angry feelings, she ate the whole candy bar, causing herself to feel angrier because she was trying to lose weight. Instead of stuffing your angry feelings with food, try confronting and expressing your anger in a healthy way. Practice forgiveness and releasing your angry feelings.

Stress Eater: According to Dr. Phil, "when you are under stress, your body releases hormones that automatically stimulate your appetite and set off cravings, prompting you to eat huge quantities of fattening food." When you feel stressed, take 15 minutes of quiet alone time or a 15 minute brisk walk instead. Evaluate your life to see what is contributing to your stress levels. Make some adjustments to eliminate the stressors from your life.

Convenience Eater: You don't have time or don't feel like making something healthy to eat, so you grab whatever is convenient – fast food or take home, chips, donuts, etc. Keep healthy and convenient foods around the house and at the office – fruit, granola bars, Lean Cuisines, string cheese, and yogurt. Ask yourself what you can do differently to slow down the pace of your life. Take a couple of hours on the weekend to make several quick and easy meals that you can throw in the oven or microwave during the week.

Tired Eater: Morning comes around or the afternoon energy runs out and you need a kick of sugar or caffeine to keep you going. You load up on cookies, cake or a Mocha Latte and you're off and running until you crash. Try getting 8 hours of sleep at night, exercising regularly, taking vitamins or taking a short cat nap. Choose instead to eat an energy bar packed with a lot of protein and carbohydrates. Sugar is a temporary high that actually increases your appetite.

No Waste Eater: Were you taught to never waste food? Were you reminded of all the poor children that had nothing to eat? Now you cannot bring yourself to leave anything on your plate or throw away any food. Make less food and put smaller portions on your plate. Give yourself permission to stop eating when you're full. Resist the temptation to finish any other family member's food. Work in a homeless shelter serving food or give food to the poor so you don't feel guilty.

Self-Disgust Eater: You look at yourself and hate what you see; you eat or deprive yourself of food to mask the feelings you have, and so starts the cycle of abuse. Work on loving yourself in every way you can – pamper yourself, repeat positive affirmations, stick up for yourself. Invest in gaining confidence and self-esteem.

Boredom Eater: This is me. I don't feel like doing laundry or cleaning the house. I'm tired of working, playing cars or watching TV. It's cold outside and so I open the food cabinet. "Hmmm, I wonder what I can eat." Fight the boredom, get creative and find something fun and different to do. Switch projects and start something new. Make a phone call to a friend. Shake up your routine, get out of the house, or lose yourself in a good book.

Fear of Intimacy Eater: Do you eat to hide yourself and avoid getting too close to someone? Sometimes reaching out to people can be a very scary and hard thing to do. Maybe you've been hurt too many times by loved ones. Excess weight caused by emotional eating is often a form of self-protection. Seek help to heal your pain. Search for supportive and loving people that you can depend on. Take baby steps to reach out and trust someone. Learn to love yourself so others can love you too.

Hopeless Eater: Have you just completely given up? Maybe you've tried too long to lose weight or given too much to your marriage, and nothing seems to change. You feel hopeless and so you just say, "Who cares? I'm just going to eat whatever I want." Or maybe you've lost your appetite altogether. Change your thoughts. Victim thoughts are destructive to your happiness and success in life – they are the equivalent to being stuck in concrete, unable to move. Even getting angry at your circumstances is better than feeling hopeless and helpless. Focus on the positive and keep a gratitude journal. Look for the bright side of everything. Actively search for the sunshine and you will find it.

"See Food" Eater: You know the saying, "I'm on a seafood diet. I see food and I eat it." Are you the type of eater that constantly grazes? If the food is in front of you, you eat it without actually thinking about it. You may or may not be hungry — it's just a habit. Habits can be broken and change can take place if you actively work on changing your patterns for a minimum of 30 days. Graze on low-fat and healthy foods. Leave the fattening foods at the grocery store. Work on being more conscious of how much food you are taking in. Keep yourself busy with fulfilling activities so your mind is not thinking of food.

Social Eater: You love to be around people and what better way to spend time with friends than going out to lunch or dinner. Socializing is great! Eating out is expensive and not always very healthy — not to mention the additional calorie intake. Add a couple of glasses of wine and you've consumed in one meal what you should have for the day. Limit your social gatherings at restaurants to once or twice a month. Start a walking group with friends. Participate in a movie or book club. Have a board game night and serve soup and salad. Socializing does not have to include eating and drinking.

Comfort Eater: Sadness or loneliness threatens to swallow you up. Depression seems to be your best friend. Food is your source of comfort. Somehow you feel better after indulging in your favorite meal and dessert. Until the feelings strike again. It's time to face your sadness or loneliness. Maybe you need to grieve the loss of someone or something. Perhaps you need to reach out more to a community of people. Developing a relationship with God may supply the consolation and companionship you need. Food cannot come close to providing the love and friendship your soul desires.

Whatever your relationship with food, ask yourself if it's a healthy one. Facing your emotions head on is the only way to heal them. Denial only causes your feelings to go away temporarily. When I watched the story of Rudine on Oprah, a recovering anorexic pleaded with her to feed her brain and give herself the nourishment that it needed. With sad-filled and hope-less eyes, Rudine simply said, "But how?" Isn't that the essential question we are all faced with when making change? How? Change starts with aware-ness. It's fueled by desire and commitment. And it ends with taking action. Take the steps you need now to develop a healthy relationship with food.

TAKE ACTION ASSIGNMENT

For the next month, keep an emotional eating journal. Every time you eat for reasons other than being hungry, pay attention to what you are feeling and record your emotions. Identify your reason for eating. After one month, look back over your journal and see if you notice any patterns in your eating. Is there one particular reason that shows up more than others? What can you do differently to address the core emotion?

CHAPTER 37
✳

Your Emotional Barometer – Release Stored Emotions before the Storm Hits

"There is no question that the things we think have a tremendous effect upon our bodies. If we can change our thinking, the body frequently heals itself." –C. Everett Koop, M.D.

✳

Barbara recently told me about an incident she experienced with her body. As she was driving, her teeth and arms began to tingle, her vision tunneled, and her heart began to pound very fast. Fortunately for her, she was close to a medical clinic. Upon arriving at the clinic, she was shocked to find that her blood pressure had soared to 190/110. Barbara is young and leads an active lifestyle, and all of her medical tests came back negative. So what happened? **Just like a barometer measures atmospheric pressure, each of us has an emotional barometer that measures our stored emotions and tension levels.** A storm is generally anticipated when the barometer is falling rapidly; when the barometer is rising, fair weather may usually be expected. In this case, Barbara's emotional barometer was falling rapidly while her blood pressure rapidly rose. Many years of unprocessed emotions finally took their toll on her.

We were created to experience many emotions – from anger and sadness to happiness and joy. Unfortunately, many of us have been conditioned to believe that certain emotions are negative and others are positive. Actually it's what we do with the emotions that makes them either negative or positive. Emotions, themselves, are just emotions. Just as a traffic light signals us to stop, slow down or go, your emotions serve the same purpose. If you are feeling angry, it is a signal that something is wrong. It could be that someone is actually disrespecting you, or you perceive that you are being mistreated. If you are feeling sad, perhaps you are missing something or someone you wish you had. Likewise, feelings of happiness and joy are signs that you appreciate an experience or your thoughts are of gratitude and abundance.

So what happens when you don't pay attention to and process your emotions? Your emotions are stored in your subconscious mind and in your body. Let me give you an example. Many years ago, at a time when my life wasn't so happy, I went for my first massage as an assignment for a college course I was taking. The massage itself was wonderful. Now you would think that I would walk out of that experience feeling great and relaxed. Surprisingly, I found myself feeling very angry. Why? Because years of angry feelings were stored in my muscles and the massage released those emotions. **If you ignore and store your "negative" emotions, they will manifest themselves in disease, health issues or other destructive outlets.** So your first step is to stop ignoring your emotions. Use them to tell you what's next. What do you need to do differently?

There are many things you can do to manage and release your emotions.

• **Speak up immediately.** Sometimes someone does something that hurts, angers, or bothers us. It can be easy, especially if it is something small, to let the issue pass without saying anything. One time I forgot to lock the doors when I left our home for a baseball game. My husband came home and found the doors unlocked. Safety of our home is very important to my husband so when I got home later that evening, he talked to me about his concerns. Had he chose to ignore the issue, he would have stored the worry inside, and eventually it would come out if he didn't address it. It is important you let others know how you are feeling so many little issues don't build into a volcano.

• **Evaluate and change your thoughts.** Our emotions come from the thoughts we have. Negative thinking can be so automatic for some people that they don't even realize what they're thinking. The other day I was feeling grumpy when it was supposed to be a fun family outing. I started to ask myself what I was thinking about. Here is what was going through my mind. "I hate the cold weather. Walking outside in this is not my idea of fun. My teenager was supposed to be on time and so now all of us have to wait on him. This is boring, just sitting here and waiting." With thoughts like that, who wouldn't feel cranky? So the next time you find yourself feeling unhappy, pay attention to your thoughts. Try changing your thoughts to something positive and see if your emotions follow.

• **Look at the boundaries in your life.** A boundary is an emotional line you draw that tells people what your limits are. Abby is a stepmother to two children. It is not uncommon for this brother and sister to argue and fight with one another. Abby is accustomed to living in a peaceful home so when her stepchildren visit and start fighting, she feels stressed and uncomfortable. So she made a new rule in her home. If the children are going to fight, they must go outside on the balcony so she doesn't have to listen to them. This boundary protects her and enables her to live the life that is important to her. Are you allowing others to step over your boundaries? Pay attention to and honor your limits. Know when to say no to protect your emotional and physical health.

• **Take time to refuel.** More often than not our emotions tell us when we are tired and emotionally drained. Pay attention to your short fuse and irritability. This is probably a sign that you need to do something to take care of yourself. Moms, more than anyone, regularly put everyone else's needs before their own. Schedule some fun and relaxation time for yourself. Call up a girlfriend and have a cup of coffee together. Indulge in a manicure or pedicure. Find a quiet place to read a good book. Spend a couple of hours engaging in your favorite hobby. This will do wonders for putting your emotions in check.

• **Laugh.** Laughter releases endorphins in your brain — the "feel good" hormone. Watch a hilarious movie or comedy skit. Read a light-hearted joke book. Do something that makes you laugh yourself silly.

• **Exercise.** My doctor has always said exercise is the best antidepressant on the market, and recent research has proved him correct. Blow off some steam by taking a brisk 30 minute walk. Go for a family bike ride around the neighborhood. Relax with a yoga class. Do a little Billy Blanks" Taebo and punch and kick to your heart's content.

• **Journal**. Take 30 minutes every morning to write in a journal anything and everything that you are feeling. Process everything that is going on in your life. You will be amazed at what can come up during the journaling process. Not only will it help you release your emotions; journaling will help you learn a lot about yourself. You may even come up with creative solutions to life's problems. One of the most creative journals I have ever seen is available on my website (**www.momnificent.com**). It's called Journey-In' - A Meditative Coloring Journal. On one side of the journal is a space for you to reflect on your emotions through writing — the other side of the journal is an intricate art design that can be used for coloring. The idea is that while you relax and color the design, you meditate on what feelings are coming up for you.

• **Prayer and Meditation.** Use prayer or meditation as an outlet to express your emotions. When I pray, I ask God to take my anger or open my heart to joy. Prayer and meditation give you the alone time you sometimes need to process your feelings. You can also listen to soothing music or sounds of nature to quiet your mind.

Weather Flash: Watch your emotional barometer and keep the storms from clouding your life.

TAKE ACTION ASSIGNMENT

What emotions might you need to release to experience optimal health? Explore your beliefs about the mind-body connection. Pick one of the eight techniques described above and commit to letting go of any stored emotions that you feel are negatively affecting your life.

PERSONAL FINANCE

CHAPTER 38
*
It's Not Money that you Want

"Don't tell me where your priorities are. Show me where you spend your money and I'll tell you what they are." —James W. Frick

*

Shannon invited her friend Michele to a Chonda Pierce comedy show. She paid $22 for her friend's ticket and drove 150 miles to the concert on her gas money. Even though they shared a fun evening together, Shannon became rather stirred up when Michele didn't offer to reimburse her for the comedy show ticket. After all, after the last concert they went to, Shannon offered to reimburse Michele for her ticket and Michele accepted.

On the surface, it would appear Shannon has a money issue, but it's not money that she wants. Shannon is financially stable and can easily afford the $22 ticket and the gasoline, but Michele has a history of self-centered and insensitive behavior. What Shannon wanted and needed from Michele was acknowledgement and love. If Michele would have offered to reimburse her for the ticket, it would have shown Shannon that she cared enough about her to ask. Shannon didn't want the $22; she wanted Michele to express her appreciation and notice the kind expression of love Shannon showed to her. As a matter of fact, Shannon would have probably declined the reimbursement had her friend offered. She wanted to give Michele a gift, but when she felt unappreciated, money became the issue.

Money, like time, is a merely a tool to get what's most important to us. There are a lot of values and personal emotional needs tied up in money. When we fight over money, we are fighting for what we value or need that money can provide. When our values are being threatened or our needs are not being met, we fight, cling and sometimes take drastic measures with our money. Let's look at some common values and needs that get tangled up with money. As you read about each of these, notice which of these values and needs represent money in your life.

Appreciation

People use money to express appreciation. We buy gifts as a way to show gratitude, care and concern. When we receive a gift from someone, we return that expression of appreciation to our gift giver. How do you use money to express appreciation? How do you feel if you spend money on someone and they don't appreciate it?

Beauty

My mother uses money to have beauty in her life. She has a beautiful home, decorated with her very own creative flair. Her clothing reflects her need to look and feel beautiful. She pays for a professional manicure so her nails look gorgeous. Beauty is an important value for a lot of women, and large sums of money are spent to beautify themselves, their children, and their homes.

Comfort

Some people don't want the luxurious house or the fancy sports car, but they do want to feel comfortable in a modest home with a reliable car. Money is a means to be able to relax and enjoy a nice lifestyle without going overboard. It allows them to be able to afford some of the activities or amenities that they enjoy without worrying about strapping themselves financially.

Control

If a person values control, money is often a tool that is used to satisfy this need. A woman or man may use money to control behavior, buy love, or attract attention. I have an uncle who was forever flaunting his wealth, in hopes of gaining respect and admiration from his family members. In addition, he used money to reward his son for acting in a way that was acceptable to him.

Family and Friends

Most moms value their family and money is a way to make sure their children are taken care of. It ensures the children get a good education, have clothing on their back and food in their tummies. Money enables one to have a good time with friends and family members, and to bond in a way that builds connection. My husband loves to entertain his family and friends, and without money, he can't afford to do that.

Freedom

For some, money spells freedom. It gives us the freedom to do whatever we want without worry. When we are financially struggling, it sometimes feels like our freedom has been taken away from us because the chains of fear drag us down. Money allows us to move freely through life, enjoying those things that are important to us.

Fun

It takes money to go on vacation. If we want to go out to dinner or go see a movie, we need money. Although there are certainly fun activities we can participate in that don't require money, most of the time there is a price we pay for fun. So for some of us, money is our answer to entertainment or recreation in our lives.

Giving

In the book, *Secrets of the Millionaire Mind*, T. Harv Eker told a story about a man who attended one of his millionaire mind seminars because he wanted to figure out how to earn $10 million a year. Now most of us would probably be wondering why someone would want to earn that much money. Well, this gentleman happened to be a very large donor to a charity that assists AIDS victims in Africa. Whether you are giving to charity, your local church or just to your friends and family, money allows us to give back to others in a way that is important to us.

Growth

There are people like myself who value personal growth. I want the money to be able to attend conferences, educational seminars or read books that inspire and encourage growth. According to Google Answers, the U.S. spent $1.14 billion on self-help and business books in 2005, and that figure continues to rise.

Happiness

What's the saying? Money can't buy happiness? Or can it? That's a question you have to answer for yourself. If you had more money, would you be happier? If so, why? If you answered no, then you probably don't value money as the avenue to your personal happiness. You might list some of these other values as the key to your happiness.

Health

Do you want to experience good health in your lifetime? Health related costs include purchasing healthy food, vitamins, exercise equipment or memberships, and good medical care. There are some countries that value health enough to offer medical care to all of their citizens. Everyone chooses to spend their money differently.

Independence
There are many women who want to declare their independence from men, and money is the way they express this need. It may be a separate banking account or a career that gives them financial independence. For some, they want the freedom to make their own decisions about money. In essence, women want to spend their money on what is important to them and avoid the value conflicts that money often brings about.

Love
One of the five love languages, as identified by Gary Chapman, is gift giving. Men and women like to give gifts as a way to express their love for one another. Most gifts cost money. Although not everyone feels this way, some people measure a person's love based on how much money he or she is willing to spend. So whether we want to give or receive love, money is often the tool that enables us to express it.

Peace of Mind
Peace of mind enables us to sleep at night and eliminate worries during the day. Now there is an unending list of things that can rob us of peace of mind, but more often than not, money tops the list for most people. BabyCenter LLC did a survey of 2400 moms. When mothers were asked what worries kept them up at night, 27% stated they worry about economic problems such as unemployment and recession. Thirteen percent of mothers said the most challenging aspect of modern day motherhood is being able to afford life with children. Financial worries are real and money can give us peace of mind.

Power
Some of the most "perceived" powerful people in the world have a lot of money. Do you equate money with power? When you think of Bill Gates, do you think of him as powerful? I don't, but other people would. People use money to throw around their power all the time. Money buys the material goods that many people associate with status – luxurious homes, high priced cars, expensive jewelry and high fashion clothing.

Respect
If you had more money, do you think people would respect you more? Unfortunately, poor people don't receive nearly as much respect as the wealthy. Would you have more self-respect if you achieved your financial goals? I know for me, I feel better about myself when I am making wise

financial choices. I value being responsible with money and I respect people who make healthy financial choices.

Security

In one introductory session with a prospective client, I asked her what money meant to her. Her answer was "Security, security, security." When we value security, it is important to us to be protected from harm. Many people view financial hardship as something to avoid at all costs. These people want a guarantee that they will always be taken care of financially. It is always possible that without money we will be sleeping on the streets or starving to death. That reality is happening all over the world, and most people don't ever want to have to experience that. Money offers the security that we won't have to suffer.

Success

I used to measure my success by how much money I made, and I have to believe that I am not the only one that has fallen into this trap. In a material society, money defines success. The more money you make, the more successful you appear to the outside world. But if success is what you want, is it possible to redefine success? I always say, "You came into this world with nothing, and you will leave this world with nothing." So what kind of legacy of success do you want to leave behind? It might be money for your loved ones, but it may be something completely different.

In this chapter, I have highlighted 18 values that we associate with money, and there are many more. The next time you find yourself wrestling with a financial decision, or having a conflict with a loved one over money, remember it's not money that you want. You are fighting for your most important values, and the relationship that money has to them.

TAKE ACTION ASSIGNMENT:

Review the list of values in this chapter and ask yourself what money represents for you. What are your top five reasons for wanting money in your life? By having a clear picture of what is most important to you, you can honor your true self with every financial decision you make.

CHAPTER 39
✳
Beware of the Money Gremlin

"Financial freedom is when you have power over your fears and anxieties instead of the other way around." —Suze Orman

✳

Most of us, at the very least, want to be financially comfortable. Some of us want to be financially wealthy. Very few, or none of us, want to struggle financially. What determines what we will experience in our relationship with money? Deep in the recesses of our minds are core beliefs about money that play an integral part in dictating the success or failure of our financial lives. More often than not, we don't even know what these beliefs are, or we are certainly not aware of the power they hold over us.

Maggie very clearly remembers the time when she and her sister went shopping with their parents for their first pair of contact lenses. Though both were teenagers at the time, they were very different when it came to selecting contact lenses. As you can probably imagine, there were many different types of contact lenses to choose from, all with different price points. Maggie's sister Laura picked the most expensive contact lens available. She was not thinking about how much money they cost or what her parents' reaction to her choice would be. Maggie, on the other hand, picked an inexpensive pair of contacts because she was concerned about the money her parents would have to spend. Maggie remembers thinking that her sister was being selfish for wanting the best money could buy. Already money beliefs were driving each of these girls' decisions. Maggie will tell you that her father regularly pounded into her his beliefs about money. The messages that were sent, or at least heard by Maggie, were: I have no voice when it comes to money; I am not worthy of nice things; you only need enough money for the basics. It's clear how these beliefs were operating in Maggie when she made her choice about which contact lenses she wanted. Did Laura receive different messages or choose to create her own beliefs?

If you are not experiencing the financial success you desire, it is likely the result of the money gremlin. The money gremlin is the compilation of money beliefs you have learned and adopted as "real" over the years.

Following are some of the common money beliefs that hold people back from achieving true financial freedom.

Rich people are selfish or greedy.

The fact of the matter is there are poor people who are selfish and greedy. There are even middle class people who are self-seeking and stingy. Your character has nothing to do with how much money you have. Some wealthy people give a lot of money to great causes in this world; some don't. The question you need to answer for yourself is: who would you be if you did have a lot of money? How could you help the world if you shared your wealth?

I'm not a numbers person.

This belief can disguise itself in many ways. Other versions of this same belief are: I'm not good with numbers; I'm not very good at handling money; I'm not good at math; I don't know what I'm doing when it comes to money; My husband is much better at handling money than I am, so he takes care of the money. All of these beliefs allow you to avoid the issue of taking owner-ship over your finances. You don't have to be the one that pays the bills, but you do need to know what is going on. If you want financial freedom, it is necessary to be in control of your money. Being in control of your money requires one to be educated about successful money practices. I have heard countless stories of women who lost their spouse, leaving them with the responsibility of managing the money. The problem is that these women don't have a clue about what they are doing, and they have a resistance to learning. Anyone can learn the basics of effective money management skills. But the belief that you're not a numbers person will certainly block the process.

I don't have the money now so I'll just charge it.

A healthier belief would be "I don't have the money right now so I will just wait." Consumer debt is a huge block to achieving financial success. Charging purchases when money is not available is an unhealthy habit to get into. Susie developed a habit of charging items she wanted but could not afford. Over a period of a few years, she had accumulated over $40,000 in debt. The credit card companies increased their interest rates and minimum monthly payments, making it impossible for Susie to keep up with the bills. Susie had to file bankruptcy to get out from underneath the debt. While bankruptcy may be an extreme solution to consumer debt, carrying consumer debt is like throwing money into the air. Why give money to a credit card company when we can learn to stop the habit of instant grat-ification?

Money is the root of all evil.

Did you catch the error in this statement? For a long time, I lived by this belief until someone pointed out the omission of the word "love." The correct statement is "the love of money is the root of all evil." Money itself does not create evil or problems. It's the person or the attitude behind the money. Money can be used for a lot of good in this world. Money is just a tool. We, as individuals, decide how we are going to use money and for what purpose.

If I don't hold tightly to my money, it will be gone.

Some people have a fear of losing their money or fear financial struggle. There is a belief that there is not an abundance of money to go around. When we operate from a place of believing there is a limited supply, fear sets in and blocks our energy. Money has energy and fear will repel money from us. Learning to let go and trust there will be enough money can be a challenging process for some, but a process worth mastering. It can be important to look at what money represents for us and ask ourselves how we can achieve this image or vision without money.

Making a lot of money is the definition of success.

That would certainly be one way to define success, but most definitely a limiting one. If we only use money as a measurement of our success, our feelings of self worth can be compromised if we don't achieve the financial success we desire. However, if we expand our definition of success to include other ideas besides financial wealth, the opportunity to experience success significantly increases. When we believe we are successful, with or without money, there is a greater chance of attracting the money we feel we deserve.

I have to have the "right" (blank) to make money.

It is not the right education, the right job, the right spouse, or the right investment that creates abundance in your life. As I shared lunch with my friend, I told her "I can't figure out what I am doing 'wrong' in my business." There was a belief that if I took the "right" action, created the "right" product, or used the "right" words to market my services, financial success would follow. My friend looked at me and said, "I don't think you are doing anything wrong. As a matter of fact, you are doing everything right." So what was wrong? I was believing that I am lacking, instead of adopting a belief that I am abundant. You have everything you need to make money if your beliefs are grounded in love and abundance.

These beliefs are certainly not the limit of what the money gremlin can tell us. The most important aspect to take away is the understanding that we can diminish the power of these beliefs and improve our relationship with money by committing to a process of self-awareness and growth. How do you define financial freedom or financial success? What beliefs hold you back from experiencing the financial abundance you desire? It is possible and necessary to rewrite the tapes that have been playing in your mind for years. Then, and only then, will you diminish the power of the money gremlin.

TAKE ACTION ASSIGNMENT

Take a journey back into your childhood. What is your earliest memory of money in your life? Remember and record as many memories as you can relating to money. Take an honest look at the patterns of money management in your life today. How are they related? Make a list of unhealthy money beliefs you feel need to be changed and rewrite those beliefs to support your financial goals. Supplement that list with healthy money beliefs that are working for you today.

CHAPTER 40

✱

Overcoming the Money Worrier in You

"Money isn't the most important thing in life, but it's reasonably close to oxygen on the 'gotta have it' scale." –Zig Ziglar

✱

It can be hard to relax about money, especially if we aren't where we want to be financially. When we speak about financial worry, there are two types of worries. There is worry over money that is grounded in real truth, and there is financial worry that comes from a fear of the unknown. Let me explain each of these in a little more detail.

Sometimes we have real reason to be worried about our finances. In the event that our expenses exceed our income, it would be quite normal to worry about where the next dollar might come from. Depending on the state of our economy, many factors can affect our financial situation. Companies downsize and lay off employees, leaving families with a significant decrease in their income. Some jobs require sales of services and goods to maintain a needed level of income. When the economy is tight and people aren't buying, it can be tough to make money. My cousin has been sitting on two pieces of property that he can't sell because of the state of the real estate market. As a result, his family is trying to maintain three mortgages. Perhaps you're strapped with a significant amount of debt and you're not sure how you're going to get out from underneath it. It could be your system of paying bills is unorganized and you're forever forgetting to pay the bills on time. Some people worry about bad credit scores because of financial choices from their past. And last, sometimes we worry because we don't have our spending prioritized in our lives.

Even though we may be doing okay financially, we still might worry about money. Sometimes past mistakes cause us to fear repeating them in the future. For instance, one of my good friends got herself into debt two times in her past. Each time there was a significant amount of debt that she and her husband had to work hard at paying back. It was such a hard time for them that she sometimes fears getting into that same place in the future. As a result, she is hyper-vigilant about her money, and worries if finances get tight.

At other times, the future and its uncertainty can cause worry. Many people worry about whether they will have enough money for retirement, or how they will put their children through college. Just last night I listened to a family member talk about retirement. She decided to retire at the age of 62, leaving her with a period of 1-1/2 years that she would be without medical insurance. This was a real concern for her and, thankfully, her employer decided to supplement her retirement income to allow for the cost of her medical insurance. Some people worry about not having a will or trust in the event of unexpected death. These may be situations we don't like to think about, but often they are a source of worry in the back of our minds.

Worry is not the solution.

Although it may be normal to worry, worrying is not the solution to our financial problems. Worry will keep you stuck, cloud your judgment and rob you of the peace you deserve. Worry causes conflict and stress in your life, and stress drains your energy. Worrying will not help make your financial situation any better.

Developing a plan is the solution.

What will help, however, is having a plan to address your financial worries.

The first step is awareness.

Before you can begin to develop a plan, there must be complete awareness of what the problems are. Let me give you some examples of what complete awareness looks like.

Example #1 – Incomplete awareness
We are in debt and don't know how to get out.

Example #1 – Complete awareness
We owe $2123.56 to Visa at an interest rate of 15%. We owe $1567.46 to Discover at an interest rate of 16.9%. We have a bill for JC Penney for $442.54 at an interest rate of 20.9%. Our home equity loan is $9765.12 and the current interest rate is 8.25%.

Example #2 – Incomplete awareness
We don't make enough money to pay our bills.

Example #2 – Complete awareness
We have exactly $4,123.60 in monthly income with both our salaries. Our current monthly expenses are $4,875.00 broken down as follows: $2125.00 for mortgage, $450.00 for groceries, $385.00 for utilities, $225.00 for telephone, etc. (Sometimes the only way to know for sure what your monthly expenses are is to track every penny you spend for a period of one month.)

The second step is education.

After you have a clear picture of what issue you are facing, it is possible that you know exactly what you need to do to develop a plan. In that case, skip the education piece. However, you might need some help in understanding how to solve your problem. Right now I am one year away from sending my teenager to college. At this point, I have no idea how I am going to pay for his college. I am not educated about what my options are. I am not familiar with financial aid, the scholarship process or even how much money is currently set aside for my son's education.

Whatever your financial situation or problem, there are resources available to help you. The internet has a wealth of free information on probably anything you would search on. There are books written to address every financial concern you may have. One book I highly recommend is *Smart Couples Finish Rich* by David Bach. This book even has a workbook that you can purchase to help you take action. Finally, there are financial planners, financial coaches, and other financial experts that can advise you. Educate yourself about what you need to do next.

The last step is to develop a plan and stick to it.

Developing a plan puts you into action and action is a step toward taking responsibility for your financial worries. One approach to not being able to pay your bills would be to worry. Another approach would be to get angry and blame yourself or other people for your financial struggles. A healthier approach to this situation would be to take an honest look at your income and expenses and use this information to create a budget that would enable you to pay your bills.

For a long time, my husband and I would worry that we didn't have a will outlining what would happen to our children and our assets should we die unexpectedly. When we went away on long trips without the children, that worry would intensify. Sometimes we would write up a piece of paper that explained who would take care of our children and give it to a relative before we boarded the plane.

Putting together a will was on our "to do" list, but we never got around to completing the task. Then one day my husband watched a commercial for LegalZoom and it inspired him to take action. He completed the will application online and received it from the company within a few days. When he got back from having the will notarized at the bank, he experienced tremendous relief because at last, the will was taken care of. This process of taking action enabled him to worry less.

In some financial situations, action taken once is enough to alleviate the worry. However, in other circumstances, it is necessary not only to develop a plan, but also to have the discipline to stick with the plan. My good friend Thea Reynolds teaches a class and offers a system for developing a budget. Her system is called Budget in a Binder' (www.budgetinabinder.com). When a couple comes to her, their finances are usually a mess. She helps them develop a plan and teaches them how to track their spending so they can set up a financial budget. Thea puts her clients into action and agrees to meet with them in another month after they have had a chance to work with the system. They meet again in the second class to review their progress and learn ways of saving money and taking responsibility for their finances. Once they leave this session, it is up to the couple to stick with their new plan. She has given them the tools they need, but they have to use self-discipline to reap the benefits.

This is where many people fall down when trying to achieve their goals, financial or other. We go into the process of change feeling optimistic and strong, and then old habits begin to resurface. Change becomes difficult, or we experience a setback, and that is when many of us give up and abandon the plan. That is why working with a coach is becoming so popular. Coaches help you face those old beliefs that are holding you back from having the life you want. They help you develop a plan, overcome the obstacles, cultivate new habits and hold you accountable until you experience the success you desire.

TAKE ACTION ASSIGNMENT

In a journal or notebook, write the answers to the following questions and take the appropriate actions.

- What are some of the real concerns you have regarding money in your life today, and in this moment?

- What future financial worries do you have or worries that are based on the fear of the unknown?

- What do you need to do to develop complete awareness of the financial problems you need to address?

- Commit to writing out a clear picture of the financial worries you want to eliminate.

- What education do you need to help you feel comfortable developing a plan for your financial worries?

- Gather the resources you need and start the process of education.

- What type of plan do you need to have in place to minimize your financial worries?

- Who can help you put together this plan?

- Who can help hold you accountable to sticking with this plan until you have experienced the success you desire? (Hint: coaches, friends, family members, mentors, and other experts)

CHAPTER 41
✳
Achieving Financial Intimacy

"Many of us have a curious relationship with money. It's a more taboo subject than our sex lives." —Eileen Ambrose

✳

When most of us think about intimacy, we think about sexual or emotional intimacy. However, in a marital relationship, financial intimacy is extremely important. Divorce typically takes place when one or both partners are not committed to the marriage, and money is one way this lack of commitment can be expressed. Money is a significant part of every couple's life and having a healthy approach to finances can dramatically improve your emotional and physical intimacy.

To achieve intimacy in any sense, we must have an understanding of one another. Each person involved should know who they are and be confident about communicating that in an authentic and loving way. When we are intimate, we are close and familiar with each other. It is the mutual sharing and giving that creates this closeness. So what does financial intimacy look like?

Understand Your Financial History
When Becky and Tom got married, they were completely unaware of how their childhood would affect their finances. Becky came from a middle class family where money was rarely an issue. Her parents provided for her financially and she never went without material possessions. Becky's mother was giving and flexible, allowing Becky to have most of what she needed and wanted. She was involved in many extracurricular activities, lived in an expensive home overlooking a lake, and had a room full of her favorite toys.

Tom, on the other hand, grew up in a working class family. His father worked three jobs just to make ends meet. Tom's mother worked also, but there never seemed to be enough money because his father had a problem with gambling. I guess you could say he wasn't a very successful gambler. Tom was subjected to conflicts about money, and there was a constant focus on pinching pennies so the family could survive.

You can probably imagine the financial differences that Becky and Tom had. Becky was used to spending money and having whatever she wanted. Tom was always worried about money, putting constant pressure on his family to conserve energy, food and money. The two differing views on money did not mix very well. The more money Becky spent, the more worried Tom was. The more constraints Tom tried to put on Becky financially, the more she wanted to spend.

The first step toward financial intimacy is understanding your financial history. What did you learn about money from the family you grew up in? Look at the financial interactions between your parents. How did each of them handle money? What beliefs about money did they pass on to you, directly or indirectly? Who handled the bills in your home? What money conflicts do you remember witnessing? What lessons about money, conscious or not, did you take away from your family of origin? Take some time to think deeply about how your childhood has financially influenced who you are today.

Communicate Honestly and Openly

The most emotionally intimate couples are the ones that can communicate honestly and openly with each other. They are not afraid to share how they feel and what they believe. Each person is accepting and listens with respect to the other person. Intimate couples take into consideration how the other person feels and they work together to reach a compromise that works for both of them.

No two people are always going to agree on money. However, if we can learn to talk about money and work together, we can still achieve financial intimacy. Share with your partner your ideas about how money should be handled in your family. Be willing to talk about your fears and worries around money. Let your spouse in on anything you remember about money from your childhood.

Financial intimacy cannot be achieved unless you are willing to listen to how your spouse feels about money as well. Your partner probably has different ideas, desires, and fears than you do. For example, he may have a need to save 20% of your money or spend his money on items that are not important to you. This does not make him wrong if you don't agree with his philosophy.

Once you have a clear understanding of what's important to both of you on the issue of money, work together to devise a plan that meets both of your needs. Decide how much money you will save or invest. Put together a budget with fixed amounts that you can spend in each category. Don't forget to allow for discretionary spending money for each of you.

No Financial Secrets

Julie had a real wake-up call when her husband handed her a magazine article on financial infidelity in marriage. She thought infidelity was about cheating on her husband, but she learned a new lesson that day. The article addressed financial secrets husbands and wives keep from each other. Whether you are hiding a $20K bonus you received from work, lying about how much something cost, or failing to disclose purchases you have made, it's all considered financial infidelity.

Just like sexual infidelity will shatter the trust in your marriage, so can financial infidelity. Julie was guilty of buying things and hiding them from her husband. She never really thought about how this behavior affected her husband. If she would lie about money, what would stop her from lying about something else? That's the way Julie's husband looked at the situation.

There should be no financial secrets in your marriage. I don't think it is necessary to report every penny that is spent to your spouse, but you shouldn't have to lie about anything either. Keep an open dialogue going about money. What is the amount of money that can be spent without permission from the other person? For example, some couples may agree that anything over $100 needs to be discussed first, especially if it's for a luxury item, as opposed to a necessary item for the family like food or clothing.

Both people in the marriage should have access to the bank accounts and bills. You should not hide credit card bills from your spouse or conceal any amount of money that is put away. I can't tell you how many women I've heard talk about how little they know about their financial situation. If your husband handles the money in your home, he should be open about everything. How much money is available for spending? What are your expenses? What does your investment portfolio look like?

Both Parties are Involved Financially

It's okay if one person handles the finances in the home, but he or she should not do it in the dark. Financial intimacy requires both parties to be involved. At the very minimum, you can discuss each month where you stand financially. Ideally, you are working together to pay the bills and making joint financial decisions.

The other day I was shocked by my husband's behavior. We had agreed we were going to use a forms company to draw up a simple will. We had started working together on my will and ran into a stumbling block. Knowing that we needed to wait until business hours to seek help, we decided we would come back to the project later. A day later I found out that he went through the online process to complete his own personal will without my involvement. I was extremely hurt by his actions because we have a child together and our money belongs to both of us. How could he make a decision without consulting me about where our child or money would go if we both died simultaneously?

In a marital relationship, your money belongs to both of you. Each person has a right to be involved in the day-to-day decisions, as well as the long-term choices that are made with your money. Sit down and pay the bills together. Visit your financial planner together. Take the time to review options together before making large financial purchases. Educate each other on a regular basis about the status of your financial picture.

Commit to Being Financially Responsible

I recently read an article about a wife who was infuriated by her husband's decision to purchase an expensive car without her permission. The couple was struggling financially to make ends meet and her husband made an irresponsible financial purchase. Financial intimacy requires us to be committed to taking responsible financial action.

Each couple needs to decide for themselves, based on their financial situation, how they define responsibility within the context of money. Some behaviors, however, are obviously not responsible and here are a few examples:

· Spending more than you bring in

· Accumulating large sums of credit card debt

· Consistently paying bills late, thus affecting your financial credit

· Making large dollar amount purchases without mutual consent

· Keeping financial secrets in the relationship

• Addictive spending habits like gambling, alcohol consumption, pornography and compulsive shopping

• Failure to educate yourself about your financial picture and future

Just like you committed to your partner to be faithful, commit to being financially responsible. Do you part to maintain a healthy financial life, and encourage your spouse to do the same.

Achieving financial intimacy in your relationship requires work, but if you work together financially, your chances at achieving financial success are much greater. Two minds committed to the same goal are always better than one.

TAKE ACTION ASSIGNMENT

On a scale of 1 to 10 (10 being highest), rate your current financial intimacy in your relationship. What is one action step you can take to increase your financial intimacy? What action step is your partner willing to take? Make a commitment to honor these steps and hold each other accountable.

CHAPTER 42
✳
7 Secrets to Having and Teaching Good Money Habits

"Once you take full responsibility for your financial health, money stops being a source of frustration and starts to flow into your life naturally."
—Cheryl Richardson

✳

How many times have you replied, "We don't have the money for that" when your child asks you to buy him something? His innocent reply is, "Get some from the machine or the bank." You think to yourself, "If only it were that easy." **Managing money is a tough concept for children to grasp, and sometimes equally as challenging for parents.** In order for your children to develop healthy money habits to take with them into adulthood, you, as their parent, must manage your money wisely and be diligent about teaching the concept of money to your children.

So what are the secrets to having a financially healthy family? I have the pleasure of working with my dear friend Thea Reynolds, who happens to be a financial planner, the creator of Budget in a Binder‘ (www.budgetinabinder.com), and an expert at managing money. Together we compiled seven secrets to having and teaching financial success in your family.

1. **Having a monthly budget to work with is a must.** If you have never sat down and figured out how much money you earn and spend, now is the time to do that. For a period of two months, record every penny you spend and assign it to a category. You can use a simple spreadsheet or a more sophisticated money management program like Quicken or QuickBooks. Our family posts all our income and expenses in QuickBooks; this makes it very easy to print budgeting reports. Typical categories include utilities, housing, entertainment, education, automobile, groceries, health and beauty, dining out, savings, etc. **Many people are amazed to discover where their money actually goes.** Just recently, I helped one of my clients post her expenses for one month. It was an eye opening experience for her. Most of the time, we don't remember how much money we are spending. Until we see it on paper, we are often oblivious to the inordinate amounts we spend in certain cate-

gories. To develop a budget for your family, you need to know how much income the family brings in and your required expenses to live. Your budget should never exceed the amount of net income you make. If you bring in $3000 per month in income, then your expenses should not exceed $3000. Assign a specific dollar amount that you will spend for each category. **Having a budget is not about limiting yourself – it is about making choices and deciding what's most important to you.** If having a fancy car is important to you, then you cut back in areas that aren't so important to you. If you want to be able to eat out once a week, then consider making cuts in your grocery expense.

• **To teach your children about budgeting, here are two exercises you can do.** At the beginning of the month or whenever the family gets paid, cash your checks and lay all the money out on the table for your children to see. Get out all your bills and work together with your children to match up the appropriate amount of money with each bill. Let them see where the money goes and how much it takes to manage a household.

Another exercise you can do with children who are a little more mature is give them a budgeted amount for a specific event, shopping excursion, or vacation. For instance, if you are taking your children to a theme park for a day, give them $75 (or whatever amount you want). Then you tell them that whatever they don't spend they can keep! Let your child pay for his own admission ticket, food, souvenirs, etc. Children will learn quickly how to manage their money. When my friend Thea went off to college, her father gave her $10,000 for the year. She was responsible for paying for her tuition, books, food and any other expenses she had to live. If she managed her money well, then she had leftover money. If she didn't, then she had to figure out how she was going to pay for her expenses. Teaching your children how to budget and manage their money is critical to their adult success.

2. **Keep your total housing cost to 30-35% of your total income.** Some people say the housing cost includes your mortgage or rent and your utilities. Others say that it includes only your mortgage or rent. Whichever formula you use, if you have a household income of $50,000 per year, then your housing expenses should not exceed $1458.00 per month.

3. **Do not carry any consumer debt.** The American culture reinforces instant gratification and that is why so many Americans have huge credit card debt. There is nothing more damaging to your financial success than credit cards. I realize credit cards may be a lifesaver for people who are

struggling financially. Believe me, I've been there. But I tell you from experience, use credit cards for emergency purposes only. If you have big ticket items you would like to spend your money on (furniture, vacation, car, remodeling), make a list of those items and put it on the refrigerator. Decide what's most important to you and start putting money away every month so you can pay cash for those items. How do you teach your children this concept? Do not let your children borrow money from you unless they can pay it back right away. If they don't have the money to buy something they want, require them to save their money until they do.

4. **Strive to put away 10% for emergency savings.** I know many people who live from paycheck to paycheck, and putting away money for savings is unheard of. Put some amount of money into a savings account on a monthly basis, even if it is just a small amount. Ideally, you should try and save 10% of your income. If you have the ability to have money deducted from your paycheck for a 401k or another retirement account, take advantage of that. Once you get used to that amount being gone, you will adjust and you'll never miss it. Open a savings account for each of your children at a very young age. Take them to the bank and encourage them to save some of their money. Let them experience the thrill of seeing their bank balance rise. Another fun way to teach kids about money is help them decorate 3 separate jars or coffee cans. Label them "Spend, Save, and Donate." Give them a weekly allowance and encourage them to contribute a certain amount to each of their jars every week.

5. **Never go over the breadwinner's income.** This is advice my mother has given me often and when I was younger, I balked. Now that I have become wiser and actually made the transition from a two income family to a one income family (with the same set of expenses), I know this is good advice. I know this can be a tough example to live by, but it is worth the effort. You never know when one person may lose their job. If your expenses don't exceed the breadwinner's income, then the rest is gravy.

6. **There should be no financial secrets between husband and wife.** Each partner in the marriage should know exactly what is happening with the family finances. Funds should be merged and each person should be accountable to the other for financial decisions. Decide between the two of you what dollar limit needs to be discussed first before purchasing. For instance, you may decide that all purchases over $300 need to be mutually agreed upon. Pay the bills together or at least communicate the financial picture after the bills have been paid. More often than not, I hear that either

the wife or the husband is completely removed from the family finances. You cannot possibly make good financial decisions unless you are knowledgeable about your financial situation on a regular basis. Too many couples divorce over money issues. Do your best to work together on money.

· Talk openly with your children about money. You do not have to share your own personal financial situation, but do not be afraid to be frank about money. One family, in helping prepare their high school age son for adulthood, gave him real facts about how much everything would cost. They helped him understand what a typical engineer makes upon leaving college, and what his expenses would average. They gave him real numbers about car payments and insurance costs. It is better to open your child's eyes to the truth than to let them be surprised and unprepared.

7. **Have an "abundance attitude."** What does this mean? Having an abundance attitude means you believe there is more than enough money to go around. There is an infinite supply of money that is available to you. Money is just a tool. It is not the answer to happiness in life. If your tendency is to hang on tight to your money, try learning to let go. When you have a giving spirit, you will be blessed tenfold.

TAKE ACTION ASSIGNMENT

Which of the seven secrets do you need to implement to have a financially successful family? Pick one baby step that you can take to implement this new habit. Tell someone you can trust what your plan is. Ask them to hold you accountable to making this change.

CHAPTER 43

✳

The Do's and Don'ts of Child Allowances

"Money management is the one subject conspicuously absent from most school curriculums, which means your child's financial education begins and ends at home. And one of the best tools for teaching your kids about managing their money is an allowance." —Marshall Loeb (former editor of Fortune *and* Money *magazines)*

✳

If you've ever wondered whether you should give your child an allowance, the answer is yes. However, I know the process of setting up an allowance plan is not that simple. So here are some do's and don'ts you'll want to read before embarking on this journey.

Do give your children an allowance.
Every parent spends money on their children. In a sense, you are managing money for them. What you don't want when your children enter adulthood is to realize they don't have a clue how to handle money. The number one reason children need an allowance is because it enables you to teach them money management skills. Unless they are handling money on a regular basis, they will not learn this very important skill.

When children are given an allowance, it allows them to make mistakes with money while the stakes are fairly low. If a child hasn't learned self-control with money, it's far less damaging to blow $10 than it is $1000. On one trip to our local Wal-Mart store, my young son had $39 to spend because he had saved his money for three months. He was just beginning to understand he could spend his money on other people. Eager to please, he had a plan to spend all his money on Pokemon cards for his new friend. This shopping excursion gave me an opportunity to talk to him about the ramifications of spending all his money on someone else, leaving none for himself. Although it seemed like a noble and generous thing to do, I thought he might later regret he left nothing for himself. We had a nice talk about finding the balance between giving to others and giving to him. He ultimately made his own decision with a little coaching from me.

An allowance gives your children the ability to think about how much things cost and whether or not a purchase is of value to them. When you pay for all your children's toys, books, and special treats, they have less appreciation for them. They don't know how much something costs, and they don't really care. However, if they have to spend their own money, they begin to care. If they have $5 to spend, they might think twice about all that candy they want. Children will have opportunities to decide if something is a good value. They will start thinking about what they get for the money they have to pay.

Lastly, an allowance teaches children the value of saving instead of giving in to instant gratification. If there is a big ticket item your child wants, she will learn that it requires her to save her allowance until she has enough money to buy what she most wants. Our 12 year old babysitter recently saved all her babysitting money for months — her reward for self-control was a brand new television for her bedroom.

Don't wait until your children are older to give allowance.
I made the mistake of waiting until my teenage son was older before I started giving him an allowance. As a result, he didn't have an opportunity to save money or learn money management skills as a young boy. He made all his mistakes with larger sums of money since he was older.

When your child is old enough to understand the concept of money, probably around the age of 3 or 4 years old, start giving him an allowance. If your child is asking for items at a store, she is old enough to understand it takes money to purchase these things. She may not know what a quarter is or what it means if something costs $2.50, but she will learn as she gets an opportunity to handle money. The earlier you can teach money management skills, the more years your children have to practice. The more practice they receive, the more successful they will be in the future.

Do give an amount that is fair.
There is no one set amount that is fair for child allowance. The cost of living varies from place to place and your neighborhood culture may be a factor you want to consider. Check around to see what other children are receiving. Look at the cost of those things you normally purchase for your children.

Obviously, what you pay a three year old is going to be different than what you would pay a 12 year old. The more maturity your child has, the more responsibility they should take for their financial purchases. The system I have used with my children is $1 per week for every one year of age. For instance, a seven year old would receive $7 per week, $364 per year, or $30.33 per month. Whatever you decide, make sure you settle on an amount that is not too overwhelming, and not too little, causing frustration for your children.

Don't tie allowance to chores.
Many parents wonder if they should tie their children's allowance to chores. My opinion is that children should be required to do chores as a result of being part of a family. If children decide they don't feel like doing chores, and you deduct all their allowance, then they are missing out on the value of having an allowance – learning to manage money. Trust me; I have tried this and it doesn't work. It would be better to enforce different consequences for chores not being completed. Make weekly chores separate from your child's allowance plan.

It is okay to use chores as a way of earning extra money, as long as their normal chores have been completed. If your child is trying to save money for something special they want, I see nothing wrong with allowing them to wash the car for $5.00. This sends a message to your children that you can earn more money by working hard. Although working hard it not the only way to earn more money, it certainly is one way. Most of the time, adults are rewarded financially for hard work.

Do have a plan for their financial responsibilities.
A valuable part of teaching your children money management skills is letting them know what they are responsible for financially. Sit down as a family and talk about what your children will be required to pay for out of their own money. Of course, you have to take into consideration how much allowance they receive on a regular basis. For instance, when a child is three or four, you might require them to buy their own candy or a small toy they want from the store.

As they get older and their allowance amount increases, gradually increase their financial responsibility. For example, a 10 year old may need to purchase her music CDs, movie or video game rentals, and special food treats she wants beyond normal meals. When your children become teenagers, the responsibility increases even more. My teenager is responsible for his recreational evenings with friends, expensive clothing beyond the twice a year clothing necessities, extra toys beyond holiday and birthday gifts and occasional gas money for the car. After your child has a job, I think it's okay to discontinue allowance. Whatever you decide for your child's financial responsibilities, write it down so there is a clear understanding between you and your child. This will eliminate a lot of arguments over money.

Don't forget to be consistent with paying allowance.
Once you decide on the amount of allowance your child will receive, and you have a plan for who pays for what, make sure you are consistent with paying. You can pay allowance on a weekly, semi-monthly or monthly basis, whichever is most comfortable for you. We pay our boys on a monthly basis, but some experts would suggest a weekly basis.

Set up a system that will help you remember to pay. Pay on the same day each week or month, much like receiving a salary from an employer. This helps your child know when to expect their allowance and how much time they have before their money supply is replenished. We wouldn't want our employers paying us whenever they remember, and it's only fair to our kids that we are consistent with their allowance. One other thing; don't forget to give your children a raise every year.

Do require your children to save and share money.
Money is not just for spending, and your children should learn to save their money and give a portion of their money to others. What you require your children to save and give is completely up to you, but experts would say 10% to 20% should be saved and shared. Personally, I require my boys to save 50% of their money. We give them a nice allowance plus they receive money from relatives as gifts.

Learning to save and invest our money is so important. When children learn the concept of saving at a young age, they are more apt to do that when they are adults. You can teach your children about the importance of giving as well. Help them understand the types of people or organizations they might be interested in giving to. Help them support causes that are aligned with their interests. For instance, if they love animals, educate them about animal organizations that may need monetary assistance. You can let them help you purchase gifts for their friends with the money that is set aside for giving. Your children can give to your local church.

One day my six year old had a lemonade stand and sold lemonade and chocolate chip cookies. The chocolate chip cookies were a big hit and he made quite a bit of money. I told him he needed to bring 10% of his earnings to church with him on Sunday. It was only 75 cents, but it helped him understand the power of giving.

Don't tell your children what to spend their money on.
I know it can be very hard to resist telling your children how to spend their money, but do your best to refrain. When you give your children the freedom to choose how to spend their money, they learn money management much quicker. At one time, my teenager had over $1100 in the bank. He was saving for a car, and then he got a girlfriend. This girl was the first girl he ever fell in love with and their love resulted in wanting matching tennis shoes and expensive clothing. I bit my tongue and gritted my teeth as I watched my teenager blow his money. He was left with $24 in the bank before he realized the damage he had done. For months, he was stranded at home with no money to take his girlfriend out and no money to have fun.

He would ask me for money and I would tell him no. I wanted him to feel the pain of the choices he made. Now he is starting all over with a new perspective on money and a different plan for managing his money. I can't tell you for sure that he will make good choices all the time, but I can tell you he won't learn if I manage his money decisions for him.

Take the opportunity while you can to teach your children some good money management skills. Using these do's and don'ts, you will be off to a good start.

TAKE ACTION ASSIGNMENT
Set up an allowance plan for your children today. Follow the tips in this chapter to come up with a detailed plan to teach your children all about managing money. Communicate your plan to your children and talk about how things will work.

CAREER AND PROFESSION

CHAPTER 44
*
A New Definition of Success

"If I have been of service, if I have glimpsed more of the nature and essence of ultimate good, if I am inspired to reach wider horizons of thought and action, if I am at peace with myself, it has been a successful day." —Alex Noble

*

How do you define success? Would you consider yourself successful? Most people define success as achieving some preconceived, future condition in their lives. If I can raise my children to be happy and confident adults, then I will be successful. Or when I make $100,000 a year, I will be a success. The problem with defining success based on an impending outcome is that by the time you reach "success," you have formed a new perception of what success means to you. And you have missed the thousands of "successful" moments in your life while trying to achieve that condition you call "success."

Success is not a destination – it is a journey. What if success meant being happy and content with your current state of <u>being</u>? This definition requires us to look at our personal desires and values – those things that are important to us. Brian Tracy, author of *Maximum Achievement*, identifies six requirements for success. These requirements are peace of mind, good health and a high level of energy, loving relationships, financial freedom, commitment to worthy goals and ideals, and a feeling of personal fulfillment or self-actualization.[10] If you take a close look at each of these items, they are all about <u>who you are</u>, not what you do.

It is healthier to develop a three dimensional view of success:
1. Be the best you can be
2. Create an action plan for what you want in the future
3. Enjoy all that life has to offer right now

Let's compare the old definition of success with the new one. Using the old definition of success, my coaching practice will be considered successful when I have a full practice, I am making six figures, and I am in high demand for speaking. I will purchase all the right tools to market my business, and model myself after all the experts. Sounds pretty empty, doesn't it?

The new definition of success would say that I am successful if I like who I am as a coach. If I have satisfying and rewarding coaching relationships with clients that I love, then I am successful. If I have a vision of what my coaching practice looks like in the future, and have a plan in place to get there, then I am successful. Because I love what I do, I am successful. This means I am successful now, and will continue to be successful as long as I am content. And if for some reason my state of contentment should change, I need to ask myself what I need to change about me to bring about happiness and success.

A Story of a Successful Mom

Sheila wrote to me one day to tell me what it meant to her to be a successful mom. This is what she said:

> As a stay at home mom of three, sometimes four, life has sent me a lot of challenges. Success has come in all shapes and sizes. When I started dating my husband, he was a single father of a three year old. I never thought I wanted children but I loved Sam as much as I loved his father. It was easy to love an adorable little red head with the biggest heart of gold. Sam and I spent a lot of time together. We have always been close. As a mother to my own children, I know that I could not love a child more than I do Sam.

> The struggle a couple goes through becoming a blended family is hard enough. We had full placement of Sam, but after a number of years his mother and father were still fighting a bitter custody battle. I decided that I would do everything I could to win over a friendship with Sam's mother. My hope was that we could be one strong family for Sam. At this point of our relationship, she had probably spoken a dozen words to me total. Sam's mother was never mean to me; she just wanted nothing to do with me. So I started by reading relationship books and praying. I would try to open up to her whenever I could.

> When I had my first baby, she came up for a function Sam had for Cub Scouts. I gave her a lot of space, but still remained friendly. She never did ask to see the baby. Things were tense to say the least, but I still felt like we could all be friends. I knew if I kept the door open and let Cindy come to me, this would work.

The situation went on like this for a long time. Placement changed and Sam was going to go stay with his mom for the school year, from here on out. It was a sad time for Tom and me. We had Sam for almost five years, so I struggled with my feelings and had to fight back my heartache. I continued to be kind to Sam's mom and pray.

I was going to pick Sam up from his mother's house that first summer before the school year started. Tom was out of town so I drove the hour to the halfway point we had shared for years to do the switch. Cindy told me she would not leave Sam with me. So I took this opportunity and asked her what had happened that she felt she could not leave Sam with me. I apologized and told her if she was ever open to talking, I would be available. I said goodbye to Sam and told her when Tom would be flying back in. I then packed up my six month old baby and drove the hour back home.

I was so defeated and angry. I struggled to put myself in her shoes. She had gone through a messy divorce and was now adjusting to being full time with Sam again. I was almost ready to give up on being her friend.

I later learned that this is when Sam, who was seven at the time, stepped in. He asked his mother why she didn't like me. He then told her how much he liked me and wished we all could be friends.

It would take an open door and her love for Sam to make the phone call I received the next day. Cindy asked me to come to her house because she had a few things to say to me. She told me I could then bring Sam home. I am not going to lie; I was afraid. I was not looking forward to a meeting with her. What was going to happen? Was she going to take out all the frustration she had with Tom on me? This meeting was what I wanted for so long so I had to get over my fear and go.

I showed up and we sat down. She wanted to share with me the struggles she had while married to Tom and throughout the divorce. I agreed to listen to her this one time. I knew she needed to share. I also knew that Tom was not a good husband to her but that he was not the man she knew anymore. She talked for a long time and I believe she healed a little. That day we decided to be friends.

It took a year and a half for me to see the fruits of my labor. I had a dream to be a strong, unified family for Sam. Nearly six years later,

Cindy and her family are not only our friends, but our family as well. She is remarried and is now a stepmother herself. As a way to knit our family together that much more, she became Godmother to one of my children. We spend time together and talk regularly as friends and co-parents. The rewards I have received from this have blessed me ten-fold. I cherish my relationships with Sam and Cindy.

Success as a mother is a constant effort of give and take. It's acting in love even in those moments when you feel like you are farthest from your goal. As Cindy as taught me by her role, success is about putting your feelings aside no matter what, and doing the right thing. One of the biggest lessons I have learned through this is that successful motherhood is about creating relationships that are healthy and solid with your children and all the people in their life. I love being a mother to all my boys. I wouldn't trade a moment of it, not even the struggles...the blessing is always just around the corner.

Now, ask yourself if you are successful. Do you have peace of mind and good health? Are you enjoying loving relationships in your life? Do you have enough money to minimize your worries? Does your life have meaning and purpose, and are you committed to becoming everything you are capable of becoming? If you answered yes to these questions, then you are successful. If you answered no to any of these questions, then what do you need to change about you to achieve personal contentment? Look at your thoughts, feelings, desires, actions, dreams, habits and personality characteristics. You have everything you need inside of you to be a raving success!

TAKE ACTION ASSIGNMENT

Define success for yourself. What makes you a successful mom? Every day, focus on every successful moment in your life and remind yourself that success is a journey, not a destination.

CHAPTER 45
✳
The Profession of Motherhood

"The hand that rocks the cradle is the hand that rules the world."
—William Ross Wallace

✳

You're at a social gathering, meeting new people for the very first time. Right in the middle of a friendly conversation, the dreaded question is presented. "So what do you do (for a living)?" Because you can't come up with a creative response fast enough, you resort to the old familiar explanation. "Oh, I don't work. I'm just a stay at home mom." You cringe inside waiting for the other person's response. Depending on this person's views, you may get a variety of replies. "It must be nice not having to work." "Don't you get bored just staying at home?" You might get a polite smile, but let's face it, a stay at home mom is not held in high regard in the world of professional careers.

But I would argue with anyone who tries to say motherhood is not a profession. And if you are a working mom, you have two careers. The skills you develop being a mom are easily transferable to any professional career, and the skills you learn on the job can be used to better manage the profession of motherhood. Following are 13 skills that will help determine the success of your organization – your family.

Being a Leader
According to the dictionary, an organization is a group of persons organized for a particular purpose. That definition would certainly include the family. I think most people would agree that the purpose of the family is to love and support one another. Although a family can have many more purposes, a family is definitely an organization, and you, as a mom, are one of the leaders of that organization. Your children are looking to you as their role model, and will seek guidance from you for many years.

Creating a Vision for the Future
Just as an organization has a vision or mission, so should your family. If you were to define who your family is and what they stand for, what would that

look like? When your children leave the home to enter into adulthood, what legacy do you want to leave them? What do you want to create in this world with your family? Part of creating your vision also includes knowing how you are going to carry that vision out. What needs to be in place to realize your mission? What steps do you need to take to craft your future? How will you overcome the obstacles that will inevitably come up? When you have a vision, you are much more likely to make your dreams come true.

Managing a Team of People

Let's face it. A family normally has at least one mom (or one dad) and one child. There may be a dad, more children, and even some other extended family members that make up your family. Nonetheless, you have a team of people that make up your organization. Imagine if you just let each member of your team do whatever they wanted and hoped it would meet the needs of the organization. You would probably end up with a team with no direction and, more likely, chaos. You have to have teamwork in your family to be at your best. A lot of activities need to be coordinated and completed in order to run a family. Each member of your team has their own individual needs, in addition to the needs of the family. All of that has to be managed. Eventually you might be able to create a self-managed team, but in the beginning, your family needs a manager. A team manager knows how to best use everyone's unique skills and personalities to get the job done.

Motivating People to Take Action

Whether you are trying to encourage your children to do their homework, motivate them to help with chores or inspire your husband to take care of the kids, you need to be able to persuade people in your family to take positive action. You can't do everything by yourself without going crazy, so you must engage your family in the process. Depending on the nature of the task, that can sometimes be difficult. Whether you use your charming personality, incentives, teaching, love, or a swift kick in the behind, something has to move your family into action. And not only do you have to motivate your family members, but you also have to keep yourself inspired. Have you ever tried to stay positive and excited about meeting the needs of your family when everyone else around you is a lump on a log? I'm sure you've been there before, and that's part of the challenge of being a mom.

Problem Solving

Have you or any of your family members ever experienced a problem? Now, of course, that's a silly question. The better question would be, how well do you cope with the problems you face in your family? How do you perceive "problems" and how do you go about solving them? In any organization, there will be challenges that need creative solutions. As one of the leaders, you need to be able to effectively manage these problems with a level head, positive energy and the ability to brainstorm ideas. Whether you are dealing with a special needs child, the challenges of disorganization, or unruly behavior in the family, you have to be able to effectively cope and solve problems without a severe disruption in your family.

Making Important Decisions
You have a lot of important decisions to make as a mom. In addition, you are responsible for members of your team that may not be capable of making good decisions. Not only do you have the responsibility of decision making; you have to teach others how to make good choices. One of my more recent challenges is helping my children make important decisions about their health, especially as it pertains to food choices. If you present kids with junk food or healthy food, most of them will select junk food. That's because they lack the knowledge they need to make a better decision. Personally, I think I made some poor decisions by introducing my kids to junk food and now I am forced to make different decisions if I want to cultivate better eating habits. It is a big responsibility to raise children to be happy, secure and productive adults, and there are a lot of important decisions that need to be made along the way.

Counseling
You didn't know you would need a PhD in psychology to raise a family, huh? Human behavior is tricky, and feelings run rampant in the average family. Moms have to manage meltdowns, tears over the dropped ice cream cone, jealousy of other siblings, and anger when children don't get their way, all while remaining calm. No easy feat. While children's emotions may be a little more exaggerated and their issues certainly different from adults, a mom needs to be skilled in counseling her family members. If you've ever talked with a psychologist, you've probably noticed they have control over their emotions. They can sit and listen to you cry, rant, and complain, and still remain cool and composed. A good counselor will help you find solutions or they will just acknowledge and validate you. Most of the time you feel better after talking with a counselor, and most of the time children feel better after talking with mom.

Conflict Resolution
One day Mindy watched her two girls fight over a baby doll. Neither girl was willing to relinquish the doll. As one girl hung on to the doll's head, the

other pulled at her feet. Within an instant, their world was turned upside down when the doll's head came off. Now Mindy had two girls crying hysterically, one from remorse over breaking her sister's doll, and the other from anger and grief over her decapitated doll. I'm sensing a need for conflict resolution. Anytime you put two individuals together for a long period of time, especially in the context of a family, you are bound to have conflict. A family consists of people with different personalities, different needs, and different values. If we are going to survive and live peacefully with one another, we have to learn how to resolve conflict. Conflict resolution requires us to be able to respect differences, listen to and express emotions, manage stress by remaining calm, and seek win-win solutions.

Good Customer Service

Being a mom is a service oriented profession. We are here to help meet the needs of the family, and to meet them with a smile (most of the time). I've always prided myself on having excellent customer service skills, but I have to admit, serving the customers in my family can get rather tiring. Mom, can you get me a glass of water? Mom, I'm hungry. Mom, can you play with me? Mom, will you read me a story? Mom, Billy took my car. Mom, I don't like that dinner. Mom, I don't want to wear that shirt. Mom, Mom, Mom! How do we provide superior customer service? I think by actually caring about your customer, even when they are a "difficult" customer. By putting ourselves in the shoes of the customer, we can better empathize with their complaints and requests.

Organizing and Prioritizing Multiple Responsibilities

As moms, we wear a lot of hats. We are doctors who heal skinned knees with kisses and Band-Aids. We are chefs who satisfy hungry tummies. Moms are teachers who teach valuable lessons. We are counselors who soothe hurt feelings. We are professional organizers who keep everyone organized. Moms are chauffeurs who transport people from one activity to another. We are dish washers and body washers. We are housekeepers mopping up spilled juice and sticky tables. And on top of all that, we are friends, wives, daughters, and volunteers. Handling all these responsibilities requires us to organize and prioritize. We become skilled at multi-tasking.

Making Efficient Use of Time

Did I mention we are also time managers? In a given day, we have to figure out how we are going to take care of everything and get sufficient sleep, all in the span of 24 hours. Some of us keep planners or family wall calendars. Others keep ongoing "to do" lists. We search for answers and consult other moms on how to better manage our time. We work at being better organized, prioritizing everything that is important, and getting rid of time wasters. And if we're really smart time managers, we figure out that we can delegate to other family members. We double our amount of time by allowing others to help us. Sometimes we even set boundaries to protect our time because time to a mom is a precious commodity.

Develop Efficient Systems

When I worked in business, one of my responsibilities was to create systems that helped the office run smoother. I might have been working on perfecting the order entry process, developing a reorder procedure for office supplies or interviewing organizations that could provide more integrated software solutions for us. Moms do the same thing. We put together morning and bedtime routines for our family. We work on simplifying the meal planning or setting up a system for chores. Moms organize their days and weeks into schedules. One mom I've worked with did laundry on Mondays, conducted public relations (phone calls, emails, play dates) on Tuesdays, lightly cleaned house on Wednesdays, paid bills on Thursdays, and ran errands on Fridays. That was the system she used to efficiently run her household. As moms, we are constantly looking for ways to refine our systems.

Working with Financial Restraints

What organization doesn't have a budget? Families are working within financial restraints as well. We only have so much money to cover all the expenses of the family, and more often than not, we usually run short. Moms have to get creative with money, searching for sales and ways to stretch the money. We might have to put aside our own desires for clothing to purchase clothing for our children. Moms search the local grocery ads to find the best deal on milk. It takes a lot of money to raise a family, and moms have to develop good money management skills if they are going to help provide for their family.

If you're a stay-at-home mom, you have plenty of skills that will transfer to the workplace should you ever make that decision. If you're a working mom, you can use what you learn at work to be a better leader at home. Motherhood is a profession that requires commitment, solid leadership skills and lots of love and compassion. And what you are investing in is one of the most valuable assets in the world – children.

TAKE ACTION ASSIGNMENT

Get out a piece of paper and write down the 13 skills listed in this chapter. Rate your skill level on a scale of 1 to 10 for each of these skills. Pick one skill you would like to develop over the next month. Seek education and guidance on how to get better at this particular skill.

CHAPTER 46
*
10 Lessons I've Learned about Life from Being an Entrepreneur

"Life is just a chance to grow a soul." —A. Powell Davies

*

When I decided to go on the journey of starting my own business, I had no idea it would be so hard. All I knew is that I wanted to make a difference in the lives of other people, I wanted the freedom to express myself through my work, and I wanted the flexibility of being in business for myself. Being an entrepreneur has been filled with ups and downs, tears and joy, but I wouldn't trade it for anything. It has been part of my purpose here on Earth, and I have learned many lessons about life on this expedition. Please allow me to share with you words of wisdom you may find helpful for your life.

1. Life is a Constant Learning Process

When I started my business, I thought I knew a lot. I worked in business for over 20 years and had a great deal of experience. I couldn't have been more wrong. The knowledge I have absorbed over the last five years is incredible. I can't even begin to count the number of books and articles I have read. And it doesn't stop there. I will be learning new ideas for as long as I am in business.

Life is no different. There is always something to learn. When we choose to be curious and intrigued with learning, we grow as individuals. Learning keeps life interesting, and keeps your mind stimulated. Have you ever noticed how life keeps handing us the same lessons over and over until we finally learn them?

My friend and I recently attended a three-day intensive seminar. After the seminar we were discussing some of the highlights and our favorite take-aways. One thing my friend mentioned was that she noticed quite a few contradictions throughout the three days. She said the trainers would say one thing and then either do something else or say something that was the opposite of what they had originally taught. To her, this was a learning opportunity. She was curious as to why she kept noticing so many contradictions. What was life trying to teach her about contradictions? How was she contradicting herself in her life?

What is life trying to teach you right now? What situations seem to be occurring again and again?

2. Be a Student of People

As an entrepreneur, you have to know your market. Who are your clients and what is important to them? You have to understand what your clients' needs and desires are. Only then can you truly serve your client. The funny thing is that people are different. I'm sure that doesn't come as a surprise to you. Although most moms have common needs and desires, moms are uniquely different. And the only way for me to meet the needs of my clients is to listen deeply to who they are and what they want.

Understanding the people in your life is no different. We all have family members, friends, coworkers and other people in our lives, and each of them has their own personality, needs, passions, style of communicating, and love language. What works for one person doesn't necessarily work for another. In order for you to have the best relationship you can with the various people in your life, it's important to study who they are. How do you need to communicate to each person to ensure your message is heard? In what way do you need to express your love so they understand you? What makes them happy or crabby? What are their triggers and how can you avoid them?

Be willing to open your awareness and learn from the mistakes you make with people. In any given moment, we have the ability to be both a student and a teacher in every relationship we have.

3. You Have to Stay Connected to People

One of the easy habits to fall into when you are an entrepreneur is hiding behind your desk away from the rest of the world. Especially if you have a work-at-home business, it can get somewhat lonely if you don't get out.

The same thing happens to busy moms. Our family becomes the center of our attention, and understandably so, but this doesn't mean we don't need to stay connected to other important people in our lives. How often are you getting out and connecting with your friends? About two months ago, I was coaching a client on the topic of friendship. She was going through what she called a "dry spell" with friends. She had a deep desire for connection and relationship with women friends, but these women friends did not seem to have the same priority. There are a lot of women out there that long to have deeper connections in their lives. I know because I talk to other women, and I am one of them as well. In a recent survey I ran, 32% of moms said, "My marriage is good, but I could use more girlfriends," and 42% said, "I feel like I need more positive relationships in my life."

It's fine to stay busy with your family, just like it is okay to be busy with your career. But making time to get out of the house or out of the office to socialize is essential to your health. As human beings, we need to be in relationship with other people so we don't feel so isolated and alone in life.

4. Surround Yourself with Positive People that Share Like Minds

Does it matter who you hang out with? You bet it does. Entrepreneurs like to hang out with other entrepreneurs. Why? Because we are on the same path in life and we can benefit from each other. You know I am not the only "mom coach" in this world and most people would view other "mom coaches" as my competition in the business world. I, however, view other mom coaches as my potential friends. As a matter of fact, the other day I spoke for over an hour on the phone with Carley Knobloch from Mothercraft Coaching. Our conversation was truly inspiring and uplifting as we shared the successes and trials of having a coaching business centered on mothers.

I'm sure you've had the experience of hanging out with someone who drains your energy, or just doesn't seem to understand who you are. On the other hand, you've probably had the privilege of sharing company with someone you felt totally connected to. When we surround ourselves with positive people that share like minds with us, we create a synergistic relationship. Synergy in our lives enables us to work together to create something greater than what we could have created on our own. If you don't know how to stay organized or deal with your latest parenting challenge, wouldn't it be nice to have synergy in your life? You and all your like-minded friends can creatively solve problems, encourage one another, and fill each other with the renewed energy needed for mothering.

5. Action is the Only Way to Move Forward

I learned an interesting fact about sharks one time when I was reading a book to my son. Most sharks can't breathe if they are not swimming, and they can't sleep for very long, if at all, or they will sink. In other words, sharks need to keep moving forward if they are going to survive. I'm glad life is not so extreme for us, but we can learn something valuable from sharks.

Taking action in our lives enables us to move forward on the goals and dreams that are most important to us. I've learned as a business owner that it's great to have a lot of creative ideas, but it doesn't help grow my business if I don't put them into action. Any great dream requires forward momentum. The people who have made the most significant impact on our world are the movers and shakers; the people that are willing to do something different to bring about change. So if you want to lose weight, have a healthier marriage, or make more money, taking action is the only answer.

And sustained action requires discipline. If you don't have the discipline to stick with a task, a goal, an activity or change from beginning to end, then you will never realize the fruits of your efforts. A successful business requires discipline and so does a successful life.

6. You Need to Get Out of Your Own Way

Nicole had dreams. She wanted to be a successful business owner. She wanted to become financially independent, and raise her two girls to be happy and healthy. Nicole wanted to write songs and use her voice to express herself. And she wanted to find a good man with whom she could settle down and build a family. Every week we would meet to develop steps she could take to help her reach her goals. I encouraged her and helped her put together a plan to overcome the obstacles that kept arising. Sometimes Nicole would show up for our weekly meetings with some success stories to share, but more often than not, we talked about why she couldn't get the tasks done she promised herself she would do. After six months, she made very little progress towards her goals, and she finally gave up.

Did Nicole lack the desire or ability to achieve her goals? No, she truly wanted to achieve her dreams and she was capable of following through, but she just couldn't get out of her own way. What I mean is that she had internal blocks that needed to be removed before she could move forward. We all encounter internal blocks that stop us from moving forward. Sometimes those blocks are temporary, and other times they are long standing.

What I've learned while owning my own business is that I am my own worst enemy. When I let fear and negative mind chatter take over, I am going to be stuck. My energy will be blocked and the creative ideas that I normally have are buried, nowhere to be found. There have been times I have sat at my computer to write, only to sit and stare at the blank screen. The little voice inside me shares all kinds of nonsense. You are not a writer. This is boring. You can't engage a reader. You're not creative enough. If I am feeding myself these messages, is it any wonder that I get writer's block?

Most of us, on a deep level, deal with self-doubt and negative self-talk. We all have limiting beliefs at times. We make assumptions that may or may not be true. We wrestle with negative emotions that drag us down. Unfortunately, all this mind junk gets in the way of us experiencing all that we are capable of being. Conquering our minds is not an easy task, but it's worth it to try. Think about what your life would be like if you could let it all go and get out of your own way.

7. You Can't Give Up on Your Dreams

Starting and building a business is hard. There is no other way to say it. In the beginning, you wear all the hats because you don't have money to hire people. You work hard and you receive very little for all your efforts. You try ideas that don't work, and you get discouraged. You worry about where the next dollar is going to come from. Sometimes you want to throw your hands up and give up. You tell yourself it's not worth it; things would be much easier if you would just go work for someone else. This is why so many businesses fail in the first five years. Entrepreneurs give up on their dreams.

You can't give up on your dreams. You have to have persistence even when you feel like you don't have any steam left. When I work with my clients, I am forever reminding them not to give up. When you try and try and still fail, it's so easy to stop trying. But that dream will still be inside of you. And chances are, if you keep trying and learning and growing, you will eventually succeed. Keep your eye on the prize, whatever that may be, and be determined. Don't ever give up on what's important to you.

8. Sometimes You Have to Let Go

I know it seems contradictory to tell you to keep trying, but in the same breath to let go. But it works. I cannot tell you how many times I have worked and tried so hard, only to be discouraged and ready to throw in the towel. I surrender and walk away, and amazing opportunities come my way. It's true we can try too hard. Sometimes when we try so hard, we have a tendency to control, especially when things are not going as planned.

Controlling and fighting blocks our energy. One of the main reasons individuals struggle with losing weight is because they fight the process. Many overweight people don't want to change their eating habits. They don't like to exercise, and they fight inside themselves with what they want to do and what they feel they should do. I can't tell you how many women say to me, "I have to lose weight or I have to exercise." My reply is always, "No you don't. You can stay at that weight." When you feel like you don't have a choice, your tendency is to fight and rebel. Give yourself the choice to stop trying and you might find you want to do the very thing you were fighting. Or better yet, what you were working so hard to achieve might just flow to you naturally.

9. Capitalize on Your Strengths and Let Others Do the Rest

When you first start a business, you do everything because you can't afford to hire anyone to help you. In the beginning, I taught myself how to design a website. I did my own homemade brochures and business cards. I was the accountant, the coach, the administrator, the marketing representative, the speaker, the salesperson, the copywriter, the graphic designer, the writer, and anyone else I had to be. Am I good at all these roles? I'm not bad, but most of these roles are not my area of strength or passion. Eventually, I got to a point where I could afford to hire other people to do some of these tasks, and they did them much better than I could.

When you come to a place in your life when you can begin to let go and admit your limits, you can then capitalize on your strengths and let others do the same. There is a certain level of freedom we experience when we focus on what we do best and stop trying to master tasks we don't naturally excel in. Why fight against who you are at your core? To admit you are not naturally organized or you lack structure is not an admission of failure, but rather a sign of strength. It takes self-assurance to ask for help in an area of challenge for you.

We are all gifted at different things, and life works much better when we pull together as a team and take advantage of each individual's strengths. Let a housecleaner do what she does best if you can't find time to clean. Allow your husband to step in and take over with the children if you struggle to be patient. Hire a professional organizer to help you organize your home if organization is not one of your strong points. And don't feel guilty about it. I realize that budget constraints can sometimes interfere with hiring help, but you can be creative with how you get help. What do you have to offer another individual in exchange for something they have? How might you trade tasks with another co-worker so that each of you benefits? Focus on what you do well and life will be much easier and more enjoyable for you.

10. Follow Your Heart and Fulfillment Will Come

I became an entrepreneur because I decided to follow my heart and honor my true self. Prior to owning my own business, I worked in the business world for over 20 years. One of the things I was very good at was identifying when I felt happy and when I was unhappy. Even though I was in a thinking world, I stayed close to what my heart was trying to tell me. At times, I would try and think my way out of a situation, and it rarely worked if my head and heart were disconnected. When I followed my heart and acted on its promptings, personal fulfillment would come.

One of my clients, Denise, has been working for the same company for 17 years. She has been relatively happy at her job, but since she became a mom, three years ago, her heart has been tugging at her. She has not been satisfied with her job, but she is able to temporarily talk her heart out of leaving. Denise's mind can come up with a hundred reasons why she should stay, but in the end, this nagging feeling of being unfulfilled does not go away. When I ask her what would make her happy, she cannot answer. It's not that she doesn't know the answer; it's just that her head clouds her judgment. She analyzes her situation and tries to think her way to the right answer. There is nothing wrong with thinking, but sometimes we have to transcend our ego to find our true path in life.

When you can tap into your heart and trust what it is telling you, you are more likely to follow the path that is right for you. Some people would argue that you can't trust your feelings. I would argue that you can't always trust your mind either. Eva Broch Pierrakos summarizes my point nicely, "When you feel and experience your real self, you will not fear and consequently overemphasize your ego faculties. Nor will you leave unimportant underde-veloped ego faculties to slumber, untended."[11] In other words, when you have a healthy balance between head and heart, your intuitive self will always point you in the right direction.

There is no continuity or order to these life lessons. I offer them as impor-tant but random thoughts, and invite you to reflect on how you might apply them to your own life, career, or family.. Or you can take a moment to reflect on your own life lessons you've learned over the years.

TAKE ACTION ASSIGNMENT

Which of these life lessons, if any, do you relate to? How might you apply them to your life today? If none of these lessons touch a chord with you, what life lessons might you be struggling to learn right now?

CHAPTER 47
✱
Evaluating Your Job Satisfaction

"Contentment means different things to people, but when it comes to your career, it's not about being laid back, giving in or doing with less." —Jeff Garton (Leader of the worldwide Campaign to Retire Job Dissatisfaction at www.careercontentment.com)

✱

There is nothing worse than going to work everyday dissatisfied. At a minimum, we are spending 40 hours of our week working. Considering we are sleeping about 29% of the time, this means we are at work for at least 1/3 of our lives. If we are not satisfied with the career we have chosen or the company we are working for, a significant part of our lives is being compromised. And because job dissatisfaction permeates the rest of our lives at home, the impact is actually much greater.

In the last five years before I left the business world and decided to become a life coach, I was miserable with my job. Every morning when that alarm went off, I dreaded getting up. I knew I had to sit in bumper-to-bumper traffic for one hour before I would even reach the office. Once I was at the office, I routinely went through the motions of work that did nothing to inspire me. I was surrounded by people with negative attitudes, and I was fighting every day to remain positive. Even though I dreaded the hour long commute back home, I couldn't wait for the clock to tell me I had worked eight hours and I could leave.

It wasn't that the company I worked for was a bad company, and not everyone was a drag to be around. It's just that it wasn't what I wanted to do with my life. My job did not support my truest self. Now there are always going to be days or periods that we feel unhappy with our job, but that doesn't necessarily mean we are in the wrong place. It's chronic dissatisfaction that we need to be concerned with. You can use the six questions below to evaluate whether or not you are in the right job for you.

Are your values aligned with the company's mission and values?

Every company has a mission and core values they represent. Monsanto Corporation is a large agricultural company in the United States. Their mission is to "apply innovation and technology to help farmers around the world produce more while conserving more." To the outside world, we can see that they value innovation, conservation, productivity and making the world a better place by making sure farmers can meet the needs of humanity.[12] Inside the corporation, there are also unspoken values that the company represents. Only people who work for Monsanto have an idea of what those values might be.

It is not only necessary for you to be clear about your company's mission and values; you must also know what you value most. Sometimes our dissatisfaction can be the result of value conflicts. Those conflicts may be with the company's overall mission and direction, or you may be conflicted about the way in which the company operates. For instance, if you place a high value on family, and your company does not display flexibility toward the demands of parenting, you will be unhappy because of the inner conflict you feel every time you need to put your family ahead of your career.

It's also possible you don't have an interest in the mission of the company. You may not necessarily disagree with it, but it might not represent anything that is important to you. If you don't have an interest in improving the health of human beings, you probably don't want to work in the healthcare industry. Pay attention to your interests and values. Make sure the career and company you choose is aligned with what's most important to you.

Do you feel you are making a valuable contribution to the big picture?
Human beings need to feel like they are part of something. Very few people want to work for no reason. We need to have a purpose for doing what we do. Having a purpose gives us meaning in our lives. For us to feel we are making a valuable contribution to the big picture, we need to know what the big picture is. Sometimes organizations fail to communicate the big picture to employees; often only senior management is privy to this information. It's not uncommon for employees to wonder why they are doing what they're doing because they don't always understand the big picture. It can be frustrating if we are left in the dark about how important our work is to the company's overall objectives. When it's clear to you why your work is important, then you feel valuable, and feeling valuable increases your job satisfaction.

In addition to knowing the big picture, you need to perceive your work as valuable, and the company needs to reinforce this belief. In the company I worked for before I left the business world, there was a high value placed on salespeople. It was extremely clear to the salespeople that their work was valuable. They understood they were contributing significantly to the big picture. The administrative personnel, however, did not feel valued. We were expected to drop everything we were doing to meet the demands of the salespeople. It didn't matter what we had going on and our work was not considered as important as the work of the salesperson. Unfortunately, this is a common complaint that is often unaddressed by organizations.

Even though a company might see your contribution as valuable, your belief in your own value will significantly affect your job satisfaction. If you don't value customer care, it's likely you won't perceive customer service skills as valuable. How you feel about your own work performance will also impact how you perceive your value. We will often project what we feel about ourselves onto another individual or company. So stay tuned in to your own inner beliefs about your value.

Do you enjoy the relationships with your co-workers and management?
Sometimes we spend more time at work than we do at home. Being immersed in unhealthy relationships at work is no different than being in an unhappy marriage at home. It's not fun. If you are going to spend all day at your job, it's extremely difficult to be happy if you don't enjoy who you work with.

My mother is forever complaining about the people she works with, and the management at the company. Everyone around her is complaining about the company all the time. They are competitive salespeople who pay little attention to what is moral or fair. Some are lazy and don't care about doing a good job, and her boss is callous and controlling. The relationships in the company are the number one source of my mother's discontent with her job.

If you can't get along with your co-workers and boss, the problem lies within you, the other person, or the combination of the two of you put together. Do some honest self-evaluation and ask yourself what you can do to improve relationships. What relationship skills might you need to work on? If you have given a fair effort to making things work, and the situation doesn't improve, it's time to move on. While it's unlikely you will find a company that doesn't have at least one difficult employee, it's totally possible to find a job where you can enjoy the people you work with.

What is your opportunity for growth?

It is not everyone's desire to experience upward growth in their career. Some people are perfectly content doing something they enjoy doing, and place little value on growth. It could be their focus is on growing in some other area of their lives, or status quo is more important than growth. Some people perceive change as stressful and prefer to keep their lives as stress-free as possible.

However, if you are one who values growing, it's important that the company you work for offers opportunities for growth. I was the type of person who needed to be constantly growing. As soon as I mastered one skill, I was ready to learn a new one. Fortunately for me, I had a boss who understood my need for intellectual stimulation, and he was happy to give me projects that stretched me and satisfied my boredom.

Sometimes our job dissatisfaction comes from not being challenged at work. Before you move on to another company, be proactive about finding opportunities for growth at the company you work for. Ask your boss if there are projects you could help him with. Inquire about openings in different departments. Seek personal growth seminars and classes that the company is willing to pay for. All of these will satisfy your need to learn something new.

You've heard of people having a mid-life crisis and changing careers completely. Sometimes that happens. It's okay to work in one profession for 20 years and decide to try your hat at something completely different. The other day I spoke with my husband about a doctor who recently joined his company. It seems the guy didn't want to be a doctor anymore. He went back to school for his MBA and was now working as a clinical educator for a company that sold blood tests. Life is short. If you have an itch to try a new career, don't let anything stop you. It could be you find your dream career.

How satisfied are you with what you are doing?

That's a fair question. If you are an accountant, I hope you enjoy working with numbers. Your personality and your interests should match the tasks you are doing at work. If you hate talking on the telephone, avoid being a receptionist. How do you know if you enjoy what you are doing? You will feel energized by your work. Time will pass quickly because you will be engrossed in what you're doing.

Sometimes people will say they don't enjoy doing what they are doing, but they don't know what they would like to do. If that's you, it's okay. It is a great opportunity to try new things. Patricia came to me for a coaching session because she needed some guidance about figuring out what she wanted to do for work. She had started several jobs that she was initially excited about, only to find out later that she didn't enjoy these things anymore. Patricia was distressed because she was considering becoming a professional organizer, but was afraid she would lose interest in that as well. Even with significant soul searching, we can't really know for sure if we will enjoy something until we try it.

If you are clear about what you enjoy doing, you have the major work done. You only need to find a company that will help you utilize those skills. If, on the other hand, you are unsure about what you enjoy or what you do best, a great book I can recommend is "Unique Ability" by Catherine Nomura and Julia Waller. This book will help you identify what you love to do.

In your eyes, are you being fairly compensated?

While money is not everything, it certainly is part of the package. It is one of the reasons we work. No one wants to be grossly underpaid. Know what your skills are worth. What is the rest of the industry paying for what you do? It is true that some companies don't pay their employees what they're worth. They either don't have the money or they don't value their employees. If you feel you're being underpaid, check around. Put your resume out or inquire with people you may know with other companies. Don't stay with a company that is underpaying you, or you will feel resentful and will not do your best work.

If there are other ways for you to be compensated for your work, try to negotiate a benefits package that will work for you. Request that you work fewer hours for the same pay. Ask for increased vacation time or more flexibility with your work hours. Consider negotiating a work at home position for one or two days of the week so you avoid the commute. There are a lot of creative ways to be fairly compensated for your skills and your time.

The bottom line: your job satisfaction is a significant piece of your overall well-being. It affects all other areas of your life. How satisfied you are with your work can positively or negatively contribute to your stress level, your happiness, your fulfillment in life, and ultimately, your health. In other words, it's worthy of your attention.

TAKE ACTION ASSIGNMENT

On a scale of 1 to 5, with 5 being completely satisfied, rate your satisfaction in each of the six areas mentioned in this chapter. What is one thing *you* can change to increase your job satisfaction? Put a plan in place to make this change.

CHAPTER 48

✳

Everyone is a Leader, So How Will You Lead?

"When leaders take back power, when they act as heroes and saviors, they end up exhausted, overwhelmed, and deeply stressed." –Margaret J. Wheatley

✳

For as long as I can remember, people have asked the question "Are you a leader or a follower?" There was an attempt to categorize or label people based on their ability to lead other people. What if I were to tell you that everyone is a leader? Would it change your perception of who you are, or would you continue to think of yourself as a follower because that is what you've believed all your life?

If you are a parent, then you are definitely a leader. You are a leader of a very important organization – your family. Leadership is what helps us move people into action, including ourselves. So the question is not whether you are a leader, because you are. The question we have to answer for ourselves is how well do we lead? How effective are you in motivating and inspiring yourself and other people in your life?

Bruce Schneider at iPEC Coaching says, "our leadership ability determines whether or not our children do their homework, and how well they do it; how well we negotiate the purchase of a new car or home; how we communicate with anyone we do business with; how we develop mutually supportive and sustaining relationships, and most importantly, how much energy we can muster to motivate ourselves to take action – sometimes life-altering action – to live our most powerful, productive, and purposeful lives."[13]

Evaluating Leadership Characteristics

In my lifetime, I have had the fortunate opportunity to be around a lot of inspiring leaders. I've also had the experience of being exposed to people who, though in leadership positions, were not motivating or inspiring enough for me to want to follow. As a leader myself, in my home and business life, I have paid particular attention to what leadership characteristics are effective in inspiring other people. Below are seven traits that I feel are worthy of mention.

A Heart of Goodness

An inspiring leader genuinely cares about other people. She has a giving spirit. When leaders are more concerned about what they can receive from people than what they can give, others have a tendency to avoid them. None of us want to be in a relationship where someone is continually taking from us and giving nothing in return. A great leader doesn't take advantage of other people – her mindset is one of equality and respect for all human beings.

A heart of goodness means a leader is helpful and wants others to succeed. Leadership is not about being on top but instead creating a team atmosphere where everyone is recognized for their individual contributions. It's not about having an environment of winning and losing. An inspiring leader wants to create an opportunity for everyone to win.

An effective leader operates out of a good heart. There is nothing deceiving or manipulative in her actions. I once had a boss who had a lot of admirable qualities, but he was at times evasive and secretive. He withheld significant truths from customers in order to obtain the business. As a result, a part of me always wondered how much I could trust him. If we can't trust a leader, we will not likely follow his lead.

When thinking about inspiring our children to do what we want them to do, we will be much more effective if we are kind and giving. Although using power and authority over our children may work in the short term, in the long run, they won't have as much respect for us.

A Life in Motion

Most people are inspired by people who take action. Most all of my clients have come to me because they are struggling to take important action in their lives. They want to do something different, and they are looking to me to help motivate them to achieve their goals. I am the leader they are hoping will inspire them to move forward. Instead, I teach them to be encouraging leaders for themselves.

All the good things that happen in this world are because people take action. Companies create products that help change people's lives. Non-profit agencies support important causes. Authors and songwriters entertain people and touch people's lives, often to a point of life-altering change. Local churches gather volunteers to help people in need.

Think about all the great leaders that have made significant changes in our world. Mother Teresa ministered to the poor, sick, orphaned and dying for over 40 years. Martin Luther King was instrumental in organizing and leading non-violent protests for civil rights. His "I Have a Dream" speech motivated a lot of people to take action. Oprah Winfrey, a global leader in the self-help industry, has brought lots of problems to the public eye and has organized charities and fund raising for victims of poverty worldwide. Effective leaders know that nothing happens until you take action.

A Foundation of Positive Energy
When I think of people who have positive energy, I think of individuals who are physically, mentally, emotionally and spiritually strong. They are not necessarily in perfect shape, but there is a glow about them that only comes from inner strength. Let's face it. Healthy leaders are inspiring. Most of us want to experience at least some semblance of good health, and we look to leaders as examples of how to achieve that.

Who are you more likely to follow? Would it be someone who has a negative disposition or someone with a positive and strong attitude? I am much more effective with my family when I use positive energy with them. It is more likely you will receive cooperation and action when you approach people in an emotionally healthy way.

People will be inspired by a leader they feel safe with. Individuals will not be motivated to take action if their leader is likely to crumble under pressure, or give up because of fear. This negative energy will filter down to all people under his or her leadership. Even if you are leading yourself, how likely will you be to move forward if you are caught up in unhealthy emotional and mental patterns?

To be an effective leader, we must all manage our physical, emotional, mental and spiritual health. We need to take care of our physical bodies by getting proper sleep, exercising regularly and maintaining a healthy diet. It's important to release negative emotions that are dragging us down, and change destructive thought patterns to support mental health. And there is a certain power, strength and peace that only come from having a healthy spiritual life. When we take care of our whole being, we will radiate positive energy, and this energy will propel us forward and attract what we want in life.

An Approach of Preparedness and Organization

When I worked in the food industry, I worked for a Vice President of Marketing that we lovingly called "Dagwood," after the famous cartoon character from "Blondie." Matt was always running late. His office was an unending disorganized mess, and he was forever frantically searching through papers to find what he was looking for. While he struggled to get on top of his work life, Matt's customers and employees constantly waited for him. As intelligent and creative as he was, it was sometimes difficult to take him seriously. His lack of preparation and organization interfered with his ability to take action without feelings of stress. Matt was forever at war with time.

An effective leader is an excellent time manager. Your perception of time and how you use your time directly affects the success you experience in your life. Successful leaders understand that time is a gift and they choose how they are going to use their time. They choose to relax and do nothing just as easily as they choose to complete a task.

Being prepared and organized requires thoughtfulness. We have to take the time to think about what we need to get done, what is most important to us, and what our plan of action will be to accomplish our goals. We cannot communicate our vision, and lead others to success, if we are not prepared and organized in our approach. I cannot expect my children to be successful with their schoolwork if I don't teach them to organize themselves and prepare for projects and tests in advance.

A Demeanor of Elegance and Poise

It could be me, but I have always been inspired by people who carry themselves with elegance and poise. There is something about this type of demeanor that radiates confidence. A confident leader is admired and respected because she respects herself. But not many people are motivated to follow the footsteps of leaders who are unsure of themselves, because how we treat ourselves is a direct reflection of how we treat others. When you care about yourself, you care about other people.

Elegant leaders display style and beauty in their appearance, their mannerisms and their communication. You don't have to be knock-down gorgeous to be stylish and beautiful. True beauty and style comes from within. It's reflected by our commitment to self-care and healthy relationships with others. Leaders who have style and beauty care about their outward appearance, how they carry themselves and how they treat human beings. They are kind and loving to others, but also to themselves.

Leaders who have poise are mentally balanced and stable. My children respect me when I handle their misbehavior with emotional control. They need the stability of a strong leader to help bring them under control. I know it is not always easy to stay poised in every situation, but that's what makes leadership so challenging. Good and inspiring leaders are held in high regard because of their ability to practice high standards of behavior.

A Spirit of Creativity

When I first started my coach training, I remember talking to my peer coach about creativity. At the time, I was struggling to see myself as a creative individual. As I looked all around me, I was inspired by all the creative people in this world. However, in my eyes, I was someone who didn't receive the gene of creativity. The fact of the matter is we are all creative individuals, even though some of us have not yet come to believe it or embrace our unique creativity. Fortunately for me, I can now admit that I am creative.

To be an inspiring leader, you must first admit that you *are* creative, and start tapping into your own personal creativity. It's our creative energy that helps us find solutions to everyday challenges, big and small. Creativity is what enables us to generate new ideas. It allows us to be self-expressive.

Leaders need to be able to rise above the muck in life and see opportunity. Sometimes people – me included – get so caught up in their problems that they forget there are always creative solutions to every problem. A great leader has the ability to shift her perspective and open her mind to all the possibilities around her. She has access to her intuitive self and she trusts her innate creative abilities.

A Character of Wisdom and Inspiration

An effective leader has great insight; she has the ability to discern what is true and right. She is wise with her words and actions. One of the bosses I worked for had tremendous wisdom. Whatever situation I brought to him, he always stopped and listened deeply to what I was telling him. He took the time to be thoughtful about what approach he thought was best. He was reflective, had the ability to look at a situation from many different angles, and he always chose his words carefully. Because of his wisdom, I always trusted his judgment and never hesitated to take any action he suggested. I worked for him for 14 years and I had tremendous respect for him; he taught me much of what I know today about making wise business choices.

To be a great leader, you must have the ability to inspire yourself and other people to take action. Nothing gets done until people take action. What motivates people to take action? There has to be some type of emotional drive that encourages people to move. The person needs to understand W.I.I.F.M. (What's In It For Me?). Emotional drives are different for everyone because people value different things. I vividly remember a time when I was trying to motivate my husband to help me with the housework. For me, I was motivated by peace. I knew I would feel more relaxed once the house was clean. My husband, on the other hand, was motivated by something completely different. He said to me, "If I knew we were going to do something *fun* afterwards, I would be more motivated to clean."

A lot of people struggle with motivating themselves to take action. They are challenged by their own inability to remain positive and productive in spite of life's circumstances. Before you can inspire others, you must first work on encouraging yourself. When you have the ability to lead yourself effectively, others are more likely to follow your lead.

TAKE ACTION ASSIGNMENT

Which of the seven areas of inspiring leadership is your strongest asset? How can you capitalize on these strengths? In which area do you have the most opportunity for growth? What is one step you can take to increase your leadership effectiveness in this area?

CHAPTER 49
✳
Goal Setting – Getting from Here to There

"To accomplish great things, we must not only act, but also dream; not only plan, but also believe." –Anatole France

✳

It has been said that 60-80% of New Year's resolutions will be broken within the first two weeks. In other words, a lot of people have a hard time making the changes in their life they want to make. So if you are one who stopped setting New Year's resolutions because you never stuck to them, you are not alone. Personally, I am not a huge advocate of New Year's resolutions because I believe in setting and achieving personal goals all year round. For all of my adult life, I have been focused on growing and learning to be my best. I have used goal setting as a means of getting from where I was to where I wanted to be. And when I reached where I wanted to be, I set new goals to continue my growth. When will I stop growing and setting goals? Probably never. Growing and learning keeps us on the path of living, and setting goals keeps us focused on our growth. That being said, here are the top ten ways to increase your likelihood for success with achieving your goals.

1. **Focus on one or two goals at a time.**

Having a laundry list of all the things you would like to change in your life is okay, but it can also be overwhelming. Your chances for success are much higher if you stick to one or two of your most important goals. This allows you to concentrate all your energy and focus on these goals. For instance, I currently have eight business goals I'd like to achieve in the coming year. They are so radically different from one another that it would be difficult for me to try achieving all of them at one time. I would be jumping from one area of focus to another. Instead, I can be more efficient and effective if I concentrate on one or two goals at a time. Once you achieve your first set of goals, you can always set one or two more.

2. **Be realistic.**

It's okay to think big and want the best, but it is more important to succeed, so be realistic. Ask yourself whether your goals are reasonable and possible. It is probably not realistic to set the goal of never yelling at your kids again. How will you feel about yourself when your children test you on a very bad day and you yell? Certainly one can cut back on yelling and work to find alternative ways to deal with misbehavior; but an all or nothing attitude may set you up for failure, and feelings of failure can set you up for more failure. Instead, accept and honor your humanness.

3. Be specific.

Be as specific as possible when determining goals. Articulate how you will measure success and exactly what you are trying to achieve. Setting a goal to lose weight is too general. A better choice would be to set a specific and manageable goal. For example say, "I will lose 25 pounds by June 30 of this year. I will achieve my goal by exercising four times per week and maintaining a diet of no more than 1500 calories per day." Be specific when answering the what, when and how.

4. Connect to your motivation for achieving your goal.

Why do you want to achieve this particular goal? Why now? Make sure your motivation comes from your heart, and not from your head. In other words, your goal should be something you really desire, and not something you know you *should* do. For instance, I know I should drink more water, but I don't have a great enough desire to set a goal to drink eight glasses of water per day. Connect to why this goal is so important to you. Pay attention to whether you are being driven by fear or love. Do you want to get out of debt because your husband is pressuring you about the finances, or because you have an internal need to be more responsible with your money? Beware of setting goals based on what someone else in your life thinks you should do. Your goals should come from your authentic self.

5. Examine your belief in your ability to achieve this goal.

What do you believe about your ability to achieve your goals? If you have tried to reach the same goal many times before without much success, your confidence could be wavering. You could be feeding yourself negative messages without even realizing it. Be conscious and engage in positive thinking. Remind yourself that you are capable of doing anything you set your heart and mind to. Do not let other people in your life derail you. Other people will sometimes try to convince you that your goal is not important or that you are not capable of achieving it. Tell yourself every day that you have the ability to take the steps it will take to reach your goal.

6. Create a detailed plan to achieve your goal.

Let's say your goal is to eliminate the clutter in your home. But how will you start when the clutter is overwhelming? It can be helpful to break large goals into intermediate, manageable steps. Make a list of each area you need to deal with. Then break each area into even smaller segments that can be tackled easily. For instance, set time aside to clean out old clothes, then to organize sweaters, then to throw out old shoes, and finally arrange clothing by color or type. Don't forget to specify a time limit for accomplishing each of the smaller steps. Before you know it, the larger goal will be achieved.

7. Recognize that you may encounter obstacles.

Most people give up on their goals because they run into some type of obstacle along the way. Obstacles can be internal or external. Examples of internal obstacles include negative self-talk, limiting beliefs and discipline issues. Some external obstacles are lack of time, money or resources. Know in advance what hurdles you may have to conquer. Obstacles can be eliminated, but only if you are committed to achieving your goals.

8. Identify a plan of action to overcome obstacles.

If you want to give up chocolate (I would never try this!), what are you going to do when you get a craving for chocolate, or when all your friends are celebrating a birthday with chocolate cake? Maybe your plan would be to carry a sweet substitute with you at all times. Or perhaps you could involve yourself in a fun activity when the urge strikes. If your obstacles are tougher and you need more support, consider hiring a life coach to help you work through your blocks.

9. Enlist the support of an accountability partner.

As you work toward your goals, it can be very helpful to have someone in your life to be your support partner. Consider asking your partner, a friend, or a life coach to help you stick to the goals you have set. Use this person when you are struggling and set up a plan to check in regularly with him/her. As a coach, I have the privilege of trading coaching services with my peers. My coach helps me achieve my goals, overcome any obstacles, and celebrate my success. In turn, I am her accountability and support partner for helping achieve her goals.

10. Celebrate success along the way.

One of the most important things you can do for yourself is celebrate your small successes as you work toward your larger goals. Don't wait until the end to reward yourself. You deserve to be recognized for your efforts and your commitment, especially when your goals take a long time to achieve. If you don't celebrate on your journey, you will lose your motivation. So celebrate, celebrate, and celebrate!

Achieving your goals can be tough work sometimes, but it is also very rewarding. If you fall off your path, remember you can always get back on. It's okay to take a few detours. It's also okay to take a break and rest. Don't beat yourself up or give up hope. Start again where you fell down and before you know it, you will be a pro at accomplishing your goals.

TAKE ACTION ASSIGNMENT

Pick one or two goals that you would like to work on over the next 90 days. Use the tips in this chapter to help you be successful with achieving your goals. Email me your success stories at **lori@momnificent.com**.

THE Momnificent! LIFE™

HOME AND FAMILY

CHAPTER 50
✳
Motherhood is a Perfect Adventure

"A mother's happiness is like a beacon, lighting up the future but reflected also on the past in the guise of fond memories." —Honoré de Balzac

✳

How often do you think of family life as an adventure or delightful experience? If you and your children are having a good day, then you might buy into this idea. However, many of you are probably laughing hysterically now. What is delightful about the children fighting for the umpteenth time today? Sometimes I bet your family life feels like a jungle with screeching and swinging monkeys.

It can be all too easy to get caught up in trying to control what is happening in the home instead of enjoying *what is*. We were blessed with beautiful children and we are most in touch with that precious love when the house is quiet and we watch them peacefully sleeping. So how can we connect to that love and enjoyment in the midst of family life?

Spend Quality Time with your Children

Spending quality time with children requires your full and undivided attention. Oftentimes moms are so busy trying to manage everything that we have one ear to the children and our mind on a million other things. Our children talk to us and we say "uh huh" without really hearing them. We take them to their games, lessons, etc. but how much do we really interact with them? To be delighted by your children, you need to be fully connected to them. You need to listen and marvel at how truly wonderful they are. Participate in activities they love. Relish their laughter and their unique personalities. It won't be long before your children are grown and gone from the house.

My two boys are completely different. My oldest son is athletic and loves sports. This gives me the opportunity to have fun doing active things with him. Some of my best memories with my older son are the times we played baseball together. I have fun trying to strike him out and he gets a big kick out of his mother playing sports with the boys. I have taken his love of baseball and used that to connect with him emotionally. My younger son hardly has an athletic bone in his body. If I try to connect with him in the same way I do my older son, it doesn't work. He prefers to do intellectual or creative activities to keep him busy. Spending time with my younger son means I need to connect with him doing new and interesting games. We study things in books, create games with his cars, or search the magazines for all his favorite sports cars. When you tap into what your children love, they open up their hearts to you, and you see how magnificent your children truly are.

Understand Each Developmental Stage

To really enjoy your children, you need to understand who they are and what they are going through. The journey of a child to adulthood is filled with a multitude of changes. It can be helpful to get inside your child's shoes by learning about the various stages of development. For instance, when my son was 3-1/2 years old, I stripped him to get him ready for his bath. I said, "Come on, it's time for your bath." He looked at me with the meanest face he could muster and said, "NO!" It is much easier to deal with the defiance if you know that a three year old's mission is to exert his independence. Here's this little guy wanting to grow up and be independent, but he knows deep down, he is still dependent on mom, and he doesn't like that. So I picked him up and held him in front of the mirror. He exercised his most defiant "no" over and over until he started laughing.

Each stage of life, from infant to young adult, brings new behaviors and new growth. Some of the toughest years to parent are the teenage years. Parenting a teenager requires a completely different style of parenting. What you used with a toddler, preschooler, or an elementary aged child no longer works with a teenager. You can't give a teenager advice like you did when they were 10, because even though they need it, they don't want it. Teenagers have a deep desire to become independent and figure things out on their own. When I began parenting a teenager, I had to learn completely different parenting skills. Educate yourself so you know what to expect from your child in each new phase of their life. Sometimes just understanding that your child is "normal" will help you relax as a mother.

Don't Be Afraid to Discipline

No one likes being around an unruly child. Children with a lack of discipline make motherhood stressful and less than pleasurable. Our job as mothers is to raise respectful, productive and loving adults. In order to do this, we need to teach our children boundaries. They need to know what acceptable and unacceptable behavior is. You have to set limits and avoid setting up a child-centered family. Children need to understand they are a part of a family and each individual has their own needs. Help them work together with other family members to create a peaceful and loving environment. An effective and disciplined family unit is truly a wonderful adventure.

Be Intentional about Motherhood

What would make motherhood more enjoyable for you? Take the time to reflect on what needs to change in your family to increase the level of enjoyment for you. Be intentional about those changes. Maybe you want to make time to take care of yourself as a mother. Perhaps you long to be a more consistent parent. This month I am focusing on encouraging independence in my family. My motto is "everyone will do what they are capable of doing for themselves." Not only does this teach my children valuable skills, it frees me from unnecessary responsibility and gives me more time to be with my family. Setting intentions help you create a life you love.

Motherhood is always changing and what works today may not work tomorrow. To be truly effective and to enjoy the journey of motherhood, we have to be on our toes all the time. Take time on a regular basis to evaluate your family. What is the temperature of the family? What would make the experience of family life more enjoyable for everyone? Get in the habit of setting family goals and teach your children about the importance of setting personal goals by being an example of personal growth yourself.

Keep a Positive Reflection Journal

How do you want to see your children and your family life? Do you want to see motherhood as challenging or delightful? If you focus on the undesirable aspects of your family, then that is the experience you will create. If however, you can concentrate on the positive qualities of your children and your journey, you will create a rewarding family life. At the end of every day, take the time to record in a journal all the positive things your children said or did that day. Reflect on all the fun you had that day. Notice the wonderful qualities of each person in your family. Practice an attitude of gratitude every day. Sometimes when my children are challenging me, I am thankful they are healthy, intelligent and independent human beings. This helps me see the challenges in a completely new light. As a mom, it goes without saying that we will have difficult days, and there may even be days when you find yourself wondering why on earth you ever decided to have children. However, by keeping a positive reflection journal, you can remind yourself what a truly amazing journey you are on.

TAKE ACTION ASSIGNMENT

Buy yourself a beautiful journal to capture the wonderful memories of daily life as a mom. Take five minutes everyday to highlight the wonderful and life changing adventures family life offers. On your tough days, go back to your journal, read the pages and watch your mood begin to shift.

CHAPTER 51

✷

Modeling Life for your Children

"I think it's an honor to be a role model to one person or maybe more than that. If you are given a chance to be a role model, I think you should always take it because you can influence a person's life in a positive light, and that's what I want to do. That's what it's all about." —Tiger Woods

✷

Fast forward 20 years; your children might be 20, 25 or maybe even 35. It doesn't really matter how old they are. What matters is whether or not your children will be equipped with what they need to be successful adults. Now I understand that, as mothers, we don't have complete control over the choices our children will make in their adult years. However, we have more influence than you might imagine.

My 16 year old is taking an Adult Living class right now in school. Recently, I had the pleasure of reading a paper he wrote on his expectations for his adult life. It was amazing and intriguing to see how I have influenced some of the dreams he has for his life. Here are a few ideas he shared in his paper (ignore the grammar – he's still learning).

· I want to have lots of community involvement because I think that it's very important to have community involvement and it helps you as a person. I've done a lot of community stuff as a teen now, and I want to be able to continue and especially with the church because that community work is good.

· My situation that I want with my parents is to have a good relationship. I want to be able to keep the relationship strong and still communicate with them because they have been *role models* in my life and they are very important people to me.

· Three values that will be important for the basis of the relationship will be trustworthiness, caring, and responsibility. It will be trust because that is the number one essential thing that a relationship can have because with that there will be less problems and the relationship will flow a lot smoother. Caring, because you want to be able to care for your spouse because you love them, and being caring is very important for a relationship because it involves two people and support is always great when someone is down. The third one is responsibility because you have to be responsible for your actions, and you need to be responsible for what you need to do for the relationship.

Our children are listening and our children are watching us. Sometimes we might wonder if they are learning anything we are teaching, but they are. They are listening to our words, but they are especially experiencing our actions. *Who we are* in all areas of our lives is the greatest teacher our children will ever have. The way in which we choose to conduct our lives sends very subtle, but powerful messages to our children. So think about what is important to you to model in each of the following areas.

Personal Development
Are you taking care of yourself emotionally? We teach our children about boundaries, taking care of their personal needs, and personal growth by modeling these things in our own lives. What do you want your children to learn about their own personal development? When mothers come to me for coaching, I get to help them develop in ways that are important to them. Some mothers want more confidence; they have a need to find their voice and express it. Other mothers want to learn a new skill or foster their creativity. Still others want to be more organized, more focused, or be better managers of their time. In whatever ways we commit to learning and growing, our children will learn from us.

Spirituality
One weekend, I witnessed a third grade girl pray over a box of food that was being sent to starving children in other countries. In the middle of a roomful of 135 adults and children, she delivered a profoundly mature prayer with confidence and love. This young girl has learned through powerful examples what living a spiritual life means in her family. What do you want your children to understand about who they are in relationship to the Universe? What is their purpose in life?

Fun and Enjoyment
What you teach your children today about play is what they most likely will pass on to their children. Whenever a mother struggles to know how to play with her children, I normally ask her how her mother played. Normally she will tell me her mother didn't play with her. A mother who works all the

time, leaving little room for fun and enjoyment, sends a message to her kids about what she values.

Relationships

It was interesting to me that my son chose trustworthiness, caring, and responsibility as the three most important values for relationships. I certainly never intentionally set out to teach these values as a basis for a relationship, although I admit they certainly are important. What messages might you send your children about relationships? How is conflict handled in your home? Where does your marriage fall in the order of priorities? What are they learning about friendship from you?

I'll never forget a time when my child was 2-1/2 years old, lying in a hospital bed with a broken femur bone. It was late at night and he was in and out of sleep, fighting off the pain. As I sat beside his bed, I sneezed. A tiny voice said to me "Bless you." Children learn from us how to treat themselves and others in the context of relationships.

Health and Aging

According to the American Academy of Child and Adolescent Psychiatry, between 16 and 33 percent of children and adolescents are obese. The AACAP also states that when one parent is obese, there is a 50 percent chance that the children will also be obese, and if there are two parents that are obese, the chances of childhood obesity increase to 80 percent.[14] What does this tell us? Our children are watching us for examples on how to take care of their health. What do you want your children to learn about health and wellness? The best way to teach it is to model it.

Personal Finances

Many of our beliefs about money come from our childhood experiences. What did your parents teach you about money, directly or indirectly? Did you witness patterns of stinginess or abundance, spending or saving? As a child, I was given most anything I wanted. I never went without materially. As a result, I learned that money was always available. Can you imagine the surprise I had as an adult when learning to manage my own money? Giving your children opportunities to learn about money and develop healthy money habits is a wonderful gift to pass on to them.

Career and Profession

My dad put me to work at 14 years old, and my brother started working in my dad's restaurant at the age of 12. I'm not sure if my father was conscious about what he was teaching us, but one characteristic that my brother and I both share is a strong work ethic. My father was an entrepreneur for most of his working life, and my brother and I are both entrepreneurs. Somehow we settled into what our role model taught us about work. Our children don't have to follow in our footsteps. But we want to make sure we are modeling the footsteps that are authentic for us, just in case they decide to.

Home and Family

Most moms focus a lot of their energy in the area of home and family. It is not at all uncommon for us to ask ourselves what kind of home environment we want to provide for our children. We are regularly looking at what it takes to be a "good mom." The definition of "good mom" is different for all of us. It's not something you can look up in the books — it's a way of life that feels authentic to you.

I can't tell you if there is a right way or a wrong way to model life for your children. However, I can tell you that it is worth your time and effort to explore all areas of your life and ask yourself if you are living your life authentically. Your children are looking to you to answer those important questions about how to live their lives.

TAKE ACTION ASSIGNMENT

Get out a piece of paper and draw a line down the middle. On one side of the page, make a list of all the ways in which you are positively modeling life for your children. What great characteristics, values and habits are they learning from you? On the other side, list the ways in which you would like to change the way you are modeling life for your children. What specific areas can you grow in as a parent so you are a better role model?

CHAPTER 52

✳

Your Family Values – Are You Walking Your Talk?

"The family is the corner stone of our society. More than any other force it shapes the attitude, the hopes, the ambitions, and the values of the child."
—Lyndon Baines Johnson

✳

Dorothy Law Nolte, Ph.D. wrote a famous poem called "Children Learn What They Live." In her poem she says, "If children live with criticism, they learn to condemn. If children live with ridicule, they learn to be shy. If children live with shame, they learn to feel guilty." However, her poem also states," If children live with encouragement, they learn confidence. If children live with acceptance, they learn to love. And if children live with friendliness, they learn the world's a nice place in which to live!"[15] You might wonder what this poem has to do with family values. The poem suggests that children learn whatever they live with. This means that our children learn their values from the values they live with in their family. Although children can certainly learn values from other people and experiences in life, the family is undoubtedly the primary source.

Have you ever sat down and given thought to what values you want to teach in your family? If someone asked you, could you tell them the five most important values to you? How clear are your children about what the family values are? Your values speak to what is most important to you in life. They are the foundation of your family. Without a clear vision of what your values are, life is more challenging. Let me explain why.

Your family values guide your decisions. Every decision you make is based on values. If you choose not to get up for a morning jog, then you are valuing sleep over exercise in that moment. If you allow your child to stay home from school because she complains of a stomachache, then you are valuing your child's health over her education that particular morning. Many of the day-to-day decisions are made without even thinking about them, but they should all represent what's most important to you.

Sometimes, however, you'll notice some decisions are much harder to make. It's usually because you're struggling with a value conflict. I think one of the hardest decisions I ever had to make was whether I should put my older son on medication for ADHD. The value conflict I wrestled with was his physical health vs. his emotional/educational health. Until I was very clear which was most important to me, I battled with guilt and apprehension. Today I am totally comfortable with my son taking medication because I ultimately decided that his emotional and educational success was more important than the risks I may be taking with his physical health. His dad, however, has different values than me. He values his physical health over his emotional and educational success.

Your family values teach character and develop self-esteem in your children. If you think about some of the more popular and important values, you'll probably think of love, honesty, respect and peace. Each of these values, among many others, helps us develop character by giving us proper guidelines for our behavior. From the time our children are small, we give them a lot of love and teach them to love others. We expect our children to respect us as parents, and to treat other people in their lives with kindness. We try to promote peace in our homes by minimizing fighting. When our children are clear about what is expected of them, and they are given boundaries that guide them toward proper behavior, their self-esteem develops. People feel good about themselves when they exhibit strong and positive character traits.

When we don't take the time to consciously honor our values, we may be surprised at what our children learn. One Saturday afternoon, I spent some time talking with other mothers while our children enjoyed themselves at a birthday party. Sitting around the kitchen table, I listened to one mother share a story about her family's experience making scarecrows. The local park district sponsored a scarecrow event for families. The cost stated in the community brochure was $20. This mom made a special phone call before signing up for the event to clarify what the $20 covered. She was told that the $20.00 covered the expense of making one scarecrow. So she signed her family up to make one scarecrow. When she and her family arrived at the event, it was disorganized and chaotic. There didn't seem to be any accountability around keeping track of who paid for what. Although this mom only paid to make one scarecrow, both of her boys wanted to make their own scarecrow. No one was paying attention so they grabbed materials to make two scarecrows. In the middle of the experience, one of her sons shouted out, "We are making two scarecrows, but we only paid for one." Not wanting to draw attention to her family, and secretly knowing she could walk out of this place with two scarecrows for the price of one, the mom hushed her son.

I couldn't help but wonder if she was going to take this situation and turn it into a teaching opportunity for her children. Would she choose to teach honesty or dishonesty? As moms, we have many wonderful opportunities to teach the values that are most important to us, and in the process, shape the character of our children.

Values are passed on through generations. If you look at who you are today, no doubt your parents' values influenced at least a part of you. There are values you were brought up with that you want to pass on to your children. Your family values define who your family is, and give your family an identity. When I was growing up, there was no doubt that my family valued honesty. Teaching honesty permeated my family; today I pass that same value on to my children. Dishonesty is not tolerated because I want my children to know that our family stands for honesty. In giving your children a clear sense of who their family is by what you value, you are passing on to your children a piece of their identity.

Stress is the result of not living in integrity with your values. In the coaching world, we regularly talk about how well we are walking our talk. If I say honesty is important to me, then I better live an honest life. If I'm not, then I'm not walking my talk. And the result is self-induced stress. How much stress in your family can be attributed to living out of integrity with your family values?

For instance, let's say you highly value peace. If your family has frequent conflicts, then you will feel stressed much of the time. If being on time is important to you, stress will occur anytime the family is running late. Many of the disagreements in your family can be the result of value conflicts. When I look at the disagreements between my teenager and myself, it is about our difference in values. As he struggles to separate from me and become his own person, he can be self-absorbed and focused on his own needs. This can be in direct conflict with what I want him to value – family and thinking of other people. Honoring your most important values is paramount if you are going to have the family life you want.

To have a phenomenal family, everyone needs to be on the same page with the family values. So sit down and make a list of what values you want to live by. Try to pick your top five. If you're married, have your partner make his own separate list. Combine your lists and together choose 5 to 7 values that you absolutely won't compromise in your family. Schedule a family meeting and clearly communicate your family values. For example, if respect is a value you want your family to live by, then explain to your children what respect means. Give them concrete examples of what respect looks like. Being respectful means we talk to each other with kindness. It means we must ask each other if we want to borrow personal belongings. Respect means we listen to the person who is speaking.

Once everyone is clear what the family values, then start walking your talk. That means your rules will center on your values. Your decisions will be guided by your values. Each member of the family will be held accountable to living out these values. You reward and praise each other when those values are being displayed. There are consequences when the family values are compromised. And most important, mom and dad must be walking models of these values in the home.

Being clear about and honoring your values will make life easier for you. Most decisions will be effortless. You will experience less stress in your life. You will begin to live your life with more purpose and fulfillment. **And ultimately, you will pass on to your children the family values you hope one day will be passed on to future generations.**

TAKE ACTION ASSIGNMENT

After identifying your most important values, take an honest look at your life. Are these values guiding your decisions? Does your life today reflect these values? What changes might you need to focus on to walk your talk?

CHAPTER 53
✳
Happy Kids – Happy Family

"Often people attempt to live their lives backwards; they try to have more things, or more money, in order to do more of what they want, so they will be happier. The way it actually works is the reverse. You must first be who you really are, then do what you need to do, in order to have what you want." —Margaret Young

✳

When I reflect on what is most important to me as a mom, I would have to say it's raising my boys to be happy, loving and responsible adults. While this idea may not be the most important to every mom, I know enough moms to know that this is a relatively significant goal for most moms. Although we understand that happiness comes and goes, no mom wants her children to be unhappy. We have a basic need to teach our children to be kind and loving to other human beings. And we know that our children need to learn responsibility if they are going to one day become adults.

Raising our children to be happy, loving and responsible adults is a high calling. It's not easy, and there are many factors working against us. The good news is that you can accomplish this goal if you are equipped with the right tools and information. The main focus of raising happy and responsible children lies in developing their self-esteem. When children feel good about themselves, they treat others with respect, and they are happier and more cooperative. A healthy self-esteem is the greatest gift you can give your children.

When a child comes into this world, I believe he or she is automatically valuable and worthy of love. And parents truly want to love their children, but we're human and unconditional love becomes more challenging as we wrestle with the day-to-day difficulties of raising children. Sometimes we don't understand why our children act the way they do. We get frustrated by their behavior or we become scared that our parenting is not good enough. Other times we're tired and caught up in our own problems, leaving our children with only small pieces of ourselves to give.
As parents, we do what we think is best for our children based on our own

perceptions and interpretations. Sometimes we are successful and other times we're not. But, in the end, all that is really expected is that we do our best. There will always be something new to learn about parenting. We will always be given new opportunities and experiences to help us grow. So if we keep an open heart and mind, and accept that there will be good days and bad days, we will be able to accomplish whatever parenting goals we may have.

Right now, I want to focus on helping you instill a healthy self-esteem in your children so they become happy and responsible adults, and you experience happiness in your family. Following are eight significant components to building your child's sense of worth.

Focused Attention

Children need to feel loved, and one way they understand love is to spend quality time with them. How many times per day do you hear your children say "Mom"? Every time they say "mom," they are asking for your attention. Your children might want you to listen to something they want to share. They may need you to play with them. It can even mean they need your help. Sometimes our children just need to know we are there and present for them.

When we pay attention to our children, we are sending a powerful message that says, "you matter to me." If mom and dad care enough to pay attention to me, then I must be worthy of attention. There are many times that I would rather be doing something else when my son engages me to play. Sometimes I tell him no so that I can accomplish a particular task. But many times I stop what I am doing, so I can play with him and help him believe he is someone I enjoy hanging out with.

Encouragement

Not too long ago, I was frustrated with my 17 year old. I had been trying to get him to find a job so that he'd have extra spending money and could get a feel for what adult life was all about. He wasn't motivated to work, and this scared me because I want him to be responsible. The problem was that my fear was causing me to take the wrong approach with him – an approach that was actually discouraging to him.

I'm not proud to say this, but I was so caught up in making him change to alleviate my fears, that I forgot about trying to encourage him. Thankfully, my son is not afraid to speak his mind to me. He told me that he felt like I didn't believe in him. He angrily expressed that I didn't encourage him when he did do something right. He said, "Maybe I'm a late bloomer when it comes to getting a job." My son's words were a wake up call for me. He needed to find his own way, and he needed me to support him.

Sometimes, as moms, we get overly concerned with all the misbehavior in our children. We forget that sometimes the best approach is to ignore the misbehavior and encourage the behavior that we want. All human beings respond better to encouragement than to criticism. Praise your children as often as you can. Express your appreciation for all their great qualities. When we focus on what we like about our children, they will like themselves, and we will receive more of what we like.

Emotional Understanding

Our children, like us, are experiencing a number of feelings. Sometimes they feel scared and other times they feel angry. Our children feel sad and their feelings sometimes get hurt. Young children don't always know how to articulate their feelings, but they know when an adult understands them. They can feel whether or not their emotions are accepted.

When my six year old gets angry, he might stomp his foot or let out a scream. More often than not, this makes my husband angry and he sends him to a time out. Rather than acknowledging my son's anger and trying to understand it, he punishes him. This makes my son even angrier because I think, deep down, he doesn't feel accepted or understood.

Kids need us to help them process their emotions. They need to feel safe enough to express their emotions, and when we don't respond in a loving and supportive way, they shut down and get hurt. This hurt may be disguised as anger, acting out, or insecurity. When your child feels scared, let him know he is safe with you. When she feels sad and needs to cry, tell her it's okay to cry. And if your child is angry, give him space and safety to express himself appropriately. Once the emotions have been processed, you can work together to find solutions to any perceived problems.

Coping Skills

To develop healthy self-esteem in children, they need to be equipped with coping skills. Life is full of frustrations, and they need to believe they can handle whatever comes their way. How many of us moms learned conflict resolution skills, stress management, or anger management tools as children? Many of us weren't taught these specific skills; we learned by watching our parents. Sometimes our parents had strong coping skills, and other times their approach was not very healthy.

My friend spent a lot of years in therapy healing from her past and learning various coping skills she was never taught as a child. This is often the first step we need to take for our children. Then we can pass on what we've learned. My friend's daughter has the advantage of knowing how to turn her negative thoughts into positive ones. She has practiced deep breathing when she is having a hard time falling asleep. Her mother constantly talks to her about how to handle disagreements with her friends. As a result, she is blossoming into a confident little girl.

Being Useful

Being useful and needed contributes significantly to our self-esteem. It's no different for children. When children are little, they want to help us because they want to feel like they are part of the family. Being a part of something greater than ourselves helps us feel valuable. There is something we have that is valuable to someone else.

The other day I came home from the grocery store. Not only did I need help unloading all the groceries, I wanted everyone to feel like they had something significant to contribute. I assigned my teenager the task of carrying the groceries from the car to the house. I made a special effort to comment on how strong he was to carry so many groceries. It's a big deal for my teenager to feel physically strong right now. I gave my husband and younger son the job of unloading all the groceries and putting them away. I wanted my younger son to feel especially important so I told him his job was to take everything out of the bags and put the food on the counter for dad to put away. He was so proud of himself, and I can guarantee this small task was building his self-esteem.

Create a team atmosphere in your family. Let everyone know just how valuable they are to the success of the family. Teach your children to be helpful and thoughtful about other people. When you do something nice for other people, people normally express appreciation. This helps individuals to feel good about helping other people and feeling useful. One of the main reasons the elderly often feel depressed is because they feel useless in society. Human beings with healthy self-esteem want to be needed.

Gifts and Interests

Each child has his own unique gifts and interests. If we want to help our children develop their self-esteem, we need to help them tap into their own uniqueness. Children have different personalities, different strengths, and different passions. Children cannot be someone they are not, and be happy.

One way to help your children embrace their gifts is to make a list of every positive attribute, personality characteristic, and strength they have that will potentially benefit them in their lives. For instance, my son Kai is funny, athletic, good looking, intelligent, disciplined with schoolwork, persistent, emotionally strong, caring, responsible and fun. When I made a list of positive qualities for my son Ian, I acknowledged him as smart, sensitive, sociable, cute, creative, sweet, talkative, musical, fun and giving. Make a point to focus on your children's strengths and express your appreciation to them often for these qualities. This will reinforce a positive belief in them.

Expose your children to various interests so they can identify what they are passionate about. Allow them to embrace whatever they are interested in and let go of activities, sports, and hobbies they don't particularly care for. Sometimes parents have a tendency to make their children do things they think are important for them. It's true that music lessons and sports can enforce positive lessons, but if your children hate them, what's the point? There are other ways to teach the values we want them to learn. Children will learn more when they are engaged in something that is interesting and fun for them.

Positive Discipline to Enforce Limits

For children to develop a healthy and positive self-esteem, they need to learn limits. A child that is constantly getting himself into trouble because he can't follow rules is not going to be very happy with himself. To give children structure, you must have a set of family rules for them to live by. I like to use the analogy of the road and driving to best understand the benefits of having family rules in your home. *Rules provide the boundaries* for how you expect your children to behave. If you picture a highway, more often than not, you will see guard rails on the side of the road, especially in more dangerous areas. These guard rails are like boundaries – they keep you from going off the side of the road.

Family rules *teach the necessary skills and character traits* needed to develop autonomy and healthy self-esteem. Before you are allowed on the road to drive, you must learn all the rules of the road and practice operating a vehicle for a designated number of hours. You must then take two exams to test your skills. If you can demonstrate that you know how to drive and know what is expected of you on the road, then you are granted an important privilege – a driver's license. Your family rules will teach your children how to behave in this world.

Rules *keep your children safe and secure*. If you allowed your children to jump on furniture, or physically fight with their siblings, they might get hurt. Many years ago, U.S. states instituted a state law that required drivers to wear seatbelts. This law has tremendously decreased the number of injuries as a result of car accidents. Other driving laws provide safety as well. Consider a windy two-lane road that has hills and several other blind spots. When there are two solid yellow lines on the road, the rule forbids the passing of another vehicle. If we did not have that rule, we would have a lot more accidents. So, just as laws help us feel secure on the road, family rules help children feel secure – even though they sometimes challenge the rules.

Lastly, family rules *provide order and peace* for your family. Have you ever been around a family where there were no rules and the children did whatever they wanted? Chances are the environment was quite chaotic. Imagine what the roads would be like if we did not have speed limits. Some people would drive 100 miles per hour while others might drive 50 miles per hour. If we didn't require drivers to stop at stop signs or stoplights, we would have complete madness on the roads. I know I wouldn't want to go out in my car.

However you choose to enforce the family rules, make sure you use positive discipline. Discipline that demeans a child will not help build a healthy self-esteem. The purpose of discipline is to teach your child proper behavior, not punish them for misbehavior. A great book that teaches positive discipline is *8 Weeks to a Better Behaved Child* by James Windell.

Modeling Confidence
Modeling is an excellent way to teach desired behavior because the approach is all about "do what I do." Children naturally model their parents without even thinking about it. So if you want your children to have a healthy self-esteem, work on having a high self-esteem yourself. If you feel good about who you are and display confidence to your children, they will learn from you.

A child with a healthy self-esteem will be a happy kid. And happy kids help create happy families.

TAKE ACTION ASSIGNMENT

Pick one of the eight tips on developing a healthy self-esteem in your children and practice it this week. Go above and beyond to pay more attention to your children, give them encouragement, understand their emotions, help them feel useful, teach them coping skills, focus on their gifts and interests, practice positive discipline or model confidence.

CHAPTER 54

✳

The Key that Opens the Door to Extraordinary Families

"During the family cycle, there are numerous important events and transitions which take place over time. Often these events are not adequately recognized. Rituals are important and useful ways of assisting individuals and families in dealing with transitions and losses, bringing about healing and transmitting values from generation to generation. The effective use of rituals is one avenue of strengthening families and creating an environment where personal well-being is enhanced." —John D. Friesen

✳

We've started a new game in our home. Each night at the dinner table we each take turns asking another family member a question about himself. "So, Rick, how are you feeling about your interview on Monday?" "Mom, what do you want for Christmas?" Sounds like just a normal conversation, right? Well, there is a purpose to our game. We have two introverted boys who struggle with social skills. This game was created to better teach them how to communicate and take interest in other people's lives. As adults, we are all required to be able to start a conversation with a new person or communicate our concern for the important people in our lives.

What is this new game we play called? There is no formal name, but this game is an example of a family ritual, and family rituals help you create extraordinary families. According to *Webster's Dictionary*, a ritual is "any formal, customary, or ceremonial observance, practice or procedure." Family rituals help **define who your family is**. Every family has a different way of doing things and your children will come to identify certain rituals as special. As a result, they will begin to differentiate themselves from other families. Family rituals **provide comfort and security**. Think of the child that follows the same ritual every night before bed. Mom or Dad helps her get ready for bed. They read 3 books, talk about their day and end the evening with bedtime prayers. This child comes to expect this routine every night. This very ritual is what provides the trust that is needed between parent and child.

Family rituals **build family bonds**. My two boys have a special handshake they engage in to demonstrate their love for one another. It's too complicated for parents, so we don't even try to learn it. This ritual doesn't mean anything to anyone else, but it means a lot to my boys. You can count on family rituals to **generate a lot of wonderful family memories**. I very clearly remember, as a child, going every Sunday to the donut shop with my parents. We would pick up our donuts and then go park in a parking lot somewhere. I would sit in the back seat eating my donut while my parents read the newspaper in the front seat. Now, it might seem like a strange ritual, but even today, as an adult, having a donut on Sundays brings back special memories. Lastly, family rituals can be used to **teach values and practical skills**. Without even knowing it, having a family game night is teaching your children patience, cooperation, and good sportsmanship.

There are five major purposes for family rituals:

Family rituals are used to celebrate something. Rituals during the holidays are probably the most popular kind of ritual. Most families have a certain ritual they go through that helps them celebrate Christmas, birthdays, Easter, Cinco de Mayo, New Year's and other special dates. Recently, I listened to a speaker who told about a family ritual they did every year for Christmas. In her family, they had a birthday box for Jesus. It was wrapped in special birthday paper, tied with a bow, and contained a small slot on the top of the box, much like a suggestion box. This mother asked her children to write down on a piece of paper every time they did something special in honor of Jesus. The children would then put the paper in the box. On Christmas, the family would open the box and read the various gifts that were given to Jesus. She saved all the pieces of paper over the years. Some of the things her children wrote were so cute. One child said, "I shared half of my candy with Rachel." Another child said, "I made my sister's bed for two days in a row." While holidays are popular times for family rituals, what about celebrating the first day of Spring, the last day of school, golden birthdays, or report card day? The possibilities are endless.

Family rituals can be used to smooth transitions and change. When it was time for my younger son to give up his pacifier, we introduced the "Paci Fairy." We told him the Paci Fairy was going to come at night to take all his pacifiers and leave him a special toy. Before bed one evening, we gathered all his pacifiers and left them in a pile by his bed. When he woke up the next morning, the pacifiers were gone and our son had a new toy car. My son never asked for his pacifiers after that night. We all go through change in life, and family rituals can make those times of change exciting and normal. Consider introducing rituals for potty training, new births, 1st period for girls, 1st shave for boys, new drivers, and graduations.

Another purpose for family rituals is to solve a problem. There are always family problems that need to be solved. Weekly family meetings are an excellent way to address those problems. Consider having chore rituals to increase family cooperation. I know of families that will go through a silly ritual when their child is having a temper tantrum.

Family rituals should be used to help family members connect with one another. Mealtime and bedtime rituals are excellent ways to connect. Some families have family devotionals after or during dinner. They read a story from a devotional book and then talk about what they learned. Introducing family fun nights on a regular basis generates closeness. I helped one of my clients introduce a family day on Sundays. Every Sunday, the family members would take turns choosing a particular fun family activity for everyone to participate in. Sometimes they would go to the movies; other times they would go bowling. The children were so engaged that they never let their mom forget about their special family time on Sundays. My older son and I have a special way we say "I Love You." It is a hand signal we use that no one else understands. Connection in your family is critical to creating an extraordinary family.

Family rituals are great for teaching skills and values. One great way to introduce values into your home is to create a "Value of the Month" program. Decide what your top 12 values are for your family and assign each value to a month. For instance, February is a great time to teach the value of love, and November is perfect for thankfulness or gratitude. Incorporate special rituals each month that teach these values. Reading books, playing games, doing a family community project, and watching movies that pertain to that value are great ways to reinforce what you want your children to learn.

Think about the family rituals you already engage in. What rituals would be good to add to your family to create happier and closer relationships? What problems in your family need to be addressed, and how might you add a ritual to help with them? What changes or special days do you want to celebrate in your family? To get you started, I recommend having one solid ritual of connection daily. Create one modest weekly family ritual, and work in a monthly family ritual as well. Celebrate at least one family ritual for major holidays and birthdays. Remember, the purpose of creating family rituals is to equip your children with the skills and values you want them to learn, create great family relationships, and file away wonderful family memories.

TAKE ACTION ASSIGNMENT

Choose one daily, one weekly, and one monthly family ritual that you can begin to institute in your family. Also, pick one family ritual that you can start this year to celebrate a particular holiday. I encourage you to pick some new rituals that you've never done before. Get the whole family involved in choosing. You can use the chart below to get your creative ideas flowing.

Holidays	Special Days	Smooth Transitions	Connection	Problem Solving
New Year's	Birthdays	Saying bye-bye to pacifier or bottle	Dinnertime rituals	Chore Rituals
Valentine's Day	Half Birthdays	Potty training	Bedtime rituals	Family Meetings
St. Patrick's Day	Golden Birthdays	1st haircut	Special Handshakes	Monthly Goal setting
Easter	1st Day of any season	First period for girls	Special ways to say I Love You	Teaching values or desired behaviors
Independence Day	1st Day and last day of School	Graduations	Special time with Mom or Dad	Resolving unhappy feelings
Labor Day	Adoption Day	New driver	Fun Days	
Christmas	Report Card Day	Births or deaths		
Boxing Day		Moving		

CHAPTER 55

✳

Teaching Children Independence and Responsibility

"These words reveal the child's inner needs: 'Help me to do it alone.' "
—Maria Montessori

✳

Do you remember that phase in your child's life when all you heard was "I want to do it!"? You're in a hurry, and you want to help your child get dressed, but your two or three year old will have no part of that. You must wait for 15 minutes while she masters the socks and shoes. Your helpful child, at this age, wants to take out the trash, put away the silverware, bake cookies, and clean the bathroom. What on Earth happens to this independent child?

Not all children, but many, shift into a new phase. Picking up their toys is a dreadful task. Playing is so much more important than doing homework. Getting them to hang up their coat or make their bed is like pulling their two front teeth. In the teenage years, you get another glimpse of independence, but it's not exactly in the areas you might want. Teenagers insist they have all their academics, social relationships, and life in general, under control. You may think differently, but who are you? To a teenager, you're just an old fashioned and unintelligent parent.

Regardless of what children may want or think they need, parents have a job to teach responsibility and independence. It is a lifelong commitment that isn't always so easy, but here are some tips to keep you on track.

Encourage Independence by Allowing Healthy Struggle

When your child reaches an age to take on an age-appropriate activity, show your child how to do it, then let go and let your child struggle. It can be hard to watch children fight with their shoelaces, or stumble over their words in a new friendship, but it is in these moments that children are learning.

If your child becomes overwhelmed with frustration, it's okay to practice with her until she feels more confident. Take a break from the new activity and come back to it later when her emotions are calmed down. Some children are eager to try new things while others shy away from anything that seems difficult. Encourage your children to master new tasks by praising them often and minimizing criticism. The joy children feel when they gain a little more independence can be very rewarding, and a strong motivator to try new tasks in the future.

Believe in Your Child

Children need to know you believe in them. Encourage your children with positive words such as, "You are a smart girl. You can figure this out." Teach your children to think positively about themselves by modeling this behavior in yourself. The Little Blue Engine didn't give up and the reward was confidence. Confidence builds on itself, and your child will gain greater self-esteem when you encourage independence and responsibility.

My teenager wants to become a doctor, but sometimes I think he feels a little self-doubt. In one of those moments, he asked me "Do you think I have what it takes to be a doctor, mom?" My reply was "Absolutely, if you apply yourself." When our children waver in their self-confidence, they need their parents to let them know we see their best, even when they don't.

Build in Life Skills through Routines

Routines give your child practice and repetition. If, for instance, the after school routine includes putting away the lunch box and coat, having a snack, and doing homework, your child learns responsibility as a way of life. If you want your child to have good personal grooming skills, build brushing hair and teeth, and washing face into a morning and bedtime routine. When a child does the same thing over and over, he learns independence without even thinking about it.

Start your children on doing chores at a very young age. Most children want to know they are needed. A three year old can easily put out silverware for dinner or put his toys in the toy box. As a child gets older, increase the difficulty and number of chores he is responsible for. Have your children help you put together a responsibility chart and help make decisions about their chores. Practice each new chore together first so your child knows how to do it. It doesn't matter if she doesn't do the chore perfectly. Let your child know you are proud of her effort and thankful for her help.

As a child reaches the teen years, encourage him to get a job and make his own money. Work is a part of most adult routines. My father put me to work at the age of 14, and my brother worked at my father's restaurant starting at the age of 12. Today, my brother and I share one common characteristic – a strong work ethic.

Let Children Fall Down and Experience the Consequences

Resist the urge to be a helicopter parent and hover over your child. Life is full of opportunities to succeed and make mistakes. The lesson is reinforced and learning takes place when children are allowed to make mistakes. If your child makes a bad choice, let him experience the natural or imposed consequences. A "D" or an "F" on an exam sends a very clear message that the child needs to study harder. The effect is not the same when you are hounding your child to study so she doesn't fail. When your child makes the choice to extend his curfew by an hour, he loses the privilege of going out the next weekend. Guaranteed he will think twice before staying out late the next time.

So many parents want to protect their children from hurt and failure, but this does not prepare them for real life. In real life, people will hurt us. We will make choices that have significant consequences. By learning to face these challenges from an early age, our character is strengthened and we develop the confidence to get back up and try again.

Coach your Children toward Independence and Responsibility

When your child is faced with a future or past decision, ask a lot of open ended questions that encourage your child to think for himself. "What do you think you should say to your friend?" "What could you have done differently in this situation?" Giving advice teaches your children what you want and what you think is best. Coaching your children supports them in developing good decision making skills, and honoring what is best for them. It's okay if they don't make the best choice. Live and learn.

Give your children practice in solving their own problems. I know it's much easier to offer a quick solution, but this does not encourage independence. Even if it takes longer, talk through the situation and explore the different solutions and possible outcomes. This exercise will help develop their problem solving and brainstorming skills.

The goal in raising children is not to protect them from pain or undesirable circumstances, but to equip them with what they need to be responsible, independent and resilient adults.

TAKE ACTION ASSIGNMENT

As a mom, how do you think you're doing with teaching your children independence and responsibility? Which idea would you like to work harder at incorporating into your current parenting style? What might that change look like in your family?

CHAPTER 56
*
Using Routines and Daily Habits to Maximize Your Time

"Never again clutter your days or nights with so many menial and unimportant things that you have no time to accept a real challenge when it comes along. This applies to play as well as work. A day merely survived is no cause for celebration. You are not here to fritter away your precious hours when you have the ability to accomplish so much by making a slight change in your routine. No more busy work. No more hiding from success. Leave time, leave space, to grow. Now. Now! Not tomorrow!" —Og Mandinoi

*

Moms today are busy. Whether you are a stay-at-home mom, work-at-home mom, or a working mother, I know your time is limited. It takes a lot of time to manage a household, hold down a career or volunteer activities and properly care for and nurture your family. Although there are a lot of different ideas for making the best use of your time, I want to talk to you specifically about using routines and daily habits to maximize your time. I think you'll find if you can successfully put some structure into your family life, you'll be able to save significant time.

Routines

When you get ready for your day, do you go through the same sequence of events? Most people have a specific routine they follow. Some people get up, start the coffee, read the newspaper, shower and dress. Others wake up, hit the snooze three times, get up, eat breakfast, work out, shower and dress. And I am sure there are people who get up, get in the shower, dress and fly out the door. This subconscious string of tasks is called your morning routine.

The organization and structure of routines help all of us maximize our time. Although a morning routine is a great start, there are other ways to integrate routines into our lives. Think of the various times of your day that seem to get hectic or chaotic. It might be when you first arrive at the office or when you come home at the end of your day. Meal time or bedtime might be stressful. Look for a number of times during your week that beg for structure and organization. Maybe you find yourself running around every day doing errands. Perhaps the weekends fly by and you're left wondering what you accomplished.

Some examples of common routines include:

· Morning routine
· After school routine
· Meal planning routine
· Bedtime routine
· Errand routine
· End of season routine
· Vacation routine
· Chore routine
· Back to school routine
· Travel routine
· Party planning routine
· Holiday routine

When instituting new routines, I recommend starting with just one. Pick the area of your life that would most benefit from a routine, and commit to developing a specific series of tasks you will go through on a consistent basis. Decide what time the routine starts and what time it ends. Make a list of each step you will go through to complete your routine. Let's use the example of an after work routine. It might look something like this:

5:30 PM:	Arrive home
	Check messages on voice mail
	Relax for 15 minutes
	Get the children started on homework
	Start dinner
	Set the table
	Eat dinner
	Clear the table
	Do the dishes while children finish homework
7:30 PM:	Be ready to have some down time

Benefits of Routines for Children

Just like with adults, routines teach children organization. Organization is a skill that children can learn if they practice it. The structure and repetition of routines builds in organization skills that will help your children manage their life and responsibilities better. Routines will teach them to manage their time, so they can stay focused and be more productive.

Routines also help children feel more confident and secure. When there is chaos in the family, children feel insecure. The consistency of routines helps children know what is expected of them, and they feel better equipped to follow through and be successful. With routines in place, you will experience far less behavior problems as well. The end result is higher self-esteem for your children.

Lastly, routines build in autonomy for your children. When our children come into this world as babies, they depend completely on us for every need they have. As children grow older, our job as parents is to gradually teach them independence. When they leave our homes, we want our children to know how to take care of themselves. They should know how to properly groom themselves, take care of a home, take care of their clothing, manage money and other adult responsibilities. Providing routines that teach these skills is essential to their success as adults. And the more autonomous our children are, the more we save time, as moms. We are creating built-in helpers to help us manage the home.

Creating Successful Routines

A lot of people try putting routines into place, only to abandon them later. Something about the routine doesn't work out, or life gets in the way. I want you to be successful with your routines, so keep these tips in mind when developing and following through on your routines.

Remember: Start with **one new routine at a time**. Wait until this routine is operating smoothly before implementing another routine.

Make sure your routine is **clear and specific**. A complete stranger should be able to come into your life, read your routine, and follow it exactly, without any questions. Occasionally, I babysit for my best friend's little girls. At night, they have a bedtime routine they follow. It is posted on their bedroom door. The routine is so simple and clear that I can step right in and follow the sequence of tasks they go through to get ready for bed, without any previous instructions from their mom.

Be consistent with your routine, especially in the beginning. **Consistency** is what turns your routine into habit. You want your routine to be so automatic that you don't even think about it. Successfully implementing a routine requires **perseverance**. You have to remember that you are developing new habits, and that takes time. Be patient with yourself, and keep trying even if you fall off track. Many people give up after they mess up, often abandoning a good idea because there was no room for **flexibility**. A perfect example is individuals who give up on exercising because they have a bad week, and are unable to follow through on their workout routine. A difficult day or week does not mean your routine can't be successful. It simply means that your routine is more challenging to follow at this particular time. Put the past behind you and start fresh. *Your past does not have to predict your future.*

When creating your routine, make sure it is clear and specific, but **not too difficult**. The more complicated the routine, the more likely you will give up or receive resistance from other people in your life.

Avoid These "Routine" Busters

Getting Too Busy to Follow Through
Lack of Accountability
Lack of Participation from One or More Family Members
Not Being Flexible
Too Complicated
Lack of Commitment

Daily Habits

I want you to stop and think about all the habits you have in your life right now that are related to your time and organization. Let me help you get started by exploring these questions:

· What time do you get up?

· What time do you go to bed?

· How much time do you spend watching TV?

· How often do you look for things because of disorganization?

- How much time do you spend on junk mail or email?
- How often do you say yes to things you don't want to do?
- Is procrastination an issue for you?
- Do you exercise, relax and eat healthy? (yes, this affects your time)
- Are you managing your thought life? (Getting caught up in negative thinking will considerably affect your mood, level of energy, and ultimately your time.)

Sometimes, without even realizing it, we can get caught up in habits that have a big impact on our time. By integrating daily habits that help us manage our time better, we can create more time for ourselves. Pick 5-10 daily habits you can work on that will save you more time or help you better manage the time you have. Some examples might include:

- Get up at 6:30 AM during the week
- Go to bed by 10:30 PM every evening
- Limit personal phone calls to 30 minutes per day
- Limit extracurricular activities for children to one per season
- Volunteer for only one activity at a time
- Leave work by 5:30 PM every day
- Do one load of laundry per day
- Take a 20 minute brisk walk to start my mornings
- Take 30 minutes of down time in the middle of the day
- Check and handle email once in the morning, and once in the afternoon

Record your daily habits in a chart and work on each of these until they become a way of life for you. Give yourself a sticker, smiley face or check mark every day you are successful. It may sound sort of childish, but it works! You are rewarding yourself for great effort, and the chart becomes a visual of your progress. Try it for one month and see what happens.

According to the American Psychological Association (APA), routines are powerful organizers and they offer stability. Routines simplify life and reduce stress. Routines are also associated with marital satisfaction, adolescents' sense of personal identity, children's health, academic achievement and stronger family relationships.[16] Is that a strong enough argument to motivate you to develop and stay consistent with routine in your life?

TAKE ACTION ASSIGNMENT

Pick either one routine to implement or your list of daily habits to work on. For the next month, practice being consistent with your new routine or daily habits. Do not give up if you fall off track. Keep trying until you have mastered the new structure in your life. Pay attention to the benefits you and your family experience.

CHAPTER 57

✳

Surprising Ways We Communicate with our Children

"The way we communicate with others and with ourselves ultimately determines the quality of our lives." —Anthony Robbins

✳

In March of 2007, my good friend and personal life coach visited me from out of town. It was an exciting time for us because we had been coaching each other for over two years, but we had never met face to face. We enjoyed a wonderful time together at the Hearts at Home mom's conference, and even had time to spend an evening at home with my family. Once Debbie was settled back at home in New Jersey, we had a conversation about her experience with my family. She made a comment about my teenager that took me by surprise.

Debbie said, "Kai is very perceptive. He is listening to everything that is going on." I thought about the time she interacted with Kai and remembered that the majority of the time, Kai was in a different room on the computer. The rest of us were in the family room talking and watching our wedding video. I know that Debbie is highly intuitive so I certainly did not discount her perception. It got me thinking about how closely our children are watching and listening to us. So listen up and stay alert. It's not always the words we say to our children that communicate our most powerful messages.

Our most basic form of communicating with our children is in the **words we say** to them. "Suzi, please turn off the TV and do your homework now." "Hey, great job on your spelling test!" "How's your friend Tommy doing?" What we say to our children is important, and no doubt necessary, if we are going to have a relationship with them. Sometimes we say just the right words like "I love you," but other times we don't. Out of anger or frustration, we make hurtful comments that stick like glue to our children. Out of haste and busyness, we fall into a pattern of not communicating enough positive words. Our focus becomes about issuing commands or reprimands. We lecture with too many words and our children turn us off.

Dr. Todd Cartmell, the author of *Respectful Kids: A Complete Guide to Bringing out the Best in Your Child*, taught me a very valuable way to use my words to shape the behavior I want in my children. The technique he uses with many of his clients is called the "Pour it On Technique."[17] Instead of noticing the behavior you don't want in your child, pay attention to the times your child is acting the way you want. For instance, when your child is playing nicely with her brother instead of fighting, this is the time to pour it on. Go over to your child, *touch* her in some way, and use your words to *pour on the praise*. "Wow, I really like the way you are playing with your brother. You are getting along so well and you're treating him with so much respect. Great job, Nicole!" If you can discipline yourself to pour on the praise 5-10 times per day, you will work wonders in your children. All human beings respond better to positive words.

How we say our words communicates much to our children. The same words said in a playful and loving tone can mean something very different when said in an angry or irritated tone. Sometimes when I am talking to my teenager, I am trying to communicate helpful words. But when my under-tone is laced with fear or frustration, he does not feel encouraged. As a matter of fact, he feels criticized. Your tone of voice can communicate such feelings as anger, happiness, distraction, hurt, lack of interest, and even judgment. Pay attention to how you are feeling and put your tone in check before you communicate.

When we say our words, or our timing, is critical to our communication with our children. Communicating when you do not have control of your emotions is an example of poor timing. Hold your tongue and wait until you are calm. Sometimes as parents we are calm, but our children are not. Maybe they've had a bad day or they are in the middle of a frustrating moment. Ask yourself whether this is the best time to say what you want to say. Sometimes waiting until the storm blows over can make a world of difference in how our words are received.

Have you ever been on the phone with a friend sharing something about your day? You forget that Joey is in the next room listening to every word you say. In the next moment, Joey chimes into the conversation, asking for clarification on what or who you're talking about. Now, you can use this form of communication as a positive reinforcement for your child. When talking to Grandma, tell her what a great job Maggie is doing with potty training. Believe me, Maggie will hear you. However, if you don't want your children to receive your words, be careful when you are talking to other people and your children are within earshot.

The **words we don't say** are powerful communicators to our children. Sometimes we don't say enough positive and encouraging words to our children. What is this telling our children? Other times we don't communicate something important to our children, like letting a disrespectful comment they make pass us by. What are we teaching our children in this moment? The comments we don't make can work in a positive way as well. If your children make a mistake, and you see the effect it has on them, sometimes saying nothing at all is the best way to handle things. By choosing not to lecture them, you give your children space to think about what they've done. We allow them to figure out how they will rectify the situation or learn from their mistakes. Learning is much more effective in an experiential environment.

The **actions we take and the choices we make** say a lot to our children. Whether it's a sigh, a roll of the eyes, or a lie we tell a stranger on the phone, our children are watching and listening. You know the saying, "Actions speak louder than words." I was born and raised in Missouri – the Show Me State. Words mean nothing if they are not backed by actions. Show your children how you want them to behave. Show your children that you love them. Show your children what you want them to value in life. By being their role model, you are communicating your expectations to them.

The other night my five-year-old was lying down in bed with me. He knows my routine by my actions. He asked me how much longer I was going to read. I told him I was finishing up the last two pages of a chapter and then I was going to turn off the light. He said to me, "Okay, I am going to fall asleep after you say your prayers." In a very subtle but powerful way, I have communicated to my child that God and prayer are important to me.

What do you want to communicate to your children? Think about what you say, how you say it, when you communicate, the words you don't say, and your behaviors. These are all ways you can send heartfelt and encouraging messages to your children.

TAKE ACTION ASSIGNMENT

For one week, I want you to pay close attention to how you communicate with your child. Notice your child's reaction to the various ways you communicate. What did you learn about yourself and your children in regard to communication?

CHAPTER 58

✳

Zap the "Mommy Guilt"

"Guilt is anger directed at ourselves." —Peter McWilliams

✳

I remember, almost 17 years ago, bringing my son Kai home from the hospital. We had borrowed an old, brown vinyl car seat from someone we knew. I placed all 6 lbs 14 oz. of him into the car seat and suddenly burst into tears. The car seat was way too big for him. Although my hormones were definitely talking, I really felt I had failed him. What kind of mother doesn't know he needed an infant car seat? The sudden awareness that I didn't know what I was doing hit me like a ton of bricks. The nurses were gone and I was on my own.

From the moment we become pregnant until the day we die, we try to be the very best mom we can be to our children. It doesn't take long, however, before we make mistakes. Parenting doesn't go as planned. Your children do outrageous things. Accidents happen. Feelings get hurt. And the feelings of guilt inevitably follow. It doesn't matter if our children are young or grown; motherhood guilt is always a struggle.

So how can you minimize those pesky, guilty feelings?

Here are some helpful tips to help you zap the guilt and enjoy the journey of motherhood.

Avoid Comparisons

Is Kayla sitting up yet? When did Matthew start walking? My child was reading when she was four. Does your son play travel sports? What did your daughter get on the ACT exam? Comparing our children to other children is an easy trap to fall into. But it is not healthy for our children or us as moms because every child is different. Children have different strengths, weaknesses, developmental patterns and personalities. Let your children be who they are and avoid the comparison game.

Just like you shouldn't compare your children to other children, the same goes for you. Let go of any need you have to compare yourself to other moms. Todd Parr wrote a great children's book called *The Mommy Book*. In this book, he talks about how all mommies are different. Some mommies like to cook and some like to order pizza. Some mommies work in tall office buildings and some work at home. I have a friend who is the epitome of June Cleaver. Almost all her meals are home cooked. She makes all her children's Halloween costumes. She is totally organized and structured with her children's schoolwork and activities. If I compare myself to her, I am plagued with feelings of guilt. I make Hamburger Helper for my family, purchase all their Halloween costumes, and consistently fail at structure with my kids. But I'm still a great mom, and so is she. It's okay to be different.

Human Beings Have Limits

You don't have to be all things to your children and your children don't have to be all things to you. In other words, it's okay if you make mistakes, and your children deserve the same grace. One of my struggles is thinking I need to be my child's constant playmate. I have to be honest. Sometimes I don't feel like playing cars or looking at another car magazine. Sure, my child may feel disappointed when I say no, but it doesn't mean I am not a good mother. I have my limits and I need to respect them. All moms have limits. When we don't pay attention to our limits, we usually become irritable and short-tempered. Exceeding our limits can cause a vicious cycle of behaving in a way that makes us feel guilty.

Your children have limits too. Just because your child misbehaves doesn't mean you are doing something wrong. While vacationing with my family in Florida, there were days that my 3-1/2 year old acted like a little monster. He was in time out constantly. Of course, all the other little children around were perfectly well behaved. At one point, I was exasperated and I asked my aunt, "What is wrong with him?" My aunt reassured me that he is fine – he's just being a kid. It's times like this that we often question our parenting. Sometimes I think it's helpful to just understand that motherhood has its good days and bad days and it has very little to do with our ability to parent our children.

Apologize When You Are Wrong

Let's face it. Sometimes we blow it. We say or do something to our child that we immediately regret. When this happens to you, apologize immediately.

Our children then learn that we are human and we make mistakes. Children are very forgiving and forgiveness conquers guilt. There is nothing more humbling than being able to admit when we behaved in a way we know is wrong.

Right after we took the pacifier away from our preschooler, he decided he wasn't going to take naps. My son went from taking a three-hour nap every day to taking no nap at all. One day, after trying for several days and failing, I was insisting my son take a nap. I was tired and I needed a break more than he did. My little strong-willed boy was determined to stay awake. Not only was he refusing to sleep, he was also refusing to stay in his bed. His attitude was one of defiance and his fighting was wearing me down. After several attempts to make him nap, I lost my temper. I yelled at him and told him he was *going* to take a nap. In utter frustration and anger, I spanked him and stormed out of his bedroom.

The guilt smacked me in the face. I treated my son in a way I totally disagreed with. I don't believe in spanking, especially when one is angry. I immediately turned to prayer to release my anger and replace it with self-forgiveness. Then I had a long heart to heart talk with my little guy. I told him how sorry I was and explained that I was angry. He told me he was mad too. We hugged and made up. My ability to be humble had earned his forgiveness.

Be Wary of People's Judgments

Everyone has their own set of rules and values they live by. Oftentimes when people can't accept differences in other people, they impose their judgments, often resulting in attempts to instill guilt, conscious or not. At the end of the summer, I took a three-day retreat to reenergize. I went to Door County by myself and had a wonderful time shopping, watching movies, reading, and sightseeing. Upon my return home, I was faced with disapproving remarks from my mother-in-law. She couldn't understand how I could go on a vacation by myself. I knew in my heart and soul that I did nothing wrong, despite how others might have viewed the retreat.

Children are especially great at attempting to manipulate with guilt. They know our buttons and are very aware of what tugs on our heart. My teenager is very skilled at using guilt to try and get his way. He'll say, "I never get to do anything fun" or "You never spend any time with me." He knows that it's important to me that I spend time with him, so he uses that to pull on my heartstrings. Stay strong and secure with who you are as a mother and these attempts to make you feel guilty will fall by the wayside.

Our Child's Misbehavior is Not Always Our Fault

Just because we gave birth to our children does not mean we are responsible for all their behaviors. Children have a mind of their own and often don't listen to the wisdom we give. We can be the best mom and our children will still make mistakes that take us by surprise. One evening I was babysitting my friend's little baby. The evening was progressing nicely until I had to feed the baby. My three year old was sitting next to me, watching me spoon the barley cereal into the little guy's mouth. I was holding the bowl in one hand and the spoon in the other. Don't ask me what provoked my child, but in one second flat, he had smacked the bowl of cereal out of my hand. The bowl of cereal, on its way to the back of the couch, ricocheted off the baby's eyebrow, leaving a big bump on his head. Cereal was everywhere, including in the baby's eye. I now had a hysterical infant and a laughing preschooler. Call it jealousy, or call it curiosity, I can assure you I never taught my child to behave like that. Although I was horrified by my child's behavior, I knew that I was not to blame for his outburst. I am his mom, and I am responsible for teaching him right from wrong, but I cannot always control how my children behave.

Unless you are severely neglecting your child or setting a very bad example for your children, there is no reason for you to hang on to guilt. You were chosen to be the mother of your children, and He doesn't make mistakes. You are not expected to be a perfect mother and you are not expected to raise perfect children. So relax, have confidence, and enjoy the journey of motherhood.

TAKE ACTION ASSIGNMENT

You will need a balloon and a stickpin for this assignment. Think about something in your life that you feel guilty about. If you truly feel you are in the wrong, make amends to the person you have hurt. If the guilt is due to an unreasonable expectation you have set for yourself, commit to changing this expectation. When you are ready to release the guilt, I want you to blow up your balloon. While you are blowing up the balloon, visualize yourself blowing the guilt into the balloon. Tie up the balloon and get ready to zap the guilt. While you are visualizing the guilt being zapped, take your stickpin and pop the balloon. Declare the guilt gone!

CHAPTER 59
✻
Parenting Philosophies – Overcoming Your Differences

"Despite your differences, you both want what's best for the children."
—Dr. Charles Sophy

✻

If you spend any time in the parenting section of the library or your local bookstore, you will find hundreds of books on disciplining and raising your children. All the leading experts have their own ideas about what works and what doesn't. **As a parent, you have your philosophy that you bring to the table.** Your philosophy consists of your own life experiences, your values and your beliefs. When you were growing up, you learned a lot about how to parent from your own mother and father. You may come out of that life experience with plans to parent exactly the way your parents did. In this case, you were probably very pleased with your childhood experience and have a lot of fond memories of your mom and dad. It's also entirely possible that you did not respect the way you were raised, and you have decided to parent much differently than your own parents.

Your values play a significant role in the choices you make around parenting. It is totally normal to want to pass on to your children the values you believe are important. My mother, for instance, taught me that honesty is always the best policy. Today, honesty is one of the most important values that I stress with my children. You also carry with you a set of beliefs regarding children and parenting. You have beliefs about what is best for children or what expectations are reasonable at any given age. You express love for your children based on what you believe love is. And of course, you have beliefs about what the most effective form of discipline is for your children. Many moms add to their own philosophy what they learn from books and other mom friends.

Dad has another set of ideas and plans for raising his children. Most of the time, dad's ideas have not come from the many books on parenting he reads or the oodles of fathers he brainstorms with. His philosophy, too, comes from the way in which he was raised as a boy. Even the best and most agreeable parents sometimes disagree. **So what do you do when your two philosophies clash?**

Get to know one another as parents.
It is helpful to fully understand one another's philosophy on parenting. Remember, your philosophy consists of your life experiences, your values and your beliefs. Set aside time in your marriage to get to know each other on a deeper level. The goal is not to judge one another, but to listen and understand what makes each other the parent that you are. Here are some questions to get your conversations started.

· What was your mom and dad's style of parenting when you were growing up?

· How were you disciplined as a child?

· How did you know your parents loved you?

· What did you like about how your parents raised you and what didn't you like?

· What values are important for you to pass on to our children?

· What is your goal in raising your children?

· What is the easiest way for you to express love to your children?

· How would you describe your parenting style?

· How do you feel about the various forms of discipline (time out, spanking, rewards and consequences, yelling, teaching)?

· What do we have in common as parents?

· Where do we differ in our philosophies?

Talk out your differences when the children are not around.
You're in the middle of dinner, and the children are refusing to eat. They are crabby and testing your every nerve. Dad can see that you are stressed so he decides to take matters into his own hands. He yells with his loud, booming voice, "Eat your food right now or you will go straight to bed." The kids start crying. You are even angrier now because you can't stand yelling. You feel it is an ineffective way to discipline the children, and you believe it scares them. Wait until the children go to bed and have a talk with your husband.

Explain to him exactly how you feel about yelling. Listen to his side of the story and why he chose to do what he did. Do your very best to understand him and acknowledge his feelings. Then decide together what would work better for everyone in the future.

Decide how important an issue is to you.
My friend's husband takes his little girl to swimming lessons every Saturday morning. After swimming, his daughter is starving. Dad's way of ending their fun time together in the pool is to let his daughter pick something to eat from the vending machine. My friend does not want her daughter associating fun time with Dad and junk food. She believes they should come home so her daughter can eat something healthy. *Sometimes each parent needs to decide how important an issue is to them.* Use a rating scale to determine your level of importance. Ask each other, "On a scale of 1 to 10, how important is this to you?" If Dad rates his need to buy his daughter a junk food treat after swimming at an 8, and Mom rates her need for her daughter to eat healthy at a 6, then Dad wins. *Learn to give (let go of control) on issues that aren't extremely important to you.*

Understand that differences can be good.
Believe it or not, children can benefit from differences in our parenting styles. As long as children are being loved and treated with respect and fairness, it can be good for children to learn to adapt to different childrearing approaches. No two people in this world are exactly alike. Some parents are very flexible and some are quite structured. Some parents are playful and others are more serious. There are quiet and mild-mannered parents and loud and boisterous parents as well. Step back and appreciate your differences. Children who are exposed to diversity have a tendency to be well rounded and adaptable.

Combine your viewpoints and get on the same page.
The single most important thing you can do for your children and for your marriage is to get on the same page when raising and disciplining your children. Being on the same page does not mean you necessarily agree on everything. It means you support one another as parents. If Mom says there are no privileges until homework is done, the rules are the same with Dad. If Dad says curfew is at 11:30 PM, then Mom enforces this curfew. Take the time to work through your differences and put together a plan that both of you can be happy with. Unresolved differences, if left alone, will destroy your family. Decide what the house rules are going to be and how the children will be disciplined when the rules are broken. Then stick together and

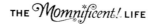

provide a united front for the benefit of your children.

Healthy parenting is taking the time to understand and accept one another as parents, instead of blaming each other for perceived differences. It means you work together to provide harmony for your family. Differences in parenting styles and philosophies are normal – learn from one another and always strive to be the best parent you can. Your children are learning from you how to parent future generations.

TAKE ACTION ASSIGNMENT

Schedule a dinner date with your partner. Take along the questions for getting to know one another better as parents. Practice giving one another the gift of listening and understanding each other as you work through the questions together.

ADDITIONAL READING

Personal Development

101 Great Ways to Improve Your Life by 101 Expert Authors including Lori Radun, The Momnificent™ Coach (New Jersey: Self Improvement Online, Inc., 2006) Available at **www.momnificent.com**

Anger Trap, The by Dr. Les Carter (San Francisco: Jossey-Bass, 2003).

Change Your Questions, Change Your Life by Marilee Adams, Ph.D. (San Francisco: Berrett-Koehler Publishers, 2004).

Compelled to Control by J. Keith Miller (Deerfield Beach: Health Communications, 1992).

Getting Things Done: The Art of Stress-free Productivity by David Allen (New York: Penguin Group, 2001).

How to Say No and Live to Tell About It by Mary M. Byers (Oregon: Harvest House Publishers, 2006).

Never Good Enough: How to Use Perfectionism to Your Advantage Without Letting it Ruin Your Life by Monica Ramirez Basco Ph.D. (New York: Simon & Schuster, 1999).

She's Gonna Blow: Real Help for Moms Dealing with Anger by Julie Ann Barnhill (Oregon: Harvest House Publishers, 2005).

Stand Up for Your Life by Cheryl Richardson (New York: Free Press, 2002).

Success Principles, The by Jack Canfield (New York: Collins, 2005).

Take Time for Your Life by Cheryl Richardson (New York: Broadway Books, 1999).

Taming Your Gremlin: A Surprisingly Simple Method for Getting Out of Your Own Way by Rick Carson (New York: Quill, 2003).

Unique Ability: Creating the Life Your Want by Catherine Nomura and Julia Waller (Toronto: The Strategic Coach, 2007).

When Pleasing Your is Killing Me by Dr. Les Carter (Nashville: B&H Publishing Group, 2007).

Spirituality / Inspiration

A New Earth: Awakening to Your Life's Purpose by Eckhart Tolle (New York: Penguin Group, 2008).

Become a Better You by Joel Osteen (New York: Free Press, 2006).

Four Agreements, The: A Practice Guide to Personal Freedom by Don Miguel Ruiz (San Rafael: Amber-Allen Publishing, 2001).

Inspiration: Your Ultimate Calling by Dr. Wayne Dyer (Hay House, Inc., 2006).

Left to Tell: Discovering God Amidst the Rwandan Holocaust by Immaculee Ilibagiza (Hay House, Inc., 2006).

Live Boldly: Cultivate the Qualities that Can Change Your Life by Mary Ann Radmacher (San Francisco: Conari Press, 2008).

One Day My Soul Just Opened Up by Iyanla Vanzant (New York: Simon & Schuster, 1998).

One Month to Live: 30 Days to a No-Regrets Life by Kerry and Chris Shook (Colorado Springs: Waterbrook Press, 2008).

Power of Intention, The by Dr. Wayne Dyer (Hay House, Inc., 2004).

Voice of Knowledge, The: A Practical Guide to Inner Peace by Don Miguel Ruiz (San Rafael: Amber Allen Publishing, 2004).

Yearnings: Embracing the Sacred Messiness of Life by Rabbi Irwin Kula (New York: Hyperion, 2006).

Fun and Enjoyment

Artist's Way, The by Julia Cameron (New York: Penguin Putman, 2002).

Make Your Creative Dreams Real by SARK (New York: Simon & Schuster, 2004).

Your Heart's Desire by Sonia Choquette Ph.D. (New York: Three Rivers Press, 1997).

Relationships

Boundaries: When to Say Yes, How to Say No to Take Control of Your Life by Henry Cloud and John Townsend (Grand Rapids: Zondervan, 1992).

Fabulous Friendship Festival: Loving Wildly, Learning Deeply, Living Fully with Our Friends by SARK (New York: Three Rivers Press, 2007).

Finding the Hero in Your Husband by Julianna Slattery, Psy.D. (Deerfield Beach: Health Communications, 2001).

Five Love Languages, The by Gary Chapman (Chicago: Northfield Publishing, 2004).

For Women Only: What You Need to Know About the Inner Lives of Men by Shaunti Feldhahn (Atlanta: Multnomah Publishers, 2004).

Love and Respect by Dr. Emerson Eggerichs (Colorado Springs: Focus on the Family, 2004).

Mom's Needs, Dad's Needs: Keeping Romance Alive Even After the Kids Arrive by Willard F. Harley, Jr. (Grand Rapids: Revell, 2003).

Who's Pushing Your Buttons by Dr. John Townsend (Brentwood: Integrity Publishers, 2004).

Health and Aging

Shrink Yourself: Break Free from Emotional Eating Forever by Dr. Roger Gould (New Jersey: John Wiley & Sons, 2007).

S.O.S. of PMS, The: Practical Help and Relief for Moms by Mary M. Byers (Oregon: Harvest House Publishers, 2008).

Writing Diet, The: Write Yourself Right-Size by Julia Cameron (New York: Tarcher, 2007).

Personal Finance

A Financial Minute: From Money Madness to Financial Freedom, One Minute at a Time by Jenifer Madson (Felton: Clear Vision Press, 2006).

Overcoming Underearning by Barbara Stanney (New York: Harper Collins Publishers, 2005).

Secrets of the Millionaire Mind by T. Harv Eker (New York: Harper-Collins, 2005).

Smart Couples Finish Rich by David Bach (New York: Broadway Books, 2002).

The Total Money Makeover Workbook by Dave Ramsey (Nashville: Thomas Nelson Inc., 2003).

Career and Profession

Coach Yourself to a New Career: A Guide for Discovering Your Ultimate Profession by Deborah Brown-Volkman (Lincoln: iUniverse, 2003).

Energy Leadership: Transforming Your Workplace and Your Life from the Core by Bruce D Schneider (New Jersey: John Wiley & Sons, 2007).

Finding Your Perfect Work by Paul and Sarah Edwards (New York: Penguin Putnam Inc., 2003).

Secrets of Millionaire Moms by Tamara Monosoff (New York: McGraw Hill Books, 2007).

What Color is Your Parachute? 2009 by Richard Nelson Bolles (Berkeley: Ten Speed Press, 2009).

What Got You Here, Won't Get You There by Marshall Goldsmith (New York: Hyperion, 2007).

Home and Family

Adolescence Isn't Terminal: It Just Feels Like It by Dr. Kevin Leman (Wheaton: Tyndale House Publishers, 2002).

Boundaries with Teens by Dr. John Townsend (Grand Rapids, Zondervan, 2006).

Family First by Dr. Phil McGraw (New York: Free Press, 2004).

Guilt-free Motherhood by Dr. Julianna Slattery (Deerfield Beach: Health Communication Inc., 2004).

Have a New Kid by Friday: How to Change Your Child's Attitude, Behavior and Character in 5 Days by Dr. Kevin Leman (Grand Rapids: Revell, 2008).

Healthy Sleep Habits, Happy Child by Marc Weissbluth, M.D. (New York: Fawcett Books, 1999).

How to Talk So Kids Will Listen and Listen So Kids Will Talk by Adele Faber (Bloomington: Collins Living, 1999).

Organizing from the Inside Out by Julie Morgenstern (New York: Henry Holt & Company, 1998).

Parent as Coach Approach, The: The 7 Ways to Coach Your Teen in the Game of Life by Diana Sterling (Oregon: White Oak Publishing, 2008).

Raising Your Spirited Child by Mary Sheedy (New York: Harper, 2006).

Scream-free Parenting by Hal Edward Runkel (New York: Broadway Books, 2007).

Teaching Your Children Values by Linda and Richard Eyre (New York: Rockefeller Center, 1993).

FOOTNOTES

1 Dr. Les Carter, *The Anger Trap: Free Yourself from the Frustrations that Sabotage Your Life* (San Francisco: Jossey-Bass, 2003).

2 "Controlling Anger – Before It Controls You," American Psychological Association, <http://www.apa.org/topics/controlanger.html>

3 J. Keith Miller. *Compelled to Control: Why Relationships Break Down and What Makes Them Well,* (Deerfield Beach: Health Communications, Inc., 1992).

4 Rick Warren, *God's Power to Change Your Life,* (Grand Rapids: Zondervan, 2006).

5 Bruce D. Schneider, *Energy Leadership: Transforming Your Workplace and Your Life from the Core.* (Hoboken: John Wiley & Sons, 2008).

6 iPEC Coaching, 1999-2008. Used by permission of iPEC Coaching and Bruce D Schneider.

7 iPEC Coaching, 1999-2008. Used by permission of iPEC Coaching and Bruce D Schneider.

8 iPEC Coaching, 1999-2008. Used by permission of iPEC Coaching and Bruce D Schneider.

9 Dr. Phil McGraw, *Family First: Your Step-by-Step Plan for Creating a Phenomenal Family* (New York: Simon & Schuster, Inc., 2004).

10 Brian Tracy, *Maximum Achievement: Strategies and Skills that Will Unlock Your Hidden Powers to Succeed* (New York: Fireside, 1993).

11 Eva Broch Pierrakos, "The Function of the Ego in Relationship to the Real Self" *Pathwork Guide Lecture* 1996: 132. The Pathwork" Foundation <http://www.pathwork.org/lectures/P132.PDF>

12 http://www.monsanto.com

13 Bruce D. Schneider, *Energy Leadership Training Manual* (New Jersey: iPEC Coaching, 2006).

14 "Obesity in Children and Teens." American Academy of Child and Adolescent Psychiatry, May 2008. <http://www.aacap.org/cs/root/facts_for_families/obesity_in_children_and_teens>

15 Dorothy Law Nolte Ph.D., "Children Learn What They Live" 1972. CharityFocus.org. 17 Jan. 2007
<http://www.charityfocus.org/blog/view.php?id=1382>

16 Barbara Fiese Ph.D.,. "Family Routines and Rituals May Improve Family Relationships and Health, According to 50-year Research Review" American Psychological Association, 8 Dec. 2002
<http://www.apa.org/releases/rituals2.html>

17 Todd Cartmell Ph.D., Respectful Kids: *A Complete Guide to Bringing out the Best in Your Child.* (Colorado Springs: NavPress Publishing Group, 2006).

ABOUT THE AUTHOR

★

Lori Radun, CEC is a certified life coach, accredited energy leadership™ coach, inspirational speaker and author of several personal and family development products. Her company, Momnificent!™, specializes in providing coaching and speaking services to mothers of all ages. Her mission is to inspire moms to live healthy, balanced and magnificent lives. She believes that when mom is at her best, the whole family is strengthened. Her clients include stay-at-home moms, working mothers, work-at-home moms, and even mothers with grown children.

Lori's focus is on helping moms:

· Develop confidence as a woman and mother
· Create and maintain healthy boundaries
· Have positive energy for herself and her family
· Develop and nurture supportive relationships in marriage and friendship
· Balance their lives
· Utilize a spiritual foundation for greater peace, hope and joy
· Practice self-care in all areas of their lives
· Be nurturing and effective parents

On her website, **www.momnificent.com**, you will find a complete array of coaching and speaking services, many personal development products, as well as tips for creating a Momnificent!™ Life Group. Please stop by to sign up for The Momnificent!™ e-newsletter and visit The Momnificent!™ Blog.

Other Products by Lori Radun, The Momnificent!™ Coach:

The Energy Equation eCourse
The Self-Care Series
Guilt-free Parenting DVD
The Five Essential R's for Families Home Coaching Program
Express Yourself! – A Guide for Finding and Creating Your Dreams
101 Great Ways to Improve Your Life
Goal Setting Online Course